HUGH MCGUIRE
AND BRIAN
O'LEARY

D1414468

Book: A Futurist's Manifesto

essays from the bleeding edge of publishing

O'Reilly Media • Boston, Massachusetts

Book: A Futurist's Manifesto

Book: A Futurist's Manifesto
Edited by Hugh McGuire and Brian O'Leary
Copyright © 2012 O'Reilly Media, Inc.. All rights reserved.

Printed in the United States of America. Published by O'Reilly Media, Inc, 1005 Gravenstein Highway North, Sebastopol, CA 95472. O'Reilly books may be purchased for educational, business, or sales promotional use. For more information, contact our corporate/institutional sales department: (800) 998-9938 or corporate@oreilly.com.

This book is available online at: http://book.pressbooks.com.

The print, ebook and web versions of this book were produced and typeset using PressBooks.com, a single-file-source book production tool that outputs EPUB, typeset PDF, and web versions of all books. For more information, visit http://pressbooks.com.

Production Editor: Dan Fauxsmith

July 2012: First Edition.

Print ISBN: 978-1-4493-0560-4 | ISBN 10: 1-4493-0560-1
Ebook ISBN: 978-1-4493-0559-8 | ISBN 10: 1-4493-0559-8

Contents

Preface

This book is the result of a belief: that "digital" fundamentally alters the mechanics of publishing books. There is much talk about this shift in the publishing world — a calendar filled with conferences, a blogosphere popping with opinion, and not a few op-eds and even books on this very topic, some many years old.

But we wanted to get beyond beliefs with this work, to get into the nuts and bolts of things. We wanted our contributors to be not just perceptive thinkers, but also doers, people who are building the kinds of tools and companies that will continue to shape publishing for years to come.

Indeed the idea for *Book* came about not so much as an idea for a book, as a way to put to real-world use a new kind of digital tool for book publishing that my small company was (and is) in the process of building: `PressBooks.com`. PressBooks is a simple, but powerful web-based book production tool, that produces ebooks, print books, and webbooks, all from one online source file. I thought I should be in the middle of it, testing it with a real publishing project.

So I pitched the idea for the book, first to my friend Brian O'Leary, who is as seasoned about book publishing as I am naive. Brian liked it, and we agreed that the best place for the book was O'Reilly Media, a publishing company known for its aggressive embrace of digital innovation.

Joe Wikert, Publisher at O'Reilly, liked it too — and we spent a good number of hours talking about how to "walk the walk" of the changes happening in publishing as we produced this book.

We're building this book — writing, editorial, copyediting, proofing, and production of the ebook (and later print) output — on a new online tool, PressBooks, and learning valuable things in the process. We released the book in three parts, and O'Reilly experimented with staged pricing with these releases. In addition, we're releasing the book for free online, and selling it as an ebook, and a print version as well.

Book: A Futurist's Manifesto is as much about the process as it is about the content. A big part of that process is you, the reader — because publishing does not stop once the book goes out into the wild. Maybe that's when publishing really begins. We'd love to get your feedback, thoughts and criticisms, and the best place for that feedback is the online version of this book, which can be found at: book.pressbooks.com.

–*Hugh McGuire.*

Introduction

The ground beneath the publishing industry trembled in 2007, when Amazon released the Kindle and Apple released the iPhone. Digital—which had wrought havoc on the music and newspaper industries—was finally coming to the consumer market for books. Certainly digital had been reshaping *reading*, and much of what we call "publishing" since at least the 1970s, but for the mass market, 2007 was when the general population started to consider that "books" might come in pixels rather than pages. In the few years since, these devices and their spawn have brought digital reading of long-form text from the realm of "it might happen sometime" to "it is happening right now," and faster than anyone predicted. Many questions have been answered, resoundingly: *Will readers read ebooks?* Yes. *Lots?* Yes. *Dedicated reading devices, or smartphones, or tablets?* Doesn't matter, as long as there is cross-device accessibility. *Browser reading?* See previous. *Shakeup in publishing?* Sorta, but the sky is still overhead.

That rapid shakeup—from print to digital buying and reading—has been massive, but it's really only a transitional phase to a radically different future.

Just a Shift?

We used to live in a paper-based model: Publishers sent print books to distributors and retailers, who sold print books to readers, who took those books home or to work and read them when and where they liked.

We are now effectively replicating this model for digital: Publishers send digital files to distributors and retailers, who sell those files to readers, who download them onto various devices and read them when and where they like.

Of course much else has happened. Pricing structures have changed (the 99-cent best-seller, as well as the agency model), the barriers to entry have crumbled (Bowker estimates 2.8 million print-on-demand and self-published print books came into being in 2010, versus an estimated 270,000 traditionally published books; Smashwords currently distributes some 30,000 ebook authors and 80,000 titles), and the role of the publisher in this disintermediated world is in question (crime writer Joe Konrath claims he does much better without a traditional publisher, and Amanda Hocking sold more than a million copies of her self-published paranormal novel through Kindle, and then went on to sign a multi-book deal with St. Martin's Press).

Or a Fundamental Restructuring?

But there is a greater shift afoot than just pricing and delivery mechanisms, and that is what this book aims to explore. We want to examine how digital changes the process of making a book, as well as what we do with it afterwards.

The move to digital is not just a format shift, but a fundamental restructuring of the universe of publishing. This restructuring will touch every part of a publishing enterprise—or at least most publishing enterprises. Shifting to digital formats is "part one" of this changing universe; "part two" is what happens once everything is digital. This is the big, exciting unknown.

What happens when all books are truly digital, connected, ubiquitous? We're starting to put the infrastructure in place now, so we can start doing things with books that have never before been possible.

What's In the Book?

This book is meant to be a guidebook for the future—a collection of essays from thought leaders and practitioners about the bleeding edge of publishing. We've organized it in three parts:

Part 1. The Setup: Approaches to the Digital Present

In this section, we explore what digital means right now for publishers, and how we need to rethink critical practical matters like design, metadata, and workflow, as well as the underlying assumptions about what a book is and what the job of a publisher might be.

Part 2: The Outlook: What Is Next for the Book?

In this section, we explore that jump into the unknown, the next phase of the "digital book." Here we look at all kinds of exotic things we can start to do with books once we truly think of them as connected, digital objects, rather than just digital copies of paper objects. This section includes pieces by Peter Brantley, Brett Sandursky, Ron Martinez, Erin McKean, Terry Jones, Hugh McGuire, and others.

Part 3: The Things We Can Do with Books: Projects from the Bleeding Edge

In this section, we'll invite those brave souls who have already plunged into the future: those who do more than think and write and talk about "the future of the book," those who have some skin in the game, with projects, passions, technologies, and enterprises struggling to explore the future now. This part includes pieces by Shana Kimball, Ian Barker, Michael Tamblyn, Kassia Krozer, and others.

Inspired by those leading the charge, this book will also practice what it preaches—it is being written and edited using a new web-based book-production system, `PressBooks.com` (full disclosure, I am the founder of

PressBooks). In fact this book was conceived as an experiment, to test out new kinds of production methods as we wrote the book. So while we've been writing and editing this book, we've also been building the book-making tool upon which it was written, edited, and from which comes the EPUB, print and web versions of the book.

We are also encouraging reader feedback throughout the writing process. The book is available for free online at http://book.pressbooks.com as well as in other formats for sale from O'Reilly, and major online retailers.

This book, like all books, is meant to start a conversation, to be part of a conversation. Feedback is encouraged. We may well be missing topics we should not have missed. We might spend too much time on the wrong topics, and we could get things wrong. But nothing is permanent, and everything is connected. Comments on what we have written or should have written help flesh out this complex discussion that surrounds all of us in publishing. We hope this book will be useful as a point of departure for thinking about what publishing can be.

You can continue reading on the web, and add your comments here:http://book.pressbooks.com/front-matter/introduction

part one.

The Setup: Approaches to the Digital Present

1. Context, Not Container (Brian O'Leary)

Brian O'Leary is a publishing consultant and principal of Magellan Media Partners, *an Adjunct Professor of Publishing at NYU, and has had held senior positions in the publishing industry, including Production Manager at Time Inc. and Associate Publisher at Hammond Inc. You can find Brian on Twitter at:* @brianoleary.

The way we think about book, magazine, and newspaper publishing is unduly governed by the physical containers we have used for centuries to transmit information. Those containers define content in two dimensions, necessarily ignoring context, defined here as tagged content, research, footnoted links, sources, and audio and video background, as well as title-level metadata.

The process of filling containers strips out context. In the physical world, intermediaries like booksellers, librarians, and reviewers provide readers with some of the context that is otherwise lost in creating a physical object.

But in our evolving, networked world—the world of "content in browsers"—we are no longer selling content, or at least not content alone.

To support discovery and utility in digital environments, we need to compete on context.

The current workflow hierarchy—container first, limiting content and context—is already outdated. To compete digitally, we must start with context and preserve its connection to content so that both discovery and utility are enhanced.

Unless we think about containers as an option and not the starting point, we remain vulnerable to a range of current and future disruptive entrants. Containers limit how we think about our audiences. In stripping context, they also limit how audiences find our content.

Further, we must organize our content in ways that make it interoperable across platforms, users, and uses. Doing so will start to open up access, making it possible for readers to discover and consume content within and across digital realms. To capture and maintain context, publishing workflows need to change.

An Emerging Threat

Here, scale is not our friend; it may well be the enemy. When disruptive technologies[1] enter a market, they don't look or feel like what we typically value. Often enough, they are cheaper, simpler, smaller, and more convenient than their traditional analogs. They can be functionally ugly, like Craigslist, or just "good enough," as is the case with Wikipedia. They can even invert the old publishing model, as the Huffington Post may have done in aggregating the work of its aspirant writers.

Today, at the outskirts of our industry, we find that smaller, more nimble digital upstarts have reversed the publishing paradigm. The new entrants start with context, which is vital to digital discoverability and trial, and use it to strengthen content. Many startups forego containers, or they create them only as a rendering of personal (consumer) preference.

Think Craigslist. Think Monster. Think Cookstr[2], a born-digital food site that started with and continues to evolve its taxonomy. Context first.

---

[1] http://bit.ly/7MCg8b
[2] http://www.cookstr.com

Increasingly, readers want convenience, specificity, discoverability, ease of access, and connection. The new entrants provide those things, making them destinations to which readers migrate. Publishers need to see these outcomes as the driving force for future sales, not as a cost or add-on to "making a book."

As barriers to entry have fallen, I've started to think more about how traditional book, magazine, and newspaper publishers can survive in a digital era. There are both new and non-traditional established entrants across most publishing segments. Their successes have pushed traditional publishers to look at ways to change business models and organize around customers.

It is time to see publishing as a whole—newspapers, magazines, and books—as part of a disrupted continuum. Digital makes convergence not only possible—it has made convergence inevitable. Marketers have become publishers, publishers are marketing arms, and new entrants are a bit of both. Customers have become alternately competitors, partners, and suppliers.

Thinking about these issues reminded me of a passage from Salman Rushdie's 1990 book, *Haroun and the Sea of Stories*. In the book[3], Haroun sets off to find stories for his father, who has lost his ability to tell tales. Along the way, Haroun comes across Iff, the Water Genie, who at first does not treat Haroun kindly. But at a low point, the Water Genie relents and starts to tell Haroun:

> … about the Ocean of the Streams of Story, and even though he was full of a sense of hopelessness and failure, the magic of the Ocean began to have an effect on Haroun. He looked into the water and saw that it was made up of a thousand thousand thousand and one different currents, each one a different color, weaving in and out of one another like a liquid tapestry of breathtaking complexity…

I'll stop there. We'll return to this story in a bit, but for the moment, I'd like to use it as a jumping-off point, a call for us to "imagine."

---

[3] http://amzn.to/yw31Xw

"Imagine" a world in which content authoring and editing tools are cheap, or even free.[4]

"Imagine" a world in which storage is plentiful[5], even virtual.

And "imagine" a world in which content can be disseminated in a range of formats, at the figurative or literal push of a button[6].

That world exists today, with literally dozens of credible, widely accessible tools and resources. These authoring, repository, and distribution tools and resources make it possible for anyone to create, manage, and disseminate content in digital as well as physical forms.

The thing is, while that world is already here, it is far from evenly distributed.

The Challenge of "Container-First"

A couple of years ago, in a discussion with Laura Dawson[7] and Mike Shatzkin[8], I sketched out a version of a somewhat basic diagram of the kinds of content best served by the use of XML. It was a two-by-two matrix that measured the number of components, or "chunks," on the y-axis and the likelihood of reuse on the x-axis. Plotted this way, the typical winners are in the upper right: genres, like cooking, that have many components, or chunks, and a higher probably of being recombined or reused.

Our problem is, we're not the only ones looking at these markets.

While publishers think of agile workflows as an opportunity to drive down the cost of making content for containers, a newer breed of "born-digital" competitors have developed workflows that start with context. These new entrants are evolving taxonomies and refining tools so that they can invade the same niches we thought we were making more efficient.

The challenge publishers face is not just being digital; it's being demonstrably relevant to the audiences who now turn first to digital to find content.

---

[4] http://www.oxygenxml.com/

[5] http://www.wordpress.org

[6] http://www.archive.org/bookserver

[7] http://www.ljndawson.com

[8] http://www.idealog.com

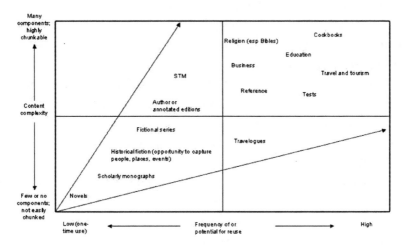

Figure 1.1. XML Readiness Matrix

New entrants—our real competition—start with the customer. They develop contextual frameworks that help them differentiate both readers and themselves. The new guys like the new tools because they are cheap, scalable, and open source. In fact, they are already exploiting tools that many traditional publishers lament are "just too hard to learn."

How did we get here? There's a reason.

In their physical forms, newspapers, magazines, and books establish the boundaries of both content and context. Historically focused on containers[9], we have become stuck using them as the primary source for digital content.

Only after we fill the physical container do we turn our attention to rebuilding the digital roots of content: the context, including tags, links, research, and unpublished material that can get lost on the cutting-room floor.

---

[9] http://bit.ly/9q4vQx

Most of that context never makes it back. We have taken to using things like title-level metadata, some search engine optimization, and occasionally effective use of syndication as proxies for something contextually rich.

Competing as we are against the "born-digital," who have built and maintain contextual connections at the level of the content itself, these proxies are not nearly enough.

Further, we treat readers as if their needs can be defined by containers. But in a digital world, search takes place before physical sampling, much more often than the reverse. Readers may at times look for a specific product, but more often they search for an answer, a solution, a spark that turns into an interest and perhaps a purchase.

Publishers are in the business of linking content to markets, but we're hamstrung at search because we've made context the *last* thing we think about.

When content scarcity was the norm, we could live with a minimum of context. In a limited market, our editors became skilled in making decisions about *what would be published*. Now, in an era of abundance, editors have inherited a new and fundamentally different role: figuring out how "what is published" will be *discovered*.

To serve that new role, we must reverse our publishing paradigm. We need to start with context and develop and maintain rich, linked, digital content.

We also need to use the tools we have (as well as ones we have yet to develop) to make containers an *output* of digital workflows, not the source of content in those workflows. This is a fundamental change to our approach, but it is the only way that I see to compete in a digital-first, content-abundant universe.

And I don't think that this change in mindset (or workflow[10]) will come easily.

Making Content Agile, Discoverable, and Accessible

Over time, we have adopted a series of mental models that constrain our ability to change. The long history of using physical containers to distribute

---

[10] http://www.magellanmediapartners.com/index.php/mmcp/article/boom_like_that/

content, for example, has led us to conflate "format" with "brand."[11]

Perhaps there was a time when the physical nature of content products—their look and feel—dominated. But in a digital era, I think that its time has passed.

In a similar way, we often speak of digital content as a derived or secondary use. The recent debate about reclaiming ebook rights for backlist titles underscores how deeply this bias runs. Who "owns" ebook rights is a different topic, but the conversation about digital versions of backlist titles has centered entirely on contractual issues. The debates are telling for the question that has not been not asked: Who owns the context that drives discoverability, use, and value in a digital realm?

In a digital era, context supports discovery, use, and reuse. Investing in context is now a requirement. Unfortunately, a product focus and an obsession with scale lead publishers to worry more about finding ways to reduce costs. In trying to make the physical object incrementally better, they optimize the creation, production, and delivery of content in a single package.

Along the way, we miss opportunities to create agile, discoverable, and accessible content.[12]

I call this situation "container myopia," paying homage to Ted Levitt's 1960 article, "Marketing myopia."[13] In the article, Levitt called on marketers to shift from a product-centered to a customer-centered paradigm. He famously showed how railroad companies failed to see that they were in the transportation business, much as publishers have struggled to see that they are in the content solutions business.

In a digital realm, true content solutions are increasingly built with open APIs, something containers are pretty bad at. APIs—application programming interfaces[14]—provide users with a roadmap that lets them customize their content consumption.

The physical forms of books, magazines, and newspapers have user interfaces that predate APIs. We've all figured out how to access the information contained in these physical products. But, the physical form

---

[11] http://bit.ly/3a3W4M
[12] http://bit.ly/d7yPQa
[13] http://en.wikipedia.org/wiki/Marketing_myopia
[14] http://en.wikipedia.org/wiki/Application_programming_interface

itself does not always make for a good user interface, something that Craigslist, the Huffington Post[15], Cookstr, and others have capitalized on.

Open up your API, I contend, or someone else will.

Many current audiences (and all future ones) live in an open and accessible environment. They expect to be able to look under the hood, mix and match chunks of content, and create, seamlessly, something of their own. Failure to meet those needs will result in obscurity, at best[16].

To illustrate that point, I want to bring you to perhaps the most hierarchical, inaccessible, closed environment I know of: an American public high school. In particular, I'd like to take you to Columbia High School[17] in Maplewood, New Jersey, where our youngest son, Charlie, is a student. The school opened in 1927, and it has not changed much since then.

Last summer, Charlie was happy to learn that he had earned a 5 on the AP Art History exam. This made him eligible to serve as a sort of teaching assistant for this year's Art History class. All he needed to do was align his free period with the scheduled slot for Art History.

I don't know how many of you have tried to parse a high-school scheduling API. It seems to rely on green-screen devices, stacks of forms, and a queuing process that means you won't have your new schedule in hand until two weeks after the start of the school year.

On a Friday in July, Charlie came home to find his junior-year schedule in the mail. His free period did *not* align. Charlie has seen his brother and sister fight the powers that be at Columbia High School, at times unsuccessfully, and he decided to pursue a different course.

Lacking access to the master schedule, he went to a free resource—*Facebook*—posted his schedule there, and asked anyone who attended Columbia High School to do the same.

By Sunday morning, he had gathered enough data to compile *his own* master schedule. With this information in hand, he rearranged his classes, filled out a homemade "change form," and sent it to the high school on Monday morning. "Please give me this schedule," it said. Problem solved.

---

[15] http://www.huffpo.com

[16] http://tim.oreilly.com/pub/a/p2p/2002/12/11/piracy.html

[17] bit.ly/MEeY7v

The Consequence of a Bad API

Stories like this one, as well as everything Kirk Biglione[18] says about DRM, have led me to see piracy as the consequence of a bad API[19]. 16-year-olds expect access, or they invent it. The future of content involves giving readers access to the rules, tools, and opportunities of contextually rich content so that they can engage with it on their own terms.

And whether they say it just like this or not, readers *want* good APIs.

Content is no longer just a product. It's part of a value chain that solves readers' problems. Readers expect publishers to point them to the outcomes or answers they want, where and when they want them. We're interested in content solutions that don't waste our time, a precious commodity for all of us.

Perhaps most daunting: Readers expect that their content solutions will improve over time. They don't care that much (or at all) about how it happens. Companies that are good at aggregating solutions will reduce the time and hassle involved in finding and buying something. Those firms have a leg up on their competitors.

Drawn from the prescient "lean consumption"[20] model that James Womack and Daniel Jones debuted half a decade ago, these ideas are evident in aggregators like Amazon. They're embodied in services like Kobo and Kindle. They're not just products—they're *solutions*.

The Emerging Role of Context

So, if containers are now an option and content must be made accessible, what is the role of context?

First, let's establish a context of our own: Freed from physical constraints, we no longer have to write to length. We can link, we can expand, we can annotate.

As low- or no-cost authoring, repository, and distribution tools and resources become freely available, it is axiomatic that ours has become and will remain an era of content abundance.

---

[18] http://www.oxfordmediaworks.com
[19] http://bit.ly/0cNrfh
[20] http://bit.ly/zfEtJH

Simply put: Content abundance is the precursor to the development (and maintenance) of context.

When there was only the Gutenberg Bible, we didn't need Dewey. When booksellers were smaller and largely independent, we didn't have much need for BISAC codes[21]. And before online sales made almost every book in print evident and available, ONIX was an unattended luxury.

Digital abundance is pushing publishers to create much more than title-level metadata. To manage abundance, publishers and their agents can (and do) use blunt instruments, like verticals, or somewhat more elegant tools, like search engines.

But when it comes to discovery, access, and utility, nothing substitutes for authorial and editorial judgment, as evidenced in the structural and contextual tags applied to our content.

Context can't be just a preference or an afterthought any more. Early and deep tagging is a search reality. In structural terms, our content fits search conventions, or it will not be referenced. And in contextual terms, our content needs to be deeply and consistently tagged, or it will face an increasingly tough time being found.

Publishers can't afford to build context into content after the fact. Doing so irrevocably truncates the deep relationships that authors and editors create and often maintain until the day, hour, or minute that containers render them impotent. Building back those lost links is redundant, expensive, and ultimately incomplete.

This isn't a problem of standards. At Indiana University, Jenn Riley and Devin Becker have vividly illustrated our abundance of contextual frameworks[22]. The problem we face, the one we avoid at our peril, is implementing these standards.

Ultimately, that's a function of workflow.

If strategy is a head, I liken workflow to a circulatory system. We all know how hard it can be to change organizational direction, but in practice, it's a matter of coordination. Decide you want to go somewhere else, and your head tells your arms and legs to swing one way or another.

---

[21] http://bit.ly/P6dfd6
[22] http://www.dlib.indiana.edu/~jenlrile/metadatamap/

If you want to change workflow, though, you are looking at the publishing equivalent of a heart transplant. And starting with context requires publishers to make fundamental changes to their content workflows.

In a digital era, how publishers work is how they ultimately compete. At a time when we in publishing struggle to create something as simple as a clean ONIX feed, planning for and preserving connections to content is a challenge of significant proportion. New entrants are already upon us, and publishers don't have much time to get this new challenge right.

Four Implications of Content Abundance

Although the precise changes in workflow will vary by publisher, certain principles apply. I think moving from a mindset of "product" to "service" or "solutions" means at least four things for publishers:

- Content must become open, accessible, and interoperable. Adherence to standards will not be an option.
- To compete on context, publishers will need to focus more clearly on using it to promote discovery.
- Because publishers are competing with businesses that already use low- and no-cost tools, trying to beat them on the cost of content is a losing proposition. Instead, they need to develop opportunities that encourage broader use of their content.
- Publishers will distinguish themselves if they can provide readers with tools that draw upon context to help them manage abundance.

Let's take each of these four things in turn, starting with "open, accessible, and interoperable content."

The current proliferation of file formats, rights management schemes, and device-specific content is unlikely to persist. Content consumers (i.e., readers) will increasingly look for content that can be accessed across multiple platforms on a real-time basis.

Content access may be provided through cloud-based services, and the bulk of what we currently think of as book sales may migrate from product to subscription sales. But, much as professionals look for standard interfaces in database products that they buy today, readers will want and come to expect similar interoperability in the content they acquire (or lease).

With respect to "using context to promote discovery": It is straightforward to understand that travel or cooking content can be made "chunkable" and offers opportunities to recombine or reuse portions of an original text. In that discussion, though, fiction often stands apart.

However, publishers such as Harlequin have already shown the value of creating context that helps promote discovery and trial. For decades, the company has carefully defined its imprints to make sure that each one delivers a specific form of romance reading. To this point, those decisions provide context at the level of a title. What's exciting now is our ability to use available tools to capture and market more than just the title-level context.

Imagine you've just finished Tracy Kidder's *Mountains Beyond Mountains*. You're struck by the book's allusions to Haiti's cultural history, and you want to learn more. Title-level data, the kind that says "people who bought *Mountains Beyond Mountains* also bought," might steer you to a book like Paul Farmer's *The Uses of Haiti*.

But a world full of contextually rich manuscripts could open a new era of discovery. Imagine the delight of a reader who could find (and even buy) a chapter of John Szwed's biography of Alan Lomax, in which the author describes in vivid terms a 1930s trip that Lomax, accompanied by Zora Neale Hurston, takes to Haiti in search of the roots of American music. In this era of abundance, delight can be the new hand-selling.

Abundance is also motivating publishers to make broader use of content. Prices, already under pressure as the popularity of digital content grows, are likely to go lower. Offering content that can be shared and loaned may help sustain a certain level of pricing, but the current practice of editing content for a single use, even a single format, is expensive and unsustainable.

In the future, tagged content will be recombined, reused, and in many cases sold as a component or chunk. We already see this in textbook publishing and in some STM markets. In a different, parallel example, Bloomberg's media efforts are built around extensive deployment of "write once, read many." As with the arguments for agile content, not every market is equally attractive, but publishers should be challenging themselves now, as any book created in the old order is one they will likely wind up retooling in the new one.

Finally, we all should think about providing readers with tools that draw upon context to help them manage abundance. The Bloomberg example applies here, as do several startups that are looking to link content with other content using metadata compiled at the level of components, chunks, or even passages.

Developing and using these tools are areas in which libraries may be able to compete and provide lasting value. Although the nature of content repositories is likely to change, abundance will only increase the demand for both context and the ability to leverage it. The skills that have been developed to direct and to teach others how to find content could provide a solid foundation for efforts to provide tools that help manage abundance.

Given these four implications, it seems clear that the publishing community will need new skill sets to compete in an era of abundance. We'll probably have to add a lot more training than we have ever done internally. Nevertheless, those aren't the toughest challenges. Changing workflow is.

I want to leave you on a stronger, happier note than that, though. Change can be hard, and we all need reasons to try something different or new. A short while ago, I asked you to leave Haroun and join me in a leap of imagination.

I'd like to travel back to the Sea of Stories, where the Water Genie is explaining to Haroun that:

> ... these were the Streams of Story, and that each colored strand represented and contained a single tale. Different parts of the Ocean contained different sorts of stories, and as all the stories that had ever been told and many that were still being invented could be found here, the Ocean of the Streams of Story was in fact the biggest library in the universe. And because the stories were held here in fluid form, they retained the ability to change, to become new versions of themselves, to join up with other stories and so become yet other stories; so that unlike a library of books, the Ocean of the Streams of Story was much more than a storeroom of yarns. It was not dead, but alive.

Like Haroun, we in publishing can sometimes become filled with a sense of hopelessness and failure.

And like Haroun, we're perched atop a tapestry of breathtaking complexity. It is a time of remarkable opportunity in publishing, one in which we are able to find and build upon those strands of stories, in context.

Yes, we face a significant challenge preparing for a very different world, but it is a challenge I think we have the insight and experience to meet. What we choose to do now will begin to determine which stories get told, as well as who writes—and publishes them.

Give the author feedback & add your comments to this chapter on the web: `http://book.pressbooks.com/chapter/context-not-container -biran-oleary`

2. **Distribution Everywhere (Andrew Savikas)**

Andrew Savikas is the CEO of Safari Books Online, VP Digital Initiatives at O'Reilly Media, and is on the Board of Directors of the International Digital Publishing Forum (IDPF). You can find Andrew on Twitter at: @andrewsavikas.

Distributing (in) the Future

Publishers working to understand the changing distribution landscape must formulate a strategic response that both responds to the present reality and provides the flexibility to adapt to multiple possible futures. There are two fundamental aspects to the changing nature of publishing: changes to the *form* of what's created and consumed, and changes to the *format* in which the content still created in traditional forms is produced and distributed (developed, packaged, and sold). This chapter focuses on the format side of the equation, so let's first define the form component so we can put it to the side.

By *form* I mean the character of the content—what length is it, what style is it presented in, and does it use text, animation, video, or some combination of the three? Examples of content forms are articles, movies, plays, games, songs, essays, and of course books. Kevin Kelly defines the form of the book nicely[1]: "A book is a self-contained story, argument or body of knowledge that takes more than an hour to read. A book is complete in the sense that it contains its own beginning, middle, and end." Nothing about the physical (or virtual) container for that book, its price, or how it is found by a reader is inherent in that definition—all of those are aspects of the book's *format.*

There are many examples of disruption for certain types of books that have been replaced by better forms for doing the same job the book used to do. Atlases, dictionaries, and telephone books will never again be the dominant way that people understand geography, word meaning, or contact information, no matter how efficiently those books can be produced or sold. (Phone books are *delivered to your door for free,* yet many people now find them nothing more than a nuisance, and have agitated for ways to opt-out of delivery[2].)

Although it is important to ask whether there is an alternate form for doing the same job that a particular book does today, this chapter is about those types of books that will remain viable as self-contained stories, arguments, or bodies of knowledge—and what the profound changes to the format in which those books are created, packaged, distributed, priced, and sold mean for publishers.

The format in which demand for books is met includes things like business model, price, supply chain, and distribution mechanism. *Form disruption* can erase demand for particular books; *format disruption* means radical changes in how continued demand for the form is met. (For an example of a form change, think newsreel; for format change, think Netflix.)

---

[1] http://bit.ly/8YoOmJ
[2] http://bit.ly/NPCyjR

Aggregation

For many in publishing, "aggregation" is a dirty word, typically tossed around in conversations that include discussions of Google, especially if the conversation involves newspapers. But aggregation is at the heart of every effective distribution system—aggregators moderate and simplify a complex network of many-to-many relationships[3], aggregating buyers and sellers at a scale neither side could achieve on its own, creating value for both sides. Supermarkets are aggregators, shopping malls are aggregators, eBay is an aggregator, Craigslist is an aggregator, and cable operators are aggregators. Jonathan A. Knee wrote about the role of aggregators in the media business in a recent issue of *The Atlantic*[4]:

> In fact, the dirty little secret of the media industry is that content aggregators, not content creators, have long been the overwhelming source of value creation. Well before Netflix was founded in 1997, cable channels that did little more than aggregate old movies, cartoons, or television shows boasted profit margins many times greater than those of the movie studios that had produced the creative content. It is no coincidence that although, say, 90 percent of the public discourse surrounding Comcast's recent $30 billion acquisition of NBC Universal involved the Conan O'Brien drama or the shifting fortunes of Universal Pictures, in reality, 82 percent of the new company's profits come in through the cable channels.
>
> The economic structure of the media business is not fundamentally different from that of business in general. The most-prevalent sources of industrial strength are the mutually reinforcing competitive advantages of scale and customer captivity. Content creation simply does not lend itself to either, while aggregation is amenable to both.

That aggregators can capture so much value in the ecosystem reinforces the notion that the value is as much (or more so) in the service provided by

---

[3] http://hbr.org/2006/10/strategies-for-two-sided-markets/ar/1
[4] http://bit.ly/myQjYB

the aggregator as in the content itself, something I wrote about in 2009[5]:

> Whether they realize it or not, media companies are in the
> *service* business, not the *content* business. Look at iTunes:
> if people paid for content, then it would follow that better
> content would cost more money. But every song costs the
> same. Why would people pay the same price for goods of
> (often vastly) different quality? Because they're **not paying for
> the goods**; they're paying Apple for the service of providing
> a selection of convenient options easy to pay for and easy to
> download.

Aggregators provide clear value to buyers and sellers, and while it is
possible to build a large and profitable business serving customers directly
(either through a direct sales channel or through vertical integration), most
publishers depend on aggregators to connect their content with a large
enough audience.

But of course aggregators are not merely benevolent actors in the
market, and both buyers and sellers understand the importance of ensuring
that no single aggregator develops too much control over either side (or especially *both* sides!) of the transaction. For publishers, that debate was long
about whether superstores like B&N or Borders (and later Amazon.com)
were gaining too much control. Managing aggregators requires a delicate
balance, as bigger aggregators can deliver a larger audience but typically
use those same economies of scale to extract more favorable pricing terms.
Ask anyone who sells to Walmart.[6]

Ideally, a content seller will seek to cultivate a rich ecosystem of
multiple aggregation points, offering a diversity of services and options
to customers. But each unique destination point introduces friction into
the supply chain needed to service it. Reducing friction is the reason
organizations like the Book Industry Study Group[7] (BISG) exist—to develop
and maintain standards and practices[8] that reduce those friction points. But
the "sameness" of an efficient ecosystem of aggregators leaves suppliers

---

[5] http://oreil.ly/9hg2hh

[6] http://hbswk.hbs.edu/item/5903.html

[7] http://www.bisg.org

[8] http://bit.ly/cjoAgq

and aggregators alike open to another threat: commoditization and its accompanying downward pricing pressure.

With sufficient choice for customers among substantially similar products, the aggregator with the biggest economies of scale can make up for a reduction in margin from lower prices on individual transactions by selling more widgets. Those economies of scale also offer the largest players the ability to use that volume to spread out the high fixed-cost investment in more efficient operational capabilities and things like algorithmic recommendation engines, reinforcing the quality of the "service" component of what customers pay for.

Injecting variety into the formats available—different business models[9], different discovery mechanisms[10], and different packaging options[11], for example—provides a hedge against consolidation and commoditization, as does any way of differentiating a more profitable sales channel that cannot easily be matched by other aggregators. The downside is that each variation in format typically introduces that channel friction. Anyone who has dealt with the metadata used by today's burgeoning ebook reseller landscape can attest to the impact of friction.

But how do you efficiently and effectively develop and cultivate the kind of rich distribution ecosystem needed to defend against any individual aggregator gaining too much control, while minimizing the cost of format friction? The rest of this chapter describes how O'Reilly Media has done it in the context of the digital disruption of the last decade, and many of the techniques described can be applied within your own business.

Digital History at O'Reilly

In the late 1990s, readers of computer books began expecting their books to behave like much of the other technical information and documentation they used to do their jobs. That is, they expected their books to be digital, searchable, and hyperlinked, like the Web. In response, O'Reilly launched a series of products called "CD Bookshelves." These were CD-

---

[9] http://www.24symbols.com/
[10] http://booklamp.com/
[11] http://bit.ly/hi7oxU

ROMs packaged in a box sized to fit on a bookstore shelf,[12] and contained HTML versions of multiple books on a related topic. Similar to the Encarta model of Encyclopedia distribution, CD Bookshelves put an electronic version of a printed text onto a reader's PC. It was O'Reilly's first real foray into "digital distribution."

At the same time, companies like Microsoft (with their nascent MSN service) and AOL were rushing to fill their walled-garden services with content that would attract subscribers, and several began reaching out to publishers to license book content. Most proposals offered a small percentage in licensing fees, not unlike the translation rights business publishers are familiar with. But if the Web was going to disrupt the book business the way it was disrupting so many other industries (travel, insurance, and investing to name a few), then digital distribution and consumption would inevitably become not just an ancillary channel, but the *primary* means of distribution and consumption. And single-digit licensing percentages would devastate any publisher's business model.

In 2001, O'Reilly partnered with Pearson Technology Group to build Safari Books Online,[13] a joint venture for distributing a library of computer books delivered on the Web for a monthly subscription. The pricing model and sales strategy developed for Safari Books Online were radically different from what its founders were familiar with, which had the side benefit of not competing directly with the existing print business.

At the time, O'Reilly books were made the same way most publishers make books: A manuscript was written in Word, then laid out in a desktop-publishing program like InDesign or FrameMaker, with metadata managed in a title database. And of course the entire production, manufacturing, and distribution workflow was optimized for selling print books at retail. Ebooks for Safari were an afterthought, the responsibility of a separate team isolated from anyone involved with making and distributing the "real" book. This made sense when digital sales were relatively small—manual rework for the needs of a small sales channel was more efficient than investing in systems or processes optimized for that channel. But by 2005, Safari Books Online had grown into the second-largest sales channel for

[12] http://oreilly.com/catalog/9780596003890
[13] http://safaribooksonline.com

O'Reilly, and there was a clear need to reevaluate the way we met demand for that channel.

On one hand, it was a channel we owned and believed in, and it was growing beyond expectations. Because it is owned by publishers, the terms are friendly, and it contributes to the diversity of aggregation points needed to hedge against dominance by any one aggregator. On the other hand, the publishing and metadata workflow in place at O'Reilly in 2005 meant substantial conversion costs and delays for getting titles into Safari. Customers were understandably frustrated when titles took days or weeks to appear in Safari, often long after they were available in print from retailers. If the new digital channels on the horizon each required the kind of rework then needed for Safari Books Online, we would be in trouble.

Several attempts were made from an operational perspective around new production tools, but all of them failed because each assumed the solution was to graft a new tool or process onto the existing workflow, because disrupting the way books were made would mean disrupting the biggest and most profitable path to market—print books, sold at retail.

The Toolchain

While much of the early Web was static documents connected to each other via hyperlinks, Web publishing quickly evolved to separate content creation from content presentation. The raw materials are captured and stored in a database, then assembled and delivered on demand, often customized for one individual. Very few web pages are presented identically to two different people; ads, navigation headings, and links to new or related information are commonly created in realtime with each request for a particular page.

A key benefit of separating content creation and storage from content presentation is that a single source can be repurposed for multiple presentation formats. This concept is pervasive within today's mobile app ecosystem. As an example, the restaurant reviews found on Yelp[14] live in a database and are dynamically delivered to desktop and mobile web browsers, as well as iPhone and Android apps, all with different interfaces and affordances, and often customized for an individual user (based on, for

---

[14] http://yelp.com

example, her location when using the service). If books were to be delivered on the Web, they needed to behave more like dynamic Web content and less like digital representations of printed books. But as long as the assumption persisted that *the printed book was the primary goal*, meeting digital demand would remain an inefficient and costly afterthought.

Was there a way to separate the content creation and storage for book content from its presentation? The answer for O'Reilly was to standardize around an XML format that we'd help create, known as DocBook XML[15]. DocBook is a *semantic markup language*, meaning it's intended for describing *what a particular piece of text is*, rather than *how it should look*. When reading text, we use visual formatting hints to infer structure—the big text at the top of a page is a heading; text formatted with italics is meant to be emphasized. What appears in its own box on the side of a page is interpreted as a sidebar of brief but related material. Indicating structure using presentation works very well when there's a single presentation, but quickly breaks down when you want to either manipulate the text for new purposes, or present it in multiple ways. And the biggest downside is that while people are great at pattern matching based on visual cues, computers remain lousy at it. Google can't effectively "look at" each web page to determine what its title is based on the relative font size or position on the page the way people do, so most web pages tell Google what their title is explicitly. You can see this yourself from your Web browser, by choosing View→Source while looking at any web page. Near the top there's text that looks like this:

```
<title>O'Reilly Media - Technology Books,

Tech Conferences, IT Courses, News</title>
```

Note that this is the same text that appears in the top of your browser window. Semantic markup like that uses computer-friendly labels to indicate the structure humans typically infer from presentation. In the case of DocBook, that means that in addition to elements like "title," there are labels for things like "chapter," "sidebar," "index," and "warning"—all of the common structural building blocks for a technical book. When everything is labeled like that, it becomes easy to apply different formatting rules

---

[15] http://docbook.org

for different presentation needs. That's accomplished through the use of stylesheets, with each one designed for a different presentation format. You see this when you view a website such as Yahoo.com[16] on your laptop and then on your smartphone or tablet. In each case, the content is substantially similar, but it's presented differently and optimized for the particular screen you are using.

Adapting that approach for books means reorienting the production process toward the "final" output of that semantically rich XML, rather than a PDF destined for the printer. Capturing the content and all of the semantic information about its structure independently of the particulars of presentation is a powerful capability, one that underpins the ability to rapidly respond to business opportunities for new distribution and presentation formats.

DocBook XML was the logical choice for O'Reilly for two main reasons. First, it is a mature, well-documented open standard, with a large ecosystem of tools and users. Second, a modified version of DocBook was already the format used for delivering content to Safari Books Online. That meant that if we could find a way to get print-friendly PDFs from DocBook, we'd be able to produce books for both of our (radically different) sales channels simultaneously from the same source files.

That large ecosystem of tools and users meant that there was already a very mature and robust set of open-source stylesheets[17] intended to do exactly what we wanted: to take a set of DocBook source files and create multiple outputs, each with its own formatting rules. We could even create multiple versions of the same output format; for example, a PDF intended for printing (with crop marks and high-resolution images) and a PDF designed for viewing digitally (with color images and hyperlinks). By customizing the stylesheets with our branding, we could deliver three different "final" outputs (print PDF, web PDF, and Safari) from the same source file at the same time, while retaining the flexibility to modify the presentation formatting independently of the content.

When EPUB[18] emerged as the standard for the growing ebook market, we partnered with Adobe to contribute changes to those open source

---

[16] http://www.yahoo.com

[17] http://docbook.sourceforge.net/release/xsl/1.75.1/doc/

[18] http://www.ipdf.org

stylesheets[19] to support output as EPUB (and with some additional processing, in Kindle-compatible Mobi format as well). That meant that as long as our production workflow resulted in a high-quality DocBook XML version of a book, we could deliver multiple print and digital versions at the same time from the same source. That's a very powerful capability in a rapidly changing market.

The toolchain was not without trade-offs. When print is just one of many output formats, you give up a degree of control over things like page and line breaks, things that many production staff have spent years fretting about. But we decided those tradeoffs were worth the substantial improvement in flexibility, especially if the assumption that print would decline relative to digital sales held.

Seizing Market Opportunities

The ability to quickly and efficiently produce multiple digital versions of a book also supported a refocus on driving direct ecommerce sales of O'Reilly ebooks. Beginning in 2008, O'Reilly began offering what we called ebook bundles[20] for new titles. Customers buying direct from oreilly.com received a web-friendly PDF, an EPUB file, and a Kindle-compatible Mobipocket file. This diversity of formats could be assembled with no additional cost or delay. The bundled offer recognized that our customers often wanted different formats for different situations—a PDF for quick searching on a laptop, but an EPUB for use on an iPhone during the morning commute.

Having all new titles automatically output as EPUB files also positioned us to quickly exploit new sales opportunities. Our partnership with Lexcycle, makers of the Stanza ereader app (a relationship that ended not long after Amazon acquired Lexcycle and development stalled), allowed us to generate hundreds of individual ebook apps from those EPUB files for sale in the App Store long before iBooks emerged. While the market for individual ebook apps for iOS has migrated toward resellers like Kindle and iBooks, we continue to sell similar EPUB-based apps in the Android Market, and we continue to sell many iOS apps to customers in countries that don't yet have access to the iBookstore. The ability to offer a bundle of

---

[19] http://oreil.ly/5B6Kc9

[20] http://oreilly.com/ebooks/

formats also means that we've been able to add Android .apk application files[21] and accessible DAISY talking book versions[22] for many titles.

Those multiple output versions are like snapshots of the underlying XML source, generated at a particular point in time. And because creating those snapshots is automated, it can be done on-demand, any time that the source XML changes. There are strong similarities to software development in that approach—programmers write and revise plain-text computer code, then "compile" that code into a program or application. Our DocBook XML is like the source code, and the output formats are like the applications. Software developers spend more time than just about anyone writing, editing, and collaborating on complex long-form text documents, so it makes sense to borrow and adapt some of the tools and techniques they use to make that task more manageable.

Most of us are now quite accustomed to getting updates to software applications, which is a reflection of the need to continuously refine and improve software to respond to customer needs, technology changes, and market dynamics. Many (though certainly not all) types of books would benefit from that capability, especially if the book is delivered digitally. If our smartphone apps can tell us when they're updated, why not our books, too? When a correction or change needs to be made to an O'Reilly book, the XML source files are modified, and the output formats are "recompiled" to include the changes. Free lifetime updates became a powerful differentiator (along with offering multiple formats) for oreilly.com as a direct sales channel.

Extending the toolchain all the way back to the authoring stage means the ability to use the same single-source, multiple-output capability well before a book is "finished." Other efforts to achieve this include the Pressbooks[23] system used for this book. Taking inspiration from systems assembled by several authors, O'Reilly built its Open Feedback Publishing System[24] to support early release and feedback for books in progress. And because we can deliver updates to customers after the purchase, many

---

[21] http://oreil.ly/P6hkOn
[22] http://oreil.ly/bkR9M1
[23] http://pressbooks.org
[24] http://ofps.oreilly.com

titles[25] also go up for sale on oreilly.com well before publication and are included in Safari Books Online as part of their Rough Cuts[26] program. This "release early, release often" attitude mirrors the philosophy of software development, and challenges the idea that many books will ever really be "done." The concept of a "networked book" is covered in this book by Bob Stein. Kevin Kelly summarizes the idea nicely[27]:

> One quirk of networked books is that they are never done, or rather that they become streams of words rather than monuments. Wikipedia is a stream of edits, as anyone who has tried to make a citation to it realizes. Books too are becoming flows, as precursors of the work are written online, earlier versions published, corrections made, updates added, revised versions approved. A book is networked in time as well as space.

As print-on-demand prices have continued to decline, we've even been able to extend that update model to print. Through a partnership with Ingram and Lightning Source[28], as updates are made to books, fresh PDFs are sent to Lightning Source so that the next order received for that title will be fulfilled with a printed book that contains the latest changes.

While the author-facing parts of the O'Reilly toolchain may still be a bit too technical for many authors (though those who do use it are quite happy[29]), projects like Pressbooks and new writing apps like Scrivener[30] are bringing the same principles of separation of content from formatting, multiple output formats "compiled" from the same source, and rapid iteration to a more mainstream author audience.

---

[25] http://oreilly.com/catalog/0636920000723

[26] http://my.safaribooksonline.com/roughcuts

[27] bit.ly/hajsQt

[28] http://bit.ly/g1WFbm

[29] http://www.apeth.net/matt/iosbooktoolchain.html

[30] http://www.literatureandlatte.com/scrivener.php

Conclusion

In addition to being able to quickly react to changes in the sales and distribution landscape, our toolchain means we can also actively nudge customers and channel partners in a direction we believe makes the most sense for us and the market at large. We have the luxury of a strong and profitable direct sales channel (though one that was built with years and years of sustained effort!), and we hold that up as the ideal from a customer experience perspective—multiple, DRM-free formats and free lifetime updates in particular. None of the major ebook resellers can match that offer, but we also know that plenty of customers will prefer to buy from Amazon, Apple, Kobo, or someone else, both in print and electronically. So anyone who buys either a print or electronic O'Reilly book anywhere can "register" that purchase with us, and for $5 they get all of those other ebook formats and the free lifetime updates. Nudge, nudge.

When I talk about what we've done at O'Reilly, it's often dismissed because we're seen as a technology company. But I can't stress enough that five years ago, even though we were publishing books about many of the technologies we eventually used for our multichannel publishing toolchain, nobody involved with actually producing, distributing, or selling those books knew any more than other publishers about multichannel publishing or a digital-first workflow. A culture that welcomed experimentation was critical, but that was as much driven by the necessity of nearly a decade of declining print sales—sales pressure many other publishers are just now starting to feel. And the tools, standards, techniques, and business opportunities available today are much more developed than they were five years ago.

Focusing a distribution strategy merely on efficiently filling existing channels with a standard set of products is only part of the challenge. A product development capability to quickly create a variety of print and digital outputs can give you the flexibility to quickly respond to new market opportunities and more effectively encourage a diverse ecosystem of aggregation points, all while hedging against the dominance of any single aggregator.

Give the author feedback & add your comments about this chapter on the web: http://book.pressbooks.com/chapter/distribution-everywhere-andrew-savikas

3. What We Can Do with "Books" (Liza Daly)

Liza Daly is Vice President of Engineering at Safari Books Online. Previously, she was owner of Threepress Consulting, *where she provided strategy and software for publishers, authors, and vendors. In 2008, she developed* Bookworm, *one of the first open-source EPUB readers, and in February of 2010 released* Ibis Reader™, *the first HTML5 ebook platform. Liza is on the Board of Directors for the* International Digital Publishing Forum. *You can find Liza on Twitter at:* @liza.

What Can You Do with a Digital Book?

You can do a lot of things with a paper book. You can read it. You can make notes in it. You can fold down corners of various pages to mark something of note or just keep track of where you are. You can easily lend a physical book to a friend. You can destroy it forever. You can even make it into art[1].

---

[1] http://www.flickr.com/photos/briandettmer/5217752891/

But what can you do with a digital book?

In the nascent electronic book era, much of the discussion covers what you *can't* do. Generally, digital books can't be lent or resold. You can't curl up with them and smell them, nor can you pass them on to grandchildren.

Many of these limitations have nothing to do with the intrinsic qualities of a digital book, but are instead a reflection of the difficult transition between an old, established medium and a new, to-date undeveloped one. We compare the physical to the digital and quickly spot the differences: digital's shortcomings.

Ebooks do not have to be mere simulacra of printed works. What are the unique qualities that being digital, especially born-digital, add to the reading experience? In what way is literature being transformed? What can we do with these new kinds of books?

The Opportunity to Upgrade

When readers open ebooks today, they have some expectation that the digital book will contain the same content it did when they last opened it. That sensibility reflects the limitations of current ereaders, not an intrinsic quality of digital media, as software clearly demonstrates. Software is, after all, text written for an audience of computers rather than people.

When software first became a consumer product in the 1980s, it was literally unchangeable. It was written on media that was write-once,[2] placed in a physical box, shrink-wrapped, and set on store shelves. Later releases of software in a box would likely include some bug fixes and minor feature additions, but conceptually, a software program was treated as any other kind of physical media—it was produced once, and if there were sufficient interest for a second edition or version, a user would be expected to purchase a completely new copy of the product.

Until computer networking became ubiquitous, there was no straightforward method for computer software to be upgraded in-place, or "patched."[3] In the 1990s and early 2000s, software updates were still done via formal release numbers and discrete new editions. The onus was

---

[2] http://en.wikipedia.org/wiki/ROM_cartridge

[3] http://en.wikipedia.org/wiki/Patch_(computing)

CHAPTER I.

Iᴛ is a truth universally acknowledged, that a single man in possession of a good fortune must be in want of a wife.

However little known the feelings or views of such a man may be on his first entering a neighbourhood, this truth is so well fixed in the minds of the surrounding

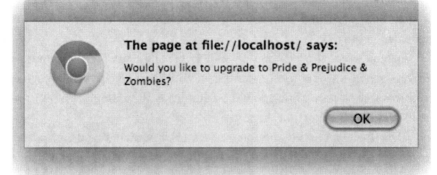

Figure 3.1. Upgrading Pride and Prejudice

on individual owners to find and acquire patches to update their own products, sometimes for free and on occasion by paying for an upgrade.

Increasingly, software designers are moving toward a versionless, seamless upgrade model. Applications now routinely notify users that a new version is available. These updates typically contain a time stamp or version number and a "change list" of bug fixes and new features. In effect, software updates have moved from a "pull" model (where users must find and then manually download updates) to a "push" model, where the user needs to play no role beyond accepting or declining the update.

Even this hands-off approach to software updates may itself be short-lived. Web browsers are beginning to continuously update without user intervention.[4] These programs are perpetually and automatically at the latest version.

Applying an updatable model to ebooks can evoke some squeamishness. The latest version of a digital book may not represent the best or most desirable version. In software, new features have been known to add new bugs or bloat the application; books could suffer a similar fate. As with software, readers may want an option to decline a proposed upgrade.

This concern grows more acute when considering fixity as it applies to scholarship. To understand an author and a work, it can be critical to have persistent access to the original version. We know that the original *Huckleberry Finn* contained offensive racist language,[5] but its use is of a time and place that demands the author's version to understand its intended message.

Digital access also makes it possible to see and perhaps access a range of versions of a single text. However, not all versions are created equal, and it is a legitimate criticism that by surfacing all versions of a text, we risk endorsing the worst of them.[6]

Nevertheless, I argue that the vast majority of digital content updates can be made ethical, innocuous, and in the service of the reader. Change lists must not be optional; it should be possible for a reader to know what is different about a new version, either through mechanical means[7] or through editorial commentary.

But there is no reason that the spectre of censorship should make us fearful of updates, edits, or upgrades. The internet is the greatest copy machine[8] ever invented; storage is plentiful. Digital preservation is an admirable goal and a tractable problem, and it can be managed while the benefits of truly "living" texts are explored.

A Chance to Interact

"Will you read me a story?"

---

[4] http://bit.ly/eYoGKI
[5] http://bit.ly/fEJXQs
[6] http://bit.ly/SQYNGL
[7] http://en.wikipedia.org/wiki/Diff
[8] http://web.archive.org/

"Read you a story? What fun would that be? I've got a better idea: let's tell a story together."
—*Photopia*, Adam Cadre

The growth of digital texts is a precursor to the advent of digital storytelling. The lessons of early game developers can teach us much about the possibilities and pitfalls of designing for true interactivity.

Transforming digital text into interactive narrative was one of the first impulses in computing. Limitations in graphics and computing capability meant that the very first games, distributed via early versions of what has become the Internet, were text-based games such as Colossal Cave (1975)[9]. Textual gaming had an initial commercial flowering, in part due to the heterogeneity of computing platforms at the time—there were dozens of consumer operating systems, each with a different set of severe constraints on memory, processor, and display.

In contrast to today's high-budget video game world, development teams in the 1980s were miniscule. Authors were generally paired with software engineers. Many classic games across all genres were coded by a single person; this model of author and implementor in small, focused teams remains viable in developing ebook-based interactivity.

In the 1980s and early 90s, game publishers experimented with form, pricing, and budget. They also exhibited tremendous anxiety about piracy[10]. Authors frequently played a direct role in early gaming, including Douglas Adams[11], Geoff Ryman,[12] and Robert Pinsky.[13]

Of these three examples, it is notable that Ryman's work, hand-coded by the author in HTML, is the only one that modern computers can still "play" (read) natively. Text games like Adams's *The Hitchhiker's Guide to the Galaxy* can be played today only because a distributed effort to reverse-engineer an obsolete but beloved technology[14] has made it possible.

---

[9] http://bit.ly/cGOgL3
[10] http://www.archive.org/details/dontcopythatfloppy
[11] http://www.bbc.co.uk/radio4/hitchhikers/stevem.shtml
[12] http://www.ryman-novel.com/info/home.htm
[13] http://www.ifwiki.org/index.php/Mindwheel
[14] http://www.gnelson.demon.co.uk/zspec/preface.html

Proprietary game engines as used in the Pinsky work are nearly impossible to run,[15] both from a legal and practical perspective.

More recently, mobile devices (including but not limited to ereaders) have resurfaced many of the same issues that challenged early computer game developers. These include platform variability (a wide range of sizes and computing capability) and an immature market with uncertain consumer expectations. A book's natural status as a cultural symbol is worth preserving, and the standardization effort around interactive ebooks,[16] suggests that viewing these artifacts as books rather than games will benefit future scholarship greatly.

A commitment to standards, however, need not limit the opportunities that digital books provide readers. These can be thought of in terms of participation, exploration and illumination.

Participate

Discussion of interactive storytelling tends to revolve around the "choose your own adventure"[17] model, in which the author writes a fixed set of narratives and the reader is given the option of exploring one or all of them. Many reject this conceit as a meaningful form of expression. "Art seeks to lead you to an inevitable conclusion, not a smorgasbord of choices," writes Roger Ebert[18] in one of his many critiques of videogames as art.

Yet extended choices is not the only way in which a participatory narrative can augment traditional storytelling. Many interactive works do not have alternate endings or choices; they may even exploit Ebert's concept of inevitable outcomes. In *Phototopia*[19] by author Adam Cadre (*Ready, Okay!*[20], HarperCollins), you do not play as the central character. The story is a series of vignettes about other people who intersect with her life. You are riding with a drunk driver who is unable to stop before running a red light. You are the father of a newborn. You are a teenage boy with a crush on a girl in your class. Interspersed with these slices of life

---

[15] http://nickm.com/writing/essays/condemned_to_reload_it.html
[16] http://idpf.org/epub/30
[17] http://www.cyoa.com/public/index.html
[18] http://bit.ly/1X4vcZ
[19] http://bit.ly/uCU5fS
[20] http://www.amazon.com/Ready-Okay-Adam-Cadre/dp/0060195584

are sequences from some kind of fantasy story, but the didactic narrative voice and dreamlike inconsistency of the settings suggest a story being told orally, made up as the narrator goes.

About halfway through the story, it is clear that these narrative pieces are being told out of order, and that when reordered, add up to tragedy. There is no opportunity for the reader/player to alter that outcome. The story, to use a derogatory term from the gaming world, is "on rails." The purpose of *Phototopia* as a work is two-fold. First, it uses the apparent agency given to the player/reader as a tease; one *should* be able to turn the car away, to magically warn the protagonist to stay a moment longer, but it is impossible. Second, you never play as the protagonist herself. Instead you see her through the eyes of people who care about her, at various times in her short life, told in the second-person, as is typical for these games. The intimacy and participatory nature of the experience means that the work can be concise and devastating in a way that would be difficult to achieve in a linear, static story.

Explore

Textual computer games with a literary bent often take the form of word-play. In The Gostak[21] by Carl Muckenhoupt, the narrative is grammatical, but nonsensical at first:

You are the gostak. The gostak distims the doshes. But you'll have to discren those glauds first.

Based on a famous illustration of syntax,[22] *The Gostak* recalls The Jabberwocky[23] but adds the pleasure of discovery. Readers do not just enjoy the wordplay—they engage with it, using trial and error and inference to solve the mystery of the words.

Crenned in the loff lutt are five glauds. A gitch tunks you from the hoggam.
>*tunk glauds*
Which do you mean, the raskable glaud, the poltive glaud, the glaud-with-roggler, the glaud of jenth or the Cobbic glaud?

[21] http://www.ifwiki.org/index.php/The_Gostak
[22] http://en.wikipedia.org/wiki/Gostak
[23] http://bit.ly/MEh3QI

>raskable

A raskable glaud is about as unheamy as a darf of jenth,
but at least it can vorl the doshery from the gitches.

Here, "tunk" is clearly a verb, and glauds is clearly a plural noun.
"Raskable" is some kind of adjective, maybe color? When used as a verb,
"tunk" provided additional information rather than causing some kind of
action, so the player will assume here that the verb is something like "look
at" or "examine."

The narrative may still be set, but in these examples, the digital text
encourages exploration in ways that can challenge and reward the reader.
By seeking direction, the reader's engagement with the text moves from
passive to interactive, while the software itself—a digital book—provides
direction and meaning in unexpected ways.

Illuminate

Text-based gaming offers a wealth of experimentation, but typing com-
mands at a computer can be frustrating. Engaging users this way is seen as
an obsolete form of interaction. Following the author/implementor model,
in 2010 I commissioned an interactive piece from game designer Emily
Short with two constraints: it must be primarily textual, but use a simple
touch-based interface.

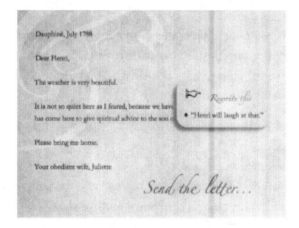

Figure 3.2. First Draft of the Revolution, Emily Short (unpublished)

First Draft of the Revolution is an epistolary story set in a parallel history in which written documents are magically linked. The reader is presented with each letter in sequence, each sentence fading in slowly to reflect the "magical" transition between sender and receiver.

The letters are at first incomplete or impetuous and cannot be sent "as-is." User interface clues (such as red text) provide hints as to which passages need to be revised. Tapping on those passages allows the reader to edit or delete them altogether. While the message of each letter is authorially fixed, readers control the tone and how much is revealed or hidden in each response.

At the time of this writing, *First Draft of the Revolution* is still being finalized, but we intend to publish it as a free EPUB book—to put it distinctly among other books, not games. At its heart are the core elements of story, set in a digital environment that allows both exploration and illumination.

Immersive and Nontrivial

Starting with the CD-ROM era of the 1990s,[24] the development of "enhanced" ebooks, usually with multimedia elements, has seemed to be a natural evolution. Yet the industry has struggled with early commercial and artistic failures, suggesting that consumers don't want or need multimedia content — such enhancements may be distracting. There is widespread concern that a multimedia ebook is not "enhanced" in any way, and that it is actually inferior to its quieter, static counterpart.

I propose that digital-only additions to texts should pass a two-fold test of utility. First, such additions should be *immersive*: they should appear to be natural extensions of the work, satisfying the curiosity of readers at the moment that these curiousities naturally arrive in the course of consuming the text.

Enhancements must also be *nontrivial*. Loading up a reference work with links to Google Maps or Wikipedia offers little value the reader could not obtain independently. Primary source material, topics not easily

---

[24] http://en.wikipedia.org/wiki/Beethoven's_Ninth_Symphony_CD-ROM

discoverable via search engines, or deeply curated dives into ancillary topics represent rewarding additions that readers will want to explore.

For example, ChessBase[25] is a database and game engine used by serious chess players worldwide. It holds thousands of historical games and provides users with a challenging artificial intelligence engine that can recommend moves based on deep searches of those games.

ChessBase is also an ebook reader of a kind in that it can consume and display the PGN format (Portable Game Notation[26]), which mixes narrative content with game notation. Players can purchase chess ebooks[27] and read them inside the engine; the games that are referenced in the book can be played interactively.

The scope of the experience is not limited to information available at the time of the ebook's publication. If a reader wants to know more about the Sicilian Defense, ChessBase data can provide a list of all tourament games that used it as recently as a matter of days.

Chess ebooks can also be *authored* in ChessBase. The ebook sold to consumers is essentially the author's manuscript and source file. This is perhaps the fullest expression of immersive reading—there is a one-to-one relationship between the authoring and reading environment, and readers engage with the content in the same context in which they will make use of it.

By comparison, *Listen to This* by music critic Alex Ross has an extraordinarily complete companion website[28] featuring audio and video clips to accompany the pieces mentioned in the text. The web-based guide is *nontrivial*, but because it is external to the ebook, it is not *immersive*. While rights issues around multimedia are murky, they should be clarified, not avoided, in pursuit of experiences that are both immersive and nontrivial.

---

[25] http://en.wikipedia.org/wiki/ChessBase

[26] http://www.lutanho.net/pgn/pgnviewer.html

[27] http://www.everymanchess.com/

[28] http://www.therestisnoise.com/listentothisaudio/

Options to Invent

> The cell phone has rapidly cemented its place as a media delivery platform for young people. In a typical day, 8- to 18-year-olds spend an average of 49 minutes either listening to music (:17), playing games (:17) or watching TV (:15) on a cell phone—and this is an average for all 8- to 18-year-olds, including the youngest children, and all of those who don't even own a cell phone."
>
> —*Kaiser Family Foundation study*[29], January 2010

In 2011, nearly every online form of self-expression enables commentary. Whether it is the erudite dialog of MetaFilter,[30] dubious comments on YouTube, or a simple binary Facebook "like," children today are growing up with media that is almost universally participatory. The next generation of authors will expect the written word to be as fluid and maleable as online video or updates on social networks. Some might take comfort in writing as a solitary pursuit, but most will embrace the cacophony of digital expression.

Production values of home videos today exceed those of big-budget network shows from only 20 years ago. I similarly expect tech-savvy or curious authors to leapfrog the tentative digital experiments of the 1980s and 1990s directly into new forms of popular expression. I encourage those of us in the publishing industry during this transitional period to enable this expression, technologically, economically, and culturally. We need to provide readers with their own options to invent, or we risk losing them to other media possibilities that do.

Give the author feedback & add your comments about this chapter on the web: http://book.pressbooks.com/chapter/what-we-can-do -with-books-liza-daly

---

[29] http://www.kff.org/entmedia/upload/8010.pdf
[30] http://metafilter.com/

4. What We Talk About When We Talk About Metadata (Laura Dawson)

Laura Dawson is Product Manager, Identifiers at Bowker. She's a 25-year veteran of the book industry, having worked in e-commerce (Barnes & Noble.com), libraries (SirsiDynix), and publishing (Doubleday and Bantam), and has worked as an independent consultant offering expertise on the digital transition for clients including McGraw-Hill, Alibris, Ingram Library Services, Bowker, and Muze. You can find Laura on Twitter at: @ljndawson.

Introduction

As Brian O'Leary noted in his previous chapter, metadata assumes a critical importance once the content is out of the container. Those of us who make our living in publishing by working with metadata regard its sudden popularity with a mix of amusement (that something previously regarded as so dry is now sexy) and exasperation (what took you so long?). In practice, metadata has been important in bookselling for many, many years. But because a book is no longer a physical object, discoverability via metadata is only just now becoming a front-office problem.

While metadata has been important for a while and is now in a new spotlight, the term still means many different things to many different people. To address that, I think it's worth revisiting what the book industry means when it says "metadata."

A Little History

We've come to think of metadata as a collection of attributes—ISBN, title, author, copyright year, price, subject category, etc. This title-level metadata started with library catalogs. Bibliographies as published monographs were, essentially, big books of metadata. "Books in Print," those large volumes that tried to list every book that could possibly be obtained, were the same. As libraries developed computerized systems and moved away from print bibliographies, MARC[1] became the standard metadata format for catalog records.

The concept of digital metadata for the commercial book world originated in the 1970s and early 1980s, when bar coding on books was introduced and EDI transactions between retailers and publishers began. Trade publishing metadata was very different from that of the scholarly and library world. It was limited, in many cases consisting only of ISBN, availability, and price, because transactions were done around a physical object, no more metadata than that was really necessary.

But the efficiency of digital metadata could not be denied. Even prior to e-commerce, retailers like Barnes & Noble and Borders rose to prominence because they made great use of computer transactions and scanners, realizing tremendous speed and logistics savings through their computer systems. Metadata—as bare-bones as it was—was a crucial element in the success of the superstore. A database of inventory (consisting of ISBN, title, author, price, status, quantity on hand, quantity on order, and where in the store the book was supposed to be shelved) allowed store personnel to know stock levels and locations of books.

---

[1] http://www.loc.gov/marc/

Metadata changed again with the development of graphic user interfaces (GUI) and the rise of Amazon. Until the early 1990s, computer systems in both libraries and bookstores were large mainframes with dumb green-screen terminals. Software based on Microsoft Windows made it easier and more intuitive to display information, supporting a lot more innovation. Launched in 1995, Amazon took full advantage of these opportunities. In fact, when the meteor of Amazon's online bookstore hit the publishing industry, it was clear that the world of metadata was never going to be the same.

Through Amazon, consumers were looking at metadata for the first time. No longer relegated to wholesalers' warehouses and library reference desks, book metadata was front-and-center on the website of "The World's Largest Bookstore." Suddenly ISBN and price were not enough.

Why not? Because in order to figure out what they were buying, whether they were even interested in buying, or what books they had to look forward to being published, consumers needed to see the metadata, too.

Consumers wanted to know as much about each book as humanly possible. They wanted cover images, robust descriptions, and excerpts. They wanted to know when a book was published or going to be published—they wanted to place orders for books before they even rolled off the presses. In response, publishers frantically began supplying *their* warehouse data. This was frequently garbled, including truncated titles, TITLES IN ALL CAPS, misspelled author names, and nonstandard abbreviations. Amazon (and eventually its competitors) hired staffs of data editors whose job it was to clean up the information received from the ever-widening array of sources.

Libraries soon followed suit, demanding Amazon-like web-based catalog software from their software providers. Books-in-Print, formerly those large volumes of titles relegated to the reference desk, produced weekly CD-ROM updates that libraries (and retailers) could subscribe to. A host of services arose to fulfill the needs of both online retailers and libraries, providing additional content that could not be reliably provided by publishers.

These suppliers included Syndetics (ultimately bought by Books-in-

Print's parent company, Bowker), Muze (now Rovi), Firebrand's Eloquence, and NetRead's Jacketcaster. The value of metadata can be seen in the longevity of the firms that help publishers manage metadata. Even after a period of enormous upheavals in the book industry in the last 15 years, all of these companies are still very strongly in business.

This is because most book sales are now happening online. Consumers are using the web to browse and search for the titles they want. And if there is insufficient (or inaccurate) metadata for those books, consumers simply will not find them. The publisher (and retailer) with the best, most complete metadata offers the greatest chance for consumers to buy books. The publisher with poor metadata risks poor sales—because no one can find those books.

By 1998, it was clear that the metadata marketplace had reached Babel-like proportions. File formats proliferated, and both data receivers and data senders were overstretched in trying to produce and ingest feeds. The number of book-selling websites and libraries that required metadata had grown so large that the Association of American Publishers called a meeting in New York City, for the first time bringing all concerned parties to the table. It was time for a metadata standard.

Thus began ONIX: ONline Information eXchange.[2] A global standard overseen by EDItEUR, ONIX is perpetually in development. The US standards body is the BISAC (Book Industry Standards And Communications) Metadata Committee, which operates within the Book Industry Study Group (BISG). ONIX, an XML data transmission protocol, quickly became the lingua franca among retailers, distributors, and publishers. Even libraries developed an ONIX-to-MARC mapping, allowing them to use ONIX records to power their online public-access catalogs (OPACs) so that library patrons could view the same information that appeared on Amazon, BarnesandNoble.com, and similar websites.

As metadata standards, ONIX and MARC held steady for about 12 years. "Metadata" came to mean a basic set of tags, or fields, that described a physical book: ISBN, title, author, price, copyright year, synopsis, subject codes, cover image, availability, excerpts, reviews, and several other bits

---

[2] http://www.editeur.org/83/Overview/

of information that make it easier for customers and patrons to decide whether or not they want to acquire a book via online means.

As the share of online book sales and lending increased, this metadata grew in importance. No longer could publishers, booksellers, or libraries rely on in-store or in-library displays to lead readers to books. Gradually, the value of metadata as a tool to drive "discovery" began to take hold, as retailers, distributors, and lenders considered how readers might discover and locate the books they wanted to read when searching in an online environment.

To this point, the metadata fields in ONIX and MARC largely described a physical product: a hardcover or paperback version of a book. To some extent, they also described ephemeral aspects of that product—what the book is about, for example. But the metadata we had been using until very recently was, by and large, developed to describe what Brian O'Leary refers to[3] as "the container"—the physical manifestation of a work.

Out of the Container

But what happens when books are set free from their containers (as O'Leary describes in his "Context First"[4] presentation)? How do we describe those products (or services)? How do you ensure that readers can find content that—at least physically—defies description?

As the market migrates from print to digital, metadata becomes an even more critical issue. Without metadata, ebooks are invisible. Because they are not present in our physical world, there is absolutely no chance that readers will bump into them serendipitously the way readers bump into print books—typically, by seeing other people reading them or catching sight of them on a bookstore table. It is possible to receive a digital book as a gift, but the giver must still discover it.

Ebooks face a discoverability problem that print books never have: they are *only* discoverable online and by word of mouth. As far as the digital reader is concerned, without good metadata, the ebook doesn't exist.

---

[3] http://www.toccon.com/toc2011/public/schedule/detail/16323
[4] http://www.toccon.com/toc2011/public/schedule/detail/16323

EPUB 3 and Metadata

Printed objects don't support efforts to coherently cull metadata; that culling is a separate process. At some stage in the supply chain, a warehouse employee holds an actual printed book in her hands and enters all the relevant data she can glean from its cover, copyright page, and title page. She flips through the book to get a page count. She weighs and measures the book. An ONIX record (magically!) gets created and sent to trading partners. The print book is then shipped separately. These "book in hand" programs have provided publishers, distributors, and retailers with foundational book metadata for years.

Fortunately, ebooks offer a possibility that print books do not: the ability to extract metadata directly from the files themselves. With EPUB 3[5] in particular, it's possible for publishers to embed relevant metadata within the file, and for their trading partners to then extract this metadata and use it as they need to. The metadata travels *with* the product, rather than separately.

EPUB is an XML format, and it's useful to remember that (as with all things XML) extensibility offers great flexibility and control—and great responsibility. Because it's possible to enhance product metadata with tags that are not necessarily part of *any* standard, it's critical to use those nonstandard elements intelligently.

Who Is Your Audience?

When an object is no longer confined by its container—in this case, book covers—describing it is challenging. As content forms evolve, it is likely that we won't always be able to say that the thing we are talking about is, in fact, a "book." Perhaps it's a database, or an online resource. This harkens back to Books in Print, which went from book to CD-ROM to website-with-an-API.

At the 2011 BISG Making Information Pay Conference in New York, Madi Solomon of Pearson described[6] her efforts to create good metadata for Pearson's biology products. These products ranged from print books to

---

[5] http://idpf.org/epub/30/spec/epub30-publications.html
[6] http://slidesha.re/10HYUb

HMTL ebooks to EPUB ebooks to databases. At the same time, Solomon notes, "lots of metadata" is not the same as "good metadata."

So what do we mean when we say "good metadata"? As with most things in the digital age, that depends on who's asking.

Librarians rely on several metadata standards: the Dublin Core,[7] Library of Congress,[8] METS,[9] MARC,[10] and (to some degree) ONIX. All of these standards help librarians describe, locate, purchase, and recommend books (and ebooks).

Distributors, wholesalers, data aggregators (such as Bowker), and retailers rely on ONIX metadata, in large part. While certainly not perfect, ONIX has proven to be reliable and extensible, evolving to meet the challenges of e-commerce, of selling print books via digital means.

However, it's still early days for the ebook trade. Many ebook retailers (who are not traditional book companies) require publishers to submit (long, wide) spreadsheets of metadata. Some of these ebook retailers do not accept ONIX at all, requiring wholly different data sets.

Some of this makes sense. Certainly digital book retailers don't need to see the nonexistent weights and measures of ebooks. Nor do page counts make much sense. But they do need to understand the length of the ebook and what sorts of copy and print rights the publisher is granting on that material. While the newest version of ONIX offers expanded capabilities for describing ebooks, ebook retailers (BarnesandNoble.com and Kobo excepted) are not using it.

The point of metadata is not that it comes in any particular format. ONIX, MARC, and spreadsheets are all just the different containers (there's that word again) for information that trading partners need. The important thing for publishers is that while trading partners will probably take different types of containers, depending on their needs, what's IN those containers is going to determine whether or not the books get sold. Is the author name spelled right? Is the title accurate? Does the description of the book really describe the book (and not simply say it's the best resource out there)? Are the subject headings accurate? Is the price right?

---

[7] http://dublincore.org/
[8] http://www.loc.gov/standards/mets/
[9] http://www.loc.gov/standards/mets/
[10] http://www.loc.gov/marc/

How I Learned to Stop Worrying and Love Metadata

Of course, the ultimate audience for metadata, whether for print or digital books, is the consumer.

Selling digitally means, of course, that it is possible to appeal to many different kinds of consumers—there's no single "consumer" anymore. Different markets require different descriptors; many books are suitable for *several* specifically targeted markets, each with its own vernacular.

As is often said, this stage of metadata development is "in its early days." In practical terms, this means there is no universally accepted standard for consumer metadata for out-of-the-container content yet. There may never be a true standard.

This idea may seem distressing, but it reflects an aspect of the digital market that allows us to think multi-dimensionally.

Because it's possible to embed metadata in an ePUB file, many metadata schemas can be embedded at once. Provided the recipient of each ePUB file has the correct schema to interpret its appropriate metadata, a file can carry as much metadata as an industry can throw at it. Although some concerns have been expressed about the bandwidth needed for successfully uploading and downloading these rich files, schemas are text-based and unlikely to clog most pipelines.

This digital flexibility makes it possible for a single ePUB file to contain a MARC metadata set, an ONIX metadata set, *and* a proprietary, consumer-friendly taxonomy that only the publisher's website can render. Barnes & Noble can ignore the MARC and proprietary schemas; Library of Congress can ignore the proprietary schema, and the publisher's website can ignore the MARC schema.

Digitization allows for abundance; standards allow for filtering. Metadata is that filter, that lens.

When thinking about metadata, it's useful to remember the parable of the blind men and the elephant.[11] In this tale, several blind men are presented with an elephant. Each uses his hands to feel a different aspect of the animal: the trunk, an ear, a tusk, a foot, the tail. Each comes up with a different descriptor of the animal: "It's like a snake," "It's sharp and

---

[11] http://en.wikipedia.org/wiki/Blind_men_and_an_elephant

hard," "It's big and floppy," "It's sturdy and heavy," "It's like a rope." Each interpretation is correct, but limited.

Metadata is that descriptor. ONIX describes a book from one point of view, MARC from another, and consumers will describe a book from a completely different point of view ("That book with the blue cover that was on Oprah yesterday"). It's important to remember that no single metadata schema describes a book to the full satisfaction of everyone involved in its creation and consumption. That schema would be horribly bloated and ultimately quite fragile.

Over the next decade, this flexibility will frame the challenge publishers and their intermediaries will face. It's okay to have multiple metadata schemas—in fact, it's necessary. It's okay to have different audiences for metadata; not everybody needs to know the same thing about a book. Much as there's no one way to describe an elephant, there's no one way to describe a book. Developing the workflows that capture and maintain the range of descriptions that "describe a book" will be critical in a world in which "discovery" increasingly means "found it online."

Give the author feedback & add your comments about this chapter on the web: http://book.pressbooks.com/chapter/metadata-laura-dawson

5. Analyzing the Business Case for DRM (Kirk Biglione)

Kirk Biglione is a seasoned digital media professional specializing in web publishing systems, social and search strategies, and user experience. Kirk frequently speaks on topics related to digital media and is a cofounder of `Medialoper`. *You can find Kirk on Twitter at:* `@kirkbiglione`.

The publishing industry's rapid transition from physical to digital products has been accompanied by a host of hotly debated issues. From ebook pricing to author royalties to release windows, it seems that every aspect of the publishing business is being reconsidered and reinvented in the digital era.

No issue has been more contentious than the debate surrounding the use of Digital Rights Management (DRM)[1] technology. The discussion surrounding DRM has been dominated by emotional and hyperbolic rhetoric on both sides of the debate. On one hand, publishers insist they can't release ebooks without some form of copy protection. On the other

---

[1] Digital Rights Management is the name used for access control technology designed to restrict the use of digital content. While DRM has come to be known as a form of copy protection the technology can limit a broad range of uses beyond copying.

hand, consumers are said to hate any form of restriction on legitimately purchased media.

Meanwhile, a growing number[2] of mostly independent publishers are doing the unthinkable: releasing ebooks without any form of copy restriction. Are these publishers completely oblivious to the obvious problem of digital piracy? Or are they taking a calculated risk that will ultimately benefit their business?

Traditionally the issues of DRM and copy restriction have been framed as a moral debate pitting IP rightsholders against a legion of invisible pirates. Although the efficacy of DRM technology in thwarting piracy is also debated, the use of DRM is also a business decision — one that will have a substantial impact on how consumers acquire and read books in the digital era.

Given the rapid shift in book sales from print to digital formats, it's time to move beyond the moral debate and take a serious look at the business impact of DRM. What is the business case for DRM, or DRM-free for that matter? What, exactly, are the issues a publisher should consider when determining when and where to use DRM to restrict access to digital content?

This chapter seeks answers to these questions and provides guidance to publishers who wish to have a deeper understanding of DRM and its impact on the emerging marketplace for digital content.

The Promise of DRM

Before we can perform a business analysis of DRM, it helps to have a better understanding of what DRM is supposed to accomplish. What, exactly, does DRM promise publishers?

The promise: DRM protects a copyright holder's investment in content by controlling access to and usage of digital content. Content owners may impose any number of restrictions, including limits on copying, sharing, selecting text, copying text, use of content in text-to-speech applications, and more.

---

[2] http://bit.ly/MoT9R

Arguably, publishers' belief in this promise has paved the way for the creation of a healthy and growing market for ebooks. Without some form of content control, none of the so-called "Big Six" trade publishers would permit digital editions of their books to be sold, and the market for ebooks would be quite different from the one we have today.

A Couple of Caveats

To publishers accustomed to the physical limitations of the print world, DRM's promise must sound like a good deal. But the promise of DRM comes with a few important caveats.

1. **The Analog Hole.** The biggest security challenge for ebook publishers is the existence of print books. High-speed scanner prices are dropping rapidly and optical character recognition[3] (OCR) software is getting better and faster. It only takes one home-brew ebook to seed the pirate networks. As long as print editions exist, there will always be pirated digital editions. No amount of DRM will stop that, though I'm sure there are some who would try to convince publishers to brook the expense of printing books on security paper.[4]

2. **DRM is easily broken.** The other limitation that simply can't be ignored is that DRM is easily cracked. Tools for stripping all popular forms of DRM are widely available at no cost. While this sort of cracking may not be a mainstream activity, as with book scanning, it only takes a single cracked ebook file to seed the pirate networks.

The real-world implication of these caveats can be seen in the widespread availability of pirated digital media products. Books that have never been released in a digital format are widely available on pirate websites. Those rogue digital editions occupy server space with the latest bestseller—books that are sold exclusively in DRM-encrypted editions.

Publishers who hope to overcome the limitations of DRM face some stiff odds. Overcoming the analog hole will entail rewriting the laws of physics, while developing an unbreakable DRM system might prove to be just as challenging.

---

[3] http://en.wikipedia.org/wiki/Optical_character_recognition
[4] http://www.mcgpaper.com/whatissecpap1.html

The game industry has invested heavily in pursuit of the perfect DRM scheme, and yet piracy persists. In 2008, Electronic Arts released the widely anticipated game Spore with extremely restrictive DRM. The result? Spore went on to become the most pirated[5] game in history.

Any business analysis of DRM needs to take into consideration the fact that DRM fails to live up to its promise in some fairly substantial ways.

Calculating the Cost of DRM

One of the first questions publishers should ask when assessing the business case for DRM is, "How much will it cost?"

Unfortunately, there's no clear-cut answer to this question. The cost of DRM depends on a number of factors. These factors include the kind and complexity of DRM, the markets where digital books will be sold, the required level of interoperability, and the level of consumer support that will be provided.

Investing in DRM

Publishers who plan to sell DRM-restricted ebooks directly to consumers must acquire DRM server technology. In today's world, that means Adobe Content Server[6] (ACS). Of the three most widely used DRM systems for ebooks, Adobe's is the only one that is available for publishers to license.

A publisher can expect to pay Adobe an initial license fee of $6,500, plus an additional fee of $0.22 per ebook sold. Adobe also collects an annual maintenance fee of $1,500 for the use of ACS.

These numbers don't include hardware costs, network costs, or professional services. Custom support will add to the expense. The range of platforms, devices, and operating systems ensure that any use of DRM technologies will be accompanied by support issues.

At first glance, it would appear that the economics of DRM favors publishers with extensive resources. However, smaller publishers may apply DRM to their books by working with a distribution partner. Companies

---

[5] http://bit.ly/4i75Fb
[6] http://www.adobe.com/products/contentserver/

like Overdrive[7] offer DRM as part of a comprehensive digital distribution service. Overdrive will even set up a publisher-branded storefront and sell DRM-encrypted ebooks directly to consumers on the publisher's behalf.

The prospect of a publisher going through a distributor to sell ebooks directly from its own website (the so-called "white label" provider) flies in the face of a belief that digital distribution will help flatten the supply chain. In practice, DRM may help established and emerging intermediaries consolidate their market power.

It's important for publishers to understand what they get when they invest in a system like ACS. Adobe's DRM technology occupies a unique position in the marketplace. While it is licensed to run on far more devices than any other form of ebook DRM, ACS has failed to emerge as a de facto standard. That's because competing proprietary DRM technologies control a majority of the ebook marketplace.

Amazon's ebook marketshare has been estimated to be anywhere between 61%[8] and 80%.[9] Even at the low end of that range, Amazon's Kindle DRM is clearly the most widely used form of ebook DRM in the US market. And the only way to sell an ebook with Kindle DRM is to sell direct through Amazon.

The same is true for Apple. While Apple has adopted the industry standard EPUB format, the company also uses its own proprietary DRM for iBooks.

Meanwhile, DRM-free publishers can sell directly to consumers for use on any device or reading system—Kindle, iBooks, Nook, and future devices yet to be invented. For these publishers, DRM limitations and licensing fees are not a consideration.

The Cost of "Free" DRM

Compared to Adobe's ACS technology, Amazon and Apple's DRM might seem like a bargain. There are no licensing costs, no maintenance fees, and no professional service or consumer support overhead.

---

[7] http://www.overdrive.com/
[8] http://oreil.ly/eEwHzK
[9] http://reviews.cnet.com/8301-18438_7-20012381-82.html

This may be one of the reasons why we haven't heard much talk about the cost of DRM. To some publishers, DRM might appear to be free, at least when selling through Amazon or Apple.

Of course, this "free" DRM comes at a cost. In the case of Apple and Amazon, the cost is 30% of each sale, limited access to each marketplace, and no information about consumers who purchase books. Publishers who require DRM accept certain limitations as part of the cost of doing business in these markets.

It's not just publishers who are limited by proprietary DRM. Independent retailers are incapable of selling DRM-restricted ebooks to consumers who have adopted the most popular ereading platforms. While the independent bookstore has long been a fixture of a healthy publishing industry, one wonders what will become of indie booksellers as consumers move to digital reading on proprietary platforms.

DRM shapes the marketplace for digital content in a very real way.

DRM Risk Factors

Presumably, publishers who use DRM do so in an attempt to mitigate the risk of digital piracy. But, as we've seen in the previous sections, DRM comes with its own risks and complications. Publishers looking to make an informed decision about the use of DRM will need to determine if the technology prevents enough piracy to offset the risks associated with a marketplace controlled by a small number of very large retailers.

In order to conduct this sort of risk assessment, publishers will need to perform certain calculations related to both piracy and the effectiveness of DRM. For publishers who haven't done extensive research on the impact of piracy on sales, these calculations will be quite challenging. And yet it's hard to imagine publishers committing to a marketplace fragmented by competing technologies without performing some form of risk analysis.

It will be interesting to see the data publishers produce to back up their current positions. I encourage publishers doing this sort of research to share the results in a public forum where the entire industry may benefit.

For publishers who sell DRM-free ebooks, the risk analysis is much different. By avoiding DRM altogether, these publishers have mitigated the risks associated with the technology. The fact that the industry is seeing a growing number of publishers take this position would seem to indicate that it is a viable approach to doing business. We have yet to hear about a single DRM-free publisher being forced out of business due to losses incurred as a result of piracy.

DRM's Impact on Publicity and Marketing

DRM's potential impact on publicity and marketing may not be immediately apparent to publishers. However, over the past decade, there have been numerous examples of DRM-related incidents that have snowballed into publicity disasters. While most of these episodes have occurred outside of the publishing world, ebooks have not been immune, as the infamous Kindle 1984[10] incident will attest. In a similar way, the Sony Rootkit[11] debacle in 2005 showed the limitations inherent in proprietary platforms.

It doesn't matter that most of these failures occurred outside of the world of publishing. Publishers have no choice but to live with the baggage of DRM's checkered past. When selling DRM-restricted ebooks, the best a publisher can hope for is that consumers won't notice. It certainly isn't something that will be actively marketed as a "feature."

As a result of these highly publicized DRM failures, consumers are growing more sensitive to any form of content restriction. It's safe to say that many consumers view DRM with suspicion at best and and outright contempt at worst. DRM-free, on the other hand, is an offer that resonates with a growing number of consumers who have been burned by DRM in the past.

DRM's Value Proposition

If DRM presents publishers with a marketing challenge, perhaps it's time for publishers to reconsider DRM's value proposition.

While I've heard publishers ask how much DRM costs, I have yet to hear a single publisher ask how DRM can be used to provide more value to consumers. It should come as no surprise that consumers view DRM as

---

[10] http://nyti.ms/MFqT56
[11] http://bit.ly/hxEC2C

a barrier that limits the use of legitimately purchased media—and that's apparently the way most publishers view it as well.

That's not to say that DRM can't create value for consumers. There are at least three ways that consumers might actually benefit from DRM:

1. **Access to more content.** This is a hidden value proposition that most consumers aren't aware of. For publishers who insist on copy restriction, their books simply would not be available in a digital format if it weren't for DRM. Furthermore, greater access is afforded by the availability of DRM-restricted ebooks through libraries.

2. **Lower prices.** Because DRM restricts the use of content, books sold with DRM constraints typically cannot be lent, copied, or shared with others. Behavioral data on what people will pay for DRM-limited media demonstrates that these books are bought at lower prices. I can think of no example where DRM would make a book *more* valuable. While the move to digital in general has meant lower prices for consumers, the use of DRM could lead to new services that offer ebooks at even lower prices. For example, DRM might be used to effectively offer limited-term access to ebooks—think rental versus purchase.

3. **New uses.** Publishers might use DRM as a tool for enabling and evaluating new content uses. These could include book rental, as suggested previously. With just a bit of imagination, it's possible to envision a wide range of new business models that use DRM as a control mechanism to facilitate short-term usage, sharing, and a range of social features. Unfortunately, in practice, it seems that DRM is mostly used to replicate and extend old business models.

Some examples of media services that have succeeded by providing consumers with an overwhelming value proposition while simultaneously restricting access via DRM:

- **Netflix**[12] provides consumers with instant streaming access to thousands of movies and television shows. Delivery is so seamless that most consumers aren't aware that the video stream they're viewing is wrapped in DRM.

---

[12] http://www.netflix.com

- **Pandora**[13] allows consumers to create custom music channels based on their favorite artists and songs. The result is a personalized radio station where consumers can hear old favorites mixed with new discoveries. As with Netflix, Pandora's DRM is entirely transparent to the consumer.
- **Steam**[14] is a digital marketplace for games as well as a gamer community. The success of Steam is remarkable considering some of the most avid anti-DRM zealots are hardcore gamers. Yet Steam wins over even the harshest critics by offering features like cross-platform access and the ability to resume saved games from any computer.

These examples succeed because they are low impact and provide high value to consumers. Acquisition of content is far easier than the alternative of acquiring pirated media, which is widely available at no cost.

Unfortunately, we have yet to see a significant movement toward similar models in the publishing world. Perhaps the closest any major publisher has come to offering a book-rental service is O'Reilly's Safari Bookshelf. It's worth noting that Safari offers limited access without using DRM. So, even where DRM may enable a new business model, it isn't necessarily the only way to get the job done.

DRM's Impact on Innovation

While DRM may be used to enable new business models, it is also commonly used to restrict access to content in ways that limit innovation.

Over the past several years, I've heard complaints from numerous innovative startups that publishers demand DRM even when alternate forms of access control are in place. When publishers do allow books to be sold without traditional DRM, they impose arbitrary content restrictions that limit functionality and create unnecessary barriers to delivering an acceptable user experience.

Reading-system developers wishing to offer customers web access to restricted content must go to great lengths to disable the user's ability to select text in the browser. While the intention is to limit copying, the

---

[13] http://www.pandora.com
[14] http://store.steampowered.com/

unintended consequence is that web-based reading systems are frequently unable to provide common services like word lookup and annotation.

Ironically, these limitations make pirated editions seem more valuable by comparison. Unnecessary content restrictions effectively limit the development of new products and services at a time when the publishing industry should be embracing innovative new uses. From a business perspective, publishers need to take a hard look at the opportunity cost imposed by DRM.

Alternatives to Traditional DRM

Given DRM's limited ability to prevent unauthorized use and its questionable impact on the marketplace, it might be worthwhile to consider alternative approaches to rights management.

Before evaluating new forms of content control, publishers will need to determine what they are hoping to accomplish by requiring DRM on ebooks. How does DRM fit into the big picture of developing new business models and providing value to consumers as they shift their reading preference from print to digital?

If the only goal is to restrict access to digital content, then publishers are focusing too narrowly on a single problem. Instead, publishers should consider a broad range of issues that are equally important. Among other things, these goals might include:

- Improving the discovery and acquisition process.
- Providing a superior consumer experience that is equally accessible across a broad range of retail outlets.
- Allowing access to content while supporting the development of innovative reading systems.

These are goals that will ultimately enable a healthy marketplace for digital content, while supporting the development of new business models that provide value to consumers and new revenue streams to authors and publishers.

With these goals in mind, publishers will be better prepared to evaluate alternative solutions to the challenge of access control. Currently available alternatives include:

- **Simple user authentication.** This most basic form of access control is used widely online to limit access to websites offering premium content and services. Access can be provided on either a time-limited basis or as a purchase for perpetual use, with content being priced accordingly. This method of access control is well suited to web-based reading systems.
- **Watermarking, also known as Social DRM.** While not technically an access control technology, watermarking attempts to minimize the sharing of digital content by embedding information about the purchaser in the media file. Each file is uniquely created for a specific consumer. The benefit of this approach is that the control technology does not interfere with interoperability, and the retail environment is not fragmented by proprietary DRM schemes.

While neither of these alternatives is perfect, they do offer the benefit of having a lower impact on consumers and the marketplace while being at least as effective as traditional DRM.

There's some indication that watermarking is emerging as a viable alternative to more restrictive technical control measures. Author J.K. Rowling will reportedly use watermarking in place of traditional DRM when she launches the Harry Potter ebook series on her Pottermore website. Watermarking allows Rowling to sell direct to her readers while supporting all of the major reading platforms.

Summary: Making Informed Decisions About DRM

The publishing industry has entered a time of unprecedented change. Assumptions that have held true in the past may no longer be relevant. As a result, it's time for publishers to reconsider default positions and think seriously about DRM's role in the publishing universe.

Because there are many different kinds of publishers, each one will have to evaluate the need for DRM in light of its own business as well as the needs of its customers. As publishers develop new products and services, they will need to take a critical look at when and how DRM is used.

At minimum, each publisher should answer the following essential questions:

- Does DRM enable new business models and uses?
- Are these new business models and uses conceivable without DRM?
- What impact does DRM have on pricing and consumer perception of value? Does DRM provide enough value to consumers to overcome associated limitations, or does it limit content in a way that makes pirated works seem more valuable?
- What barriers does DRM create to an open marketplace? How will these barriers impact traditional trading partners, including independent booksellers?
- What are the quantified risks associated with selling unrestricted content? How does this quantified risk compare against the costs and limitations associated with DRM?

Publishers who take the time to answer these questions will be better positioned to make informed decisions about DRM. That can only lead to better products, a healthy digital marketplace, and happy customers. While there is no precise formula for success in the digital era, that's a pretty good start.

Give the author feedback & add your comments about this chapter on the web: http://book.pressbooks.com/chapter/drm-kirk-biglione

6. Tools of the Digital Workflow (Brian O'Leary)

Brian O'Leary is a publishing consultant and principal of Magellan Media Partners, an Adjunct Professor of Publishing at NYU, and has had held senior positions in the publishing industry, including Production Manager at Time Inc. and Associate Publisher at Hammond Inc. You can find Brian on Twitter at: @brianoleary.

The nature, history, and business goals of publishers vary widely, making it impossible to identify a single set of tools as "preferred." Even the most limited decisions (buy this software, use these vendors) depend on a publisher's existing information technology, its appetite for change, corporate approaches to purchasing, and longer-term goals with respect to output and scalability.

Still, some decision points are common to all publishers. All will need to specify one or more word-processing software packages that editors and potentially authors will be expected to use. Most, if not all, will specify a software package to handle design, although increased use of style sheets could shift certain types of publishers away from the use of intermediate design steps that involve third-party software. That said, a given publisher may not need to use all the tools that are available, just the ones that make sense in helping to manage its authoring, repository, and distribution operations.

As content migrates to a much more robust digital environment, publishers will also need to make decisions about related services that may be licensed (title management software, production management software) or outsourced completely (content aggregation and search optimization). In some cases, like the development of a digital asset management system or sourcing digital asset distribution services, publishers can make a scale-dependent choice about whether to build it or buy the service.

Digital Workflow Tools

Broadly defined, there are 12 different types of digital workflow tools that will be commonly employed in the publishing value chain:

1. **Title management**: Typically, a centralized database that holds and manages book-specific information. The data set can include information relevant to sales, distribution, rights, and royalties, among other areas. Title management tools may be bought outright or licensed.

2. **Contracts, rights, and royalties**: Software and related systems that help publishers manage the creation of contracts, the sale of rights, and the payment of royalties.

3. **Content conversion**: Services or technologies used to convert common document formats (e.g., Microsoft Office, PDF, and HTML) into more agile formats, including EPUB and XML. Services can also include the conversion of physical materials (books, film) into more agile formats.

4. **XML tools**: Software used to create, edit, adapt, and render XML files. These tools are most often used internally.

5. **Production management**: Software and related systems that provide oversight and help manage editorial development and pre-press and production processes.

6. **Workflow management**: Software and systems used to manage tasks that can include automatic routing, partially automated processing, and integration among different functional software applications and hardware systems.

7. **Digital asset management (DAM)**: Systems and software that help publishers ingest, annotate, catalog, store, and retrieve digital assets, such as digital photographs, animations, videos, and music.

8. **Content management**: Tools used to create, edit, manage, and publish content in a consistently organized fashion. Content management software may also be used to store, control, and version publishing documents, whether works in progress or final files. The content managed may include web content.

9. **Archiving content**: Offline storage and backup systems and software.

10. **Digital asset distribution (DAD)**: Managing publishers' digital content, metadata, and promotional materials. Some DADs also provide content syndication to distribution and trading partners.

11. **Content aggregation**: Portals that provide users with a single point of access to a variety of content aggregated from within an enterprise, as well as from business or trading partners and the Web.

12. **Search**: Tools that help publishers improve the visibility and searchability of their content.

Components of a Digital Publishing Workflow

Much as different publishers will use digital tools in different ways, the various components of the publishing value chain also vary in their need for and use of digital tools.

Although organizational structures in publishing overlap with the core components of the publishing value chain, we focus here on a generalized set of definitions for these several activities. In particular, we identify six core functions:

- Content acquisition
- Contracts and agreements

- Editorial development
- Production editorial
- Operations
- Marketing, promotion, sales, and service

The activities, opportunities, challenges, and tools required for each of these six functions are addressed in the sections that follow.

Content Acquisition

Although the precise steps vary by type of publisher, most begin by soliciting, developing, reviewing, and assessing proposals. This process culminates in decisions about what to publish as well as the formats in which a particular work will be distributed.

Digital workflows offer publishers new ways to think about product planning. Although the practice is still rare, acquisition can signal the start of a period in which works can be discovered. Tagging and partial or selective release of works in progress is a practical option in digital-first workflows.

This ultimately means that event-driven publishing may migrate to a more continuous model. Seasonal releases may give way to more thematic or market-driven thinking about what products to release, and when. The key to obtaining these benefits starts with the introduction and use of XML tools, the software used to create, edit, adapt, and render XML files.

Over the last eight years, word-processing software packages and design software (most notably, Adobe's Creative Suite) have become increasingly XML-savvy. At the same time, open-source software has grown more sophisticated and accessible to authors and editors, although its effective use continues to require a working understanding of XML structure.

As software packages like Microsoft Word and Adobe InDesign have become XML-compliant, they have added features that export XML files relatively easily. However, the steps users take to structure Word and InDesign documents are not as tightly controlled, as is the case with native XML editors. As a result, publishers have found that obtaining useful XML from these commercial packages is not that easy in practice.

Other options include native XML formats (DocBook, OpenOffice.org XML, and TEI) as well as applications that support many aspects of XML (Adobe's InDesign CS and Microsoft's current versions of Office are examples). Users familiar with Word or other desktop word-processing packages sometimes struggle to adapt to DocBook's or OpenOffice.org's requirements for structure before content.

Supporters claim that the learning curve is not steep and that the downstream flexibility inherent in "tag first" is worth the investment. Because the software is available freely, it is an attractive option to test in smaller-scale and prototyping efforts.

Although the Adobe and Microsoft products can be used without implementing XML, they provide a familiar software alternative that can help publishers make a transition to XML workflows. To obtain XML from Adobe InDesign, users apply tags to parts of a document and export the document as an XML file. If properly structured, the XML can then be used to repurpose the content elsewhere.

Before a document is exported as XML, it is also possible to examine and edit the XML structure within InDesign, add attributes to elements, or even reverse the approach and map paragraph styles to tags. It is this flexibility that requires incremental control within an XML workflow, as users can approach the creation of a tagged document in a variety of ways that are visually acceptable but not XML-compliant.

Microsoft's commercial product, Office Open, is an XML-compliant file format for representing spreadsheets, charts, presentations, and word-processing documents. An Office Open document file contains mainly XML-based files compressed within a zip package. Starting with Microsoft Office 2007, the Office Open XML file formats have become the default file format of Microsoft Office, which includes the widely used Microsoft Word. While less costly and in some cases free options exist, Word's ubiquity makes it an appealing option for publishers looking to convert to XML workflows.

Publishers looking to use XML tools face some challenges. Obtaining benefits in tagging early requires them to develop metadata structures that make sense for their markets and content. These structures also require publishers to define the tag set and apply it consistently.

Decisions also need to be made about how to work with authors and freelancers without XML access. Some publishers have created an "ingestion" step that standardizes manuscripts received from outside a publishing house, while others have progressively extended their network of external resources skilled in the use of various XML tools.

Contracts and Agreements

Although the nature of contractual agreements is as broad as publishing itself, all publishers make deals with authors that establish rights, payments, and royalties. These agreements have only grown in importance (and in some cases, complexity) as demand for digital products and uses has grown.

Thinking about contracts and agreements as an opportunity to broaden the use of content downstream can promote cross-departmental interactions, reducing silos and improving the way that rights in particular are handled. New content forms will likely force publishers to streamline rights and permissions handling, moving it out of the back office and linking it to efforts to market and sell content.

Ultimately, this will lead publishers to integrate royalty tracking in ways that take new output options (print on demand, recombinant content) into consideration. The complexity of content marketing and sales will only increase over time, and the tools used to manage it will need to be both flexible and made available across a set of publishing functions.

Although the primary tools are the systems used to create, track, and report on contracts, rights, and royalties, this function will need to rely on digital asset management systems as well. While contractual data is a special form of metadata, it remains metadata, best linked to and available with the content it describes.

Publishers working to prepare for this more robust use of content will need to start by reevaluating existing processes. Publishers will need to create and maintain downstream controls that support credible decisions about rights without reverting to a central function or authority.

To the extent that adequate open standards exist, publishers can borrow from and organize around them, but an industry-wide agreement on rights standards is sorely needed. Early attempts to develop such a standard are under way, but the need is immediate and growing.

Even as the challenges of tracking and linking rights data to new content are solved, publishers will still face specific decisions about retrofitting past content, whether digital or analog, to the new models. Contract complexity, already evident in the literally millions of agreements now in place, may need to be revisited to make it possible to support a wider use of content.

Editorial Development

The editorial development function engages publishing staff to work with authors to write and deliver a working manuscript. This effort can include structuring content for use and reuse, but it always results in a working text document.

The growth of digital is opening up new possibilities for content development. Readers have expressed interest in options that include expanded editions as well as content that can be "chunked," or bought and consumed as components. As noted in the earlier section on content acquisition, customers may pay for a preview of content before it is finished.

Digital workflows support a variety of downstream benefits. Recombinant content can be identified and more easily supported from the outset. During and after the editorial development process, content can be more robustly searched, promoting consistency and integrity and improving discovery.

In addition to the XML tools described earlier, the editorial development function will need to rely on title management solutions as well as those systems dedicated to workflow management, digital asset management, and content management. In a digital environment, the need for greater sophistication in planning and managing content will put pressure on the classic editorial function, in which the manuscript alone was the primary output.

This may be the primary challenge publishers face in migrating editors from traditional roles to ones that emulate product managers. Although structural changes are required to implement agile workflows and the role of XML tools is evolving, the digital-workflow editor will need to manage everything from structural tagging through to the iterative, collaborative evolution of niche taxonomies. It's a role that will demand both training and flexibility.

Production Editorial

Production editorial staff works with internal staff and subcontractors to manage the assembly of book components. As content is increasingly fragmented and potentially sold in chunks, this work grows in both complexity and importance.

This function will continue to evolve its ability to manage versions and to more effectively maintain multiple versions. "Write-once" digital workflows, properly designed, are likely to result in fewer errors, with content that is easier to update or (when needed) correct.

Effective design and maintenance of production editorial workflows will enable smaller-scale distribution and facilitate repurposing. For many publishers, these options can become a significant source of downstream revenue, but most production editorial work today is dedicated toward optimizing the creation of a single manuscript in a single package.

As the role evolves, the critical digital workflow tools will include those employed in editorial development (title management, XML tools, workflow management, digital asset management, and content management) as well as production management, the software, and related systems that provide oversight and help manage editorial development and pre-press and production processes.

This function also faces challenges adapting to digital workflows. Moving from "write once, read once" to "write once, read many" is a big bite to for publishers to take, and the biggest leap occurs in this functional area. Existing XML tools, while promising, come with limitations as well. For some publishers, the ability of agile workflow tools to support more complex layouts remains.

Operations

If production editorial functions maintain content in ways that support downstream use and reuse, operations functions create and distribute that content in both print and other formats. For physical products, which will remain, operations staff also assumes responsibility for warehouse and fulfillment of those products.

There are a number of ways in which digital workflows provide operations functions with an opportunity to improve. Lead times to publication can be shortened, and with practice, the "print-to-web" pathway can be improved.

Building on work that started in editorial development and production editorial, operations can ultimately produce multiple digital versions from a single source (reducing reformatting expense). This benefit is realized only when traditional barriers (silos) are eliminated and content products and uses are planned across functions.

Other benefits can include lower vendor rates, which are the result of more standard workflows and greater control over formats. The risk associated with unsupported, proprietary formats is more significant than most publishers realize, and it is growing as the number of opportunities for reuse grows. Publishers using standard, open, documented file formats will be able to read (and understand) content files in the future.

In addition to some of the tools used in editorial functions (production management, workflow management, digital asset management, and content management), operations also relies on tools that support content conversion, archiving content, and content aggregation. In some cases, the tools are delivered as outsourced services, although that is largely a function of managing backlists.

Preparing for the next era of content creation and use will force publishers to confront legacy challenges. Cost-effectively retrieving data from proprietary platforms that can include InDesign and Quark is a problem that has not (and may not) be solved. This is also an area in which publishers' cost-benefit mindset has led them to favor freelance efforts. To the extent that this approach makes content less agile, outsourced work could come with hidden costs.

Marketing, Promotion, Sales, and Service

Publishers, long in the business of linking content to markets, find themselves facing an opportunity of greater breadth and depth than ever before. It's no longer a market in which publishers can promote and sell what they have produced (though they certainly can do that); it's also a market in which readers can find publishers and help them define new and different products and services.

These new offerings will demand and build upon richer linking that supports "many-to-many" marketing. Search is changing how readers discover and buy content, increasing the number of ways that publishers can build awareness. The marketing is also, increasingly, two-way, providing publishers with new ways to understand and extend the uses of the content they have created.

In addition to the classic marketing and sales tools, publishers with digital workflows can capitalize on the power of search (tools that help publishers improve the visibility and searchability of their content) as well as content aggregation (providing users with a single point of access to a variety of content aggregated from within an enterprise, as well as from business or trading partners and the Web).

As was the case in production editorial, the breadth and complexity of products challenges publishers that have optimized their marketing and sales efforts around a set of physical products. Multiple distribution channels demand simultaneous support at a time when marketing budgets are constrained and the efficiency of some traditional efforts is on the wane.

We're entering a period in which publishers need to shift how marketing, promotion, and sales work while also migrating to a new and potentially radically different product mix. This has been likened to changing the tires on a car traveling at 60 miles an hour; perhaps a bit dire, but at least directionally honest. The value of a vision of the future, even an evolving one, has seldom been higher.

Working with Vendors

Publishers approaching agile workflows for the first time may be able to obtain effective transition support and best practices from firms working in this space. Enterprise resource planning (ERP) vendors, for example, can help answer initial questions about the type and level of metadata structures that make sense for a given publisher to populate. Defining the tag set and a transition plan can be aided by ERP vendors, or those familiar with XML tools.

Reevaluating the processes used for contracts and agreements can involve ERP suppliers or those involved with title management. At this stage, some publishers also consider what (if any) existing content needs to be migrated to digital formats, giving conversion services an opportunity to weigh in with a specific, stylesheet-driven perspective.

Suppliers familiar with workflow tools can also advise publishers on the structural changes required to implement those tools effectively. In addition, they can provide a perspective on the value of open-source and commercial software options. Because managing the iterative, collaborative evolution of taxonomies is one of the challenges publishers typically face in editorial development, suppliers who have worked in this space with other publishers can offer both best practice as well as transition support to manage the workload.

Vendors familiar with digital asset management systems (DAMs) and archival systems can be useful when integrating XML, new workflow tools, and existing or planned content management systems. In some cases, ERP vendors working in this space can advise on production management systems or modules. In production editorial, the expertise of some conversion services becomes useful in understanding options to use stylesheets to manage content presentation without going to an intermediate design step (such as InDesign).

Finally, efforts to render and repurpose content can be aided by a digital asset distributor (DAD). While most publishers can benefit from a well-planned partnership with a DAD, there are a number of potentially significant conversion and content storage requirements that may be appropriate to outsource. Content conversion, for example, can be a significant challenge for medium- and smaller-sized publishers; establishing a conversion relationship with an accomplished DAD can help publishers remain focused on the value-added components of agile workflows.

————————————

Give the author feedback & add your comments about this chapter on the web: http://book.pressbooks.com/chapter/digital-workflow -brian-oleary

7. Designing Books in the Digital Age (Craig Mod)

Craig Mod is a writer, (book) designer, publisher, and developer (in whatever order makes sense for that day). Previously, he worked with Flipboard to make real many of the things he thinks and writes about here. You can find Craig on Twitter at: @craigmod.

[Editor's note: This chapter combines two essays that appeared previously, in a slightly different form, at craigmod.com.]

I. Books in the Age of the iPad

1. Defined by Content

For too long, the act of printing something in and of itself has been placed on too high a pedestal. The true value of an object lies in what it says, not its mere existence. And in the case of a book, that value is intrinsically connected to content.

Let's divide content into two broad groups:

- Content without well-defined form (**Formless Content,** Fig. 7.1)
- Content with well-defined form (**Definite Content,** Fig. 7.2)

Formless Content can be divorced from layout, reflowed into different formats, and not lose any intrinsic meaning. Most novels and works of nonfiction are Formless.

When Danielle Steele sits at her computer, she doesn't think much about how the text will look when printed. She thinks about the story as a waterfall of text, as something that can be poured into any container. (Actually, she probably just thinks awkward and sexy things, but awkward and sexy things without regard for final form.)

Content with form—Definite Content—is almost totally the opposite of Formless Content. Most texts composed with images, charts, graphs, or poetry fall under this umbrella. It may be reflowable, but depending on how it is reflowed, inherent meaning and quality of the text may shift.

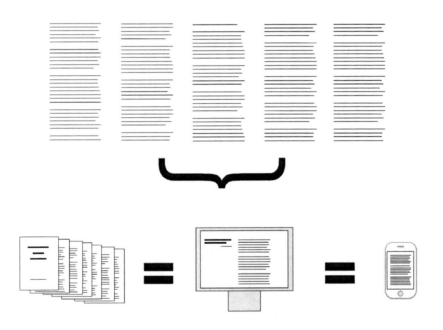

Figure 7.1. Formless Content—Retains meaning in any container

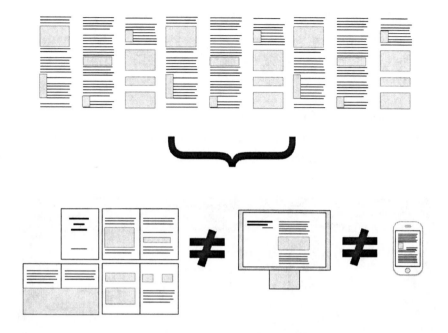

Figure 7.2. Definite Content—Shifts with the container

You can be sure that author Mark Z. Danielewski is well aware of the final form of his next novel. His content is so Definite it is actually impossible to digitize and retain all of the original meaning. *Only Revolutions*, a book loathed by many, forces readers to flip between the stories of two characters. The start of each story is printed at opposite ends of the book.

Working in concert with the author, a designer may imbue Formless Content with additional meaning in layout. The final combination of design and text becomes Definite Content.

Edward Tufte provides an extreme and ubiquitous contemporary example of Definite Content. Love him or hate him, you have to admit that Tufte is a rare combination of author and designer, completely obsessed with final form, meaning, and perfection in layout (see Fig. 7.3).

In the context of the book as an object, the **key difference** between Formless and Definite Content is the interaction between the content and the page. Formless Content doesn't see the page or its boundaries; Definite

Content is not only aware of the page, but embraces it. It edits, shifts, and resizes itself to fit the page. In a sense, Definite Content approaches the page as a canvas—something with dimensions and limitations—and leverages these attributes to both elevate the object and the content to a more complete whole.

Put very simply, Formless Content is unaware of the container. Definite Content embraces the container as a canvas. Formless content is usually only text. Definite content usually has some visual elements along with text.

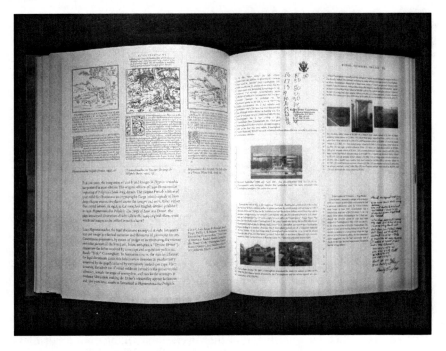

Figure 7.3. Tufte—Embracing his canvas

Much of what we consume happens to be Formless. The bulk of printed matter—novels and nonfiction—is Formless.

In the last two years, devices excelling at displaying Formless Content have multiplied, the Amazon Kindle being the most obvious. Less obvious are devices like the iPhone, whose extremely high-resolution screen, despite being small, makes longer texts much more comfortable to read than traditional digital displays.

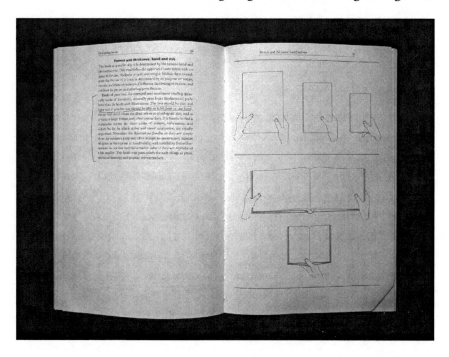

Figure 7.4. Designing Books—Awareness of physicality

These devices make it easier and more comfortable than ever to consume Formless Content in a digital format.

Is it as *comfortable* as reading a printed book?

Maybe not. But we're getting closer.

When people lament the loss of the printed book, they are usually talking about comfort. *My eyes tire more easily,* they say. *The batteries run out, the screen is tough to read in sunlight. It doesn't like bathtubs.*

These aren't complaints about the text losing meaning. Books don't become harder to understand or confusing just because they are digital. The complaints are generally directed at the quality of the reading experience.

The convenience of digital text—on demand, lightweight (in file size and physicality), searchable—already trumps that of traditional printed matter in many ways. Because technology is closing the gap (through advancements in screens and batteries) and beginning to offer additional features (note-taking, bookmarking, searching), digital reading will inevitably surpass the comfort level of reading on paper.

The formula used to be simple: Stop printing Formless Content; only print well-considered Definite Content. The iPad changes this.

2. The Universal Container

We love our printed books—we physically cradle them close to our heart. As digital reading has migrated away from computer screens, the experience of reading on a Kindle, iPhone, or iPad has begun to mimic this familiar maternal embrace. The text is closer to us, the orientation more comfortable. The seemingly insignificant fact that we touch the text actually plays a very key role in furthering the intimacy of the experience.

The Kindle and iPhone are both lovely, but they handle only text well. These devices are not nearly as effective for more complex layouts.

The iPad changes the experience formula (see Fig. 7.5). It brings the excellent text readability of the iPhone and the Kindle to a larger canvas. It combines the intimacy and comfort of reading on those devices with a canvas *both* large enough and versatile enough to allow for well-considered layouts.

With the iPad, a 1:1 digital adaptation of Definite Content books is now possible (see Fig. 7.6). However, I don't think this is a solution we should blindly embrace. Definite Content in printed books is laid out specifically for that canvas, that page size. While the iPad may be similar in physical scope to those books, duplicating layouts would be a disservice to the new canvas and modes of interaction introduced by the iPad.

Take something as fundamental as pages, for example. The metaphor of flipping pages already feels boring and forced on the iPhone and on the iPad. The flow of content no longer has to be chunked into "page"-sized bites. One simplistic reimagining of book layout would be to place chapters on the horizontal plane, with content on a fluid vertical plane (see Fig. 7.7).

In printed books, the two-page spread was our canvas. It's easy to think similarly about the iPad. Let's not. The canvas of the iPad must be considered in a way that acknowledges the physical boundaries of the device, while also embracing the effective limitlessness of space just beyond those edges.

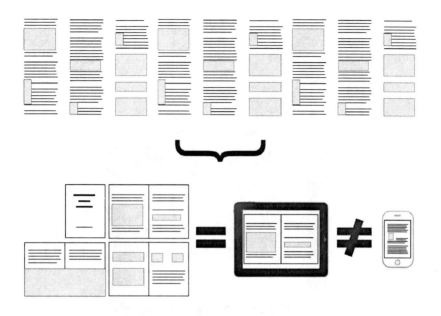

Figure 7.5. The New Equation—Retaining structural meaning in digital form

We're going to see new forms of storytelling emerge from this canvas. This is an opportunity to redefine modes of conversation between reader and content. And that's one hell of an opportunity if making content is your thing.

So, are printed books dead? Not quite.

The rules for digital devices that provide a platform for Definite Content are still ambiguous. We have not yet had enough time with these devices to confidently define them. I have, however, spent six years thinking about materials, form, physicality, content and—to the best of my humble abilities—producing printed books.

So, for now, here's my take on the print side of things moving forward.

Ask yourself, "Is your work disposable?" For me, in asking myself this, I only see one obvious ruleset:

- Formless Content goes digital.
- Definite Content gets divided between the iPad and printing

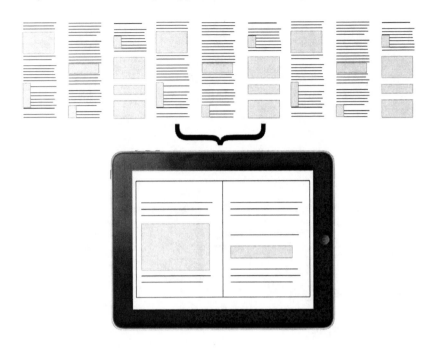

Figure 7.6. Definite Content 1:1 with iPAD—A first

Of the books we do print—the books we make—they **need rigor**. They need to be books where the object is embraced as a canvas by designer, publisher, and writer. This is the only way these books as physical objects will carry any meaning moving forward.

I propose the following to be considered whenever we think of printing a book:

- The Books We Make **embrace their physicality**, working in concert with the content to illuminate the narrative.
- The Books We Make are **confident in form and usage of material**.
- The Books We Make **exploit the advantages of print**.
- The Books We Make are **built to last** (see Fig. 9a and Fig. 9b).

The result of this is:

- The Books We Make will feel whole and solid in the hands.
- The Books We Make will smell like now-forgotten, far-away libraries.

Figure 7.7. Vertical Chapters—Breaking the habit

- The Books We Make will be something of which even our children—who have fully embraced all things digital—will understand the worth.
- The Books We Make will always remind people that the printed book can be a sculpture for thoughts and ideas.

Anything less than this will be stepped over and promptly forgotten in the digital march forward.

Goodbye disposable books.

Hello new canvasses.

II. Post-Artifact Books and Publishing

1. The book, a system

Once we start thinking of books—both Formless Content and Definite Content—in the context of new digital reading tools, it becomes clear that

Figure 7.8. The Infinite Content Plane

we need to start thinking differently about what books *are* and how they are produced. We need to reconsider not just the mechanisms of production—replacing one tool or system with another, as you might shift from a pencil to a ball-point pen. Instead, we need to reconsider the whole approach to the process of making a book into the thing it is: the creation, the consumption, and everything that happens around and in between.

Books are not really fixed objects. Books are systems.

Books emerge from systems. Book themselves are systems, the best of which are as complex as is necessary, and not a bit more. And once complete, new systems develop around their content.

To understand where books and publishing are moving, it is critical to understand the following three systems that contribute to the making of a book:

- the **pre-artifact** system
- the system of the **artifact**

Figure 7.9. Not Disposable—From 1871

- the **post-artifact** system

In the **pre-artifact** system, the book or story or article is conceived and made. It is a system full of (and fueled by) whiskey, self-doubt, confusion, debauchery, and a general sense of hopelessness. Classically, it is a system of isolation, involving very few people. The key individuals within the classic manifestation of this system are the author and the editor. A publisher, perhaps. A muse. But generally, not the reader. The end product of this system is what we usually define as "the book"—the Idea made tangible.

The **artifact**—*the book*—too, is a system. Classically, it is an island unto itself, immutable, a system self-contained. The artifact requires great efforts to extend beyond the binding. When finished, it becomes a souvenir of a private journey.

Finally, the **post-artifact** system. This is the space in which we engage with the artifact. Again, classically this is a relatively static space.

Figure 7.10. Not Disposable—From 1871

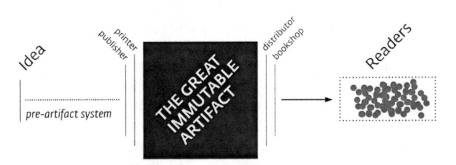

Figure 7.11. Classic Publishing—Two+ years between Idea and Reader. A lonely, isolated pre-artifact system. An immutable non-networked artifact. A near non-existant post-artifact system.

Isolated. Friends can gather to discuss the artifact. Localized classes can be constructed in universities around the artifact. But, generally, there is an overwhelming sense of disconnection from the other systems.

Digital changes this.

Digital removes the book from the **pre-**, **artifact**, and **post-** systems. Most fundamentally, digital removes isolation. The corollaries: an increase in connectivity, a mutability of artifact, continuous engagement with readers, and most excitingly, a potentially public record of change, comment, discussion—*digital marginalia*—layered atop the artifact, adding to the artifact, and redefining "complete."

With the connection of these systems, our classic definition of a literary artifact no longer applies. And our common understanding of publishing systems is irrevocably disrupted.

2. Pre-artifact systems

With the emergence and growing adoption of the Kindle and the iPad, publishers, writers, readers, and software-makers have concerned themselves with shoehorning the old-media image of a book into new media. Everyone asks, "How do we change books to read them digitally?" But the more interesting question is, "How does digital change books?" And, similarly, "How does digital change the authorship process?"

This authorial shift is critical to the understanding of the new **pre-artifact** system.

With digital impermanence (a new kind of ephemerality) comes two concepts key to the future of storytelling and books:

1. We can continuously develop a text in real time, erasing the preciousness imbued by printing. And because of this …
2. Time itself becomes an active ingredient in authorship (in contrast to authorship happening in a seemingly timeless place, a finished product suddenly emerging).

Wikipedia is a fully realized example of how digital drastically affects authorship. By creating a system that allows collective edits in real time, Wikipedia has embedded iterative writing into its foundation. Nothing on

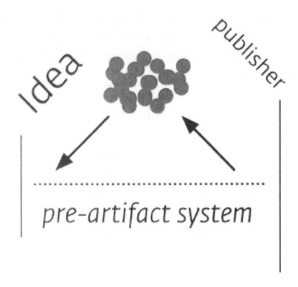

Figure 7.12. The injection of readers early into the authorial process.

that site is precious. No letter, word, sentence, or article is immune to reconsideration. And yet, by tracking changes on a micro scale, they have built trust around a continuously evolving system.

Consider the physical analog to Wikipedia: the encyclopedia set. In the early naughts, it would have been difficult to imagine that a website written and edited by hundreds of thousands of people, constantly mutating, could have possibly formed the replacement for that dusty set of leather bound books on your bookshelf. And yet, not only has Wikipedia replaced the physical encyclopedia for many of us, it has surpassed it in usefulness, quality, timeliness, and perhaps most significantly, convenience. The core editorial ethos of the physical encyclopedia still informs Wikipedia, but the ways in which content is created, shared, and edited are born from digital.

Take a set of encyclopedias and ask, "How do I make this digital?" You get a Microsoft Encarta CD. Take the philosophy of encyclopedia-making and ask, "How does digital change our engagement with this?" You get Wikipedia.

Figure 7.13. Jame Bridle's The Iraq War, the entire Wikipedia editorial history for the Iraq War entry, printed, and bound—the pre-artifact system manifested physically.

When we think about digital's effect on storytelling, we tend to grasp for the lowest-hanging imaginative fruits. The common cliche is that digital will "bring stories to life." Words will move. Pictures will become movies. Narratives will be choose-your-own-adventure. While digital does make all of this possible, these are the changes of least-radical importance brought about by digitization of text. These are the answers to the question, "How do we change books to make them digital?" The essence of digital's effect on publishing requires a subtle shift toward the query, "How does digital change books?"

A FEW EXAMPLES. As much as it may pain literary purists to admit, blogs have been laying the foundation for this kind of on-the-fly contemporary book writing for over a decade. 37Signals' title, *Getting Real*, was composed over the course of years on their blog, Signal vs. Noise.RSS subscribers to Signal vs. Noise had been reading *Getting Real* without knowing it. Heck, 37Signals had been writing *Getting Real* without knowing it.

Consider that they sold 30,000 PDFs at $19 a piece. That's over half a

Figure 7.14. Getting Real, by 37Signals

million dollars in revenue (profit, really—there are no distribution costs or middle men) for a book that was authored publicly. And this was in 2006.

Figure 7.15. The Shape of Design, by Frank Chimero

Frank Chimero has been sketching a book live. It's his blog. He's been working hard at fleshing out ideas around creativity and design for years now. And he's built up such a community of supporters, they paid him $100,000 in February 2011 to go deeper. *The Shape of Design* promises to continue exploring the narrative threads on his site. To formalize.

In Spring of 2010, **Ashley Rawlings** and I ran a campaign to crowd-fund the production and publication of the second edition of **Art Space**

Figure 7.16. Art Space Tokyo

Tokyo. We raised $24,000 in a month and shared the entire process in painstaking detail for others to replicate.

Figure 7.17. Annabel Scheme, by Robin Sloane

Robin Sloan has been writing and releasing short stories in digital formats for the grateful many of us fans. He is now returning to dive deeper into those pieces that had particular resonance with his intended audience—fleshing out shorter works into full-length novels.

Amanda Hocking writes a blog. She has also published several of her novels independently on the Amazon Kindle platform. They've done well. In the past year, she's sold over a million Kindle books directly.

John from **I Love Typography** has been writing a publication live. It's—

Figure 7.18. My Blood Approves, by Amanda Hocking

Figure 7.19. Codex

surprise! —his blog. And now he, too (with the help of editor Carolyn Wood and friends) is formalizing his ideas into the bona-fide journal, Codex. Beautifully produced, masterfully edited, Codex is a collection of thoughtfully curated pieces on typography. A compendium of John's love for type wrapped, marketed, and priced in a way that takes advantage of his amazing community, it leverages changes to the classic publishing system to make it self-sustainable.

Seth Godin has been so deeply influenced by his blog's readership and the strength of his community that he threw his hands up and flat-out started his own publishing company. Domino comes from ideas that

Figure 7.20. Domino Project (from Seth Godin)

emerged in front of the audience he was ultimately trying to reach. It's a beautiful example of a sustainable ecosystem emerging from wholesome conversation.

The list continues indefinitely. To be even more hyperbolic: We are amidst an undeniable, fundamental change to authoring processes. The friction and distance between you and your readership? Gone.

... the subtle editorial push and pull by the number of page views and comments.

The "live iteration" born from these changes frees authors from isolation (but still allows them to write in isolation). The audience and author become conversant sooner. Writers can gauge reader interest as the story unfolds and decide which topics are worth further exploration. 37Signals, Frank, John, Robin, Amanda, and Seth refined their authorial philosophy before an audience of tens (if not hundreds) of thousands of readers. It is easy to imagine the subtle editorial push and pull offered up by the number of page views and comments they received on each blog entry. These frictionless, often indirect reader actions brought by digital to the **pre-artifact** system can manifest in the final authorial output.

Richard Nash of Soft Skull publishing fame, and more recently, founder of literary startup Cursor, has placed this pre-artifact system squarely in his sights. On why the disruption of the pre-artifact system is so necessary—hell, even morally required—he says:

We have tended to speak of the model of publishing for the last
hundred years as if it were a perfect one, but look at all the indie presses that arose in the last 20 years, publishing National
Book Award winners, Pulitzer winners, Nobel winners. What
happened to those books before? They weren't published! They.
Were. Not. Published. Sure, some were, but most? Nope. We
cannot know how much magnificent culture went unpublished
by the white men in tweed jackets who ran publishing for
the past century but just because they did publish some great
books doesn't mean they didn't ignore a great many more . . .
So we're restoring the, we think, the natural balance of things
in the ecosystem of writing and reading.

His new imprint, Red Lemonade, is built to elicit conversations around
books, often before they're complete. Certainly a terrifying notion for
many, but it is also an inevitable product of the opening of the pre-artifact
system. And like many things inevitable in the evolution of entrenched
methodologies, you can either bemoan and lament and eulogize the old, or
become an active participant in the shaping of the future.

Of course, no author is obligated to embrace or engage these changes.
But these changes do raise the question: just where does the digital artifact
begin and end? When is it "completed"?

3. The fall of the great immutable artifact

The digital book is a strange beast. Intangible and yet wholly mutable,
everywhere and nowhere: we own it, but yet, don't. Its qualities mimic
physical books only on a meta-level.

*Have you ever edited and sent files to a printer to be reproduced several
thousand times? It's terrifying.*

To truly understand how strange and special they are, it helps to have
experience with their analog cousins. Have you ever made a physical
book before? What I mean is, have you ever edited and sent the files to
a printer to be reproduced several thousand times? It's terrifying. There
is a pervasive hopelessness to the entire process. You know there must
be mistakes. Check page numbers and punctuation a hundred times still,

and by the sheer magnitude of molecules composing a book, you will miss something.

So submitting that file to be printed is to place ultimate faith in the book. To believe—*because you must for the sake of sanity!*—that this is the best you can do given the constraints. And you will have to live with the results forever.

This is what makes physical so weighty. So precious. No matter how much you prepare, if you haven't executed well, any misstep will be writ a thousand times over.

When someone says "book," this is what we think of *(but, curiously, we may be one of the last generations to think this)*. A very specific physicality. We imagine the thick cover. The well-defined interior block. We feel the permanence of the object. Inside, the words are embedded in the paper. What's printed there today will be the same stuff tomorrow. It's reliable.

With digital, these qualities of printed books listed above become artificial. There is no thick cover constraining length. There are no additional printing costs for color. There is no permanence; the once sacred, unchanging nature of the text is sacred no longer. Updating digital text is trivially easy. When you look at the same digital book tomorrow, it may very well be different from the version you read today.

Outside of these obvious superficial differences, there are two qualities to digital artifacts that make them drastically different from physical artifacts:

1. They have a deep, interwoven connection with the **pre-** and **post-**artifact systems.
2. They exist in the classical "complete" form for only the briefest of instances.

The connection with the **pre-artifact** system is obvious. For example, the "artifact" output of a Wikipedia entry is a continued iteration—the product of a highly specialized **pre-artifact** system.

The artifacts emerging from Domino owe nearly everything to the existence of a pre-artifact system—the vetting of ideas on a blog, the conversation with readers.

Once a physical artifact is "completed," printed, boxed, and shipped, it is done. It can't change. We may scribble notes in the margins of our copy, but the next person to pick up a different copy won't see those notes. They get the same blank, "complete" edition we got.

For only the briefest of instances—*seconds, perhaps, for popular authors*—does the digital edition of a book exist in this static, classic, "complete" form. The moment a Kindle edition of a book is downloaded and highlighted, it has been altered. The next person to download a copy of that book might be downloading the "complete" form plus all associated marginalia. And the greater the integration of systems of marginalia, the greater the impact that subsequent conversations around the book will have on future readers.

The digital artifact, therefore, is a scaffolding between the pre- and post- artifact systems.

FORMATS.   This scaffolding between systems is defined in formats. EPUB, HTML, Mobi, and iOS applications are the most popular. The most pervasive digital book format is undeniably HTML. EPUB and Mobi are effectively subsets of HTML. And woven into EPUB3 is the promise of robust HTML5, CSS3, and enhanced Javascript capabilities.

The most popular digital formats file into three neat categories. They are:

- *Formless*: ePub, Mobi, HTML
- *Definite*: PDF, EPUB3 (HTML5/CSS3)
- *Interactive*: iOS/Android, EPUB3 (HTML5/CSS3)

Formless and *definite* are concepts I outlined at length in the first part of this chapter. Formless refers to content that has no inherent visual structure, and for which the meaning doesn't change as the words reflow. Think paperback novels.

Definite refers to content for which the structure of the page—the juxtaposition of elements—is intertwined with the meaning of the text. Think textbooks.

Interactive is, of course, for works that necessitate some interactive component: video, non-linear storytelling, etc.

There is overlap between these categories, which is why we see some formats appearing more than once—EPUB3, for instance. You may need to have control over both the visual structure of a page as well as the interactivity it suggests.

iOS applications could fill all three categories, but it's a tool not best suited for the job. We've seen this in iPad magazine design and distribution during 2010. Most of those magazines could have been PDFs or HTML5 documents, and readers would have been better for it (smaller downloads; selectable, searchable, resizable, "real" text; etc.).

EPUB3 to rule them all?

EPUB3 seems poised to be the one format to rule them all. Why?

1. Already, EPUB is light and well defined.
2. Documents produced with it are inherently composed of real text and naturally integrate with accessible distribution systems like iBooks, Kindle, or as direct downloads from publishers.
3. Moving forward, it will align with the latest HTML5 layout capabilities and allow embedding of robust JavaScript functionality for interactivity.

If the pre-artifact system incubates the artifact and the digital artifact glues the pre- and post-artifact systems together, then of just what, precisely, is the post-artifact system composed?

4. The Post-Artifact System

Reading the changes from left to right:

- Engagement with readers (*the building of community and conversation*) begins immediately in the **pre-artifact** system.
- The two-year disconnect between **Idea** and **Readers** is minimized to hours, days, or weeks.
- The line between **Publisher** and **Author** is blurred.
- If you choose to print, **The Great Immutable Artifact** is now only **The Immutable Artifact.**
- The production time (*from finished manuscript to readers' hands)* of a digital artifact is significantly less than that of a physical book.
- The classic authority of access to distribution is heavily deemphasized in digital. Digital distribution channels such as Amazon's

Kindle store and Apple's iBooks store are universally accessible. Anyone with an EPUB file can reach critical, global points of sale.

- A true networked **post-artifact** system of additive conversation and marginalia exists only digitally.

This, now

As I stated before, we will always debate:

the quality of the paper, the pixel density of the display;
the cloth used on covers, the interface for highlighting;
location by page, location by paragraph.

This is not what matters. Surface is secondary.

The ditch-digging,
the setting of steel,
the pouring of concrete for the foundation of the future book.
This is what requires our efforts.

Clearly defined scope of these systems,
clearly defined open protocols.
These are what require our discussion.

Tools with simple, quiet, clean, interfaces
organically surfacing our changing relationship with text.
These are what we need to build.

All of these efforts combined, these systems integrated,
these tools made well and deliberately.
This is the future book,
our platform for post-artifact books and publishing.

Give the author feedback & add your comments about this chapter on the web: http://book.pressbooks.com/chapter/2-book-design-in -the-digital-age-craig-mod

part two.

The Outlook: What Is Next for the Book?

8. Why the Book and the Internet Will Merge (Hugh McGuire)

Hugh McGuire builds tools and communities where book publishing and the web intersect. He is the founder of `PressBooks` (on which this book has been built), and `LibriVox.org`, a community of volunteers that has created the world's largest free library of public domain audiobooks. You can find him on Twitter at `@hughmcguire`.

Sometime last year, I had a moment that felt like a profound revelation, and as with all such revelations of mine, I got me to Twitter and posted there:

> The distinction between "the internet" & books is totally totally arbitrary, and will disappear in 5 years. Start adjusting now.

It seems almost trivial as far as epiphanies go now, but still at the time it was a kind of shocking realization. If you think about "books"—which are, more or less, collections of words, sentences, and images arranged in a particular way—and compare them to, say, websites—which are, more or less, collections of words, sentences, images, audio, and video, arranged

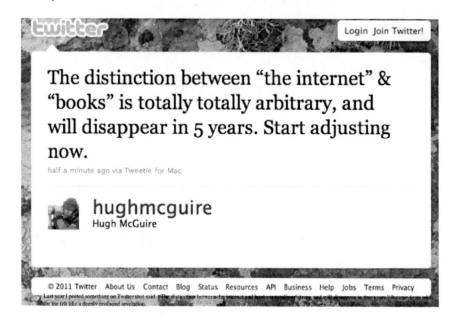

Figure 8.1. The Distinction Between Books and the Internet Is Arbitrary

in a particular way—there is a jarring distinction that presents itself. We have decided, for mostly historical reasons, that collections of words and sentences of one kind go into a "book" and collections of words and sentences of another kind go onto the "Internet."

Figure 8.2. Books vs the Internet

And the question we must ask is: Why, exactly, have we decided things should be this way? Why is it that only certain kinds of words and sentences are supposed to get sent to printers, stamped in ink on a page, stuffed and bound between covers, and sold in physical stores? (Or, sold through a Kindle, for that matter?) Why is it that other kinds of words and sentences are instead supposed to get typed into a keyboard, sent to a server somewhere, and then transmitted in one way or another to appear on the screens of computers and smartphones of readers around the world? What is the distinction between these kinds of words?

One answer came, from a fellow Twitterer, Darrian G. Walter[1], in response to my initial post.

Figure 8.3. The Internet is Ego and Noise

There are two powerful ideas behind this point of view. One has to do with quality of work and attention to detail. Books, this position claims, contain "important" work.

Whereas the Internet? The Internet is the domain of celebrity gossip, flamewars, self-obsessed or half-crazed bloggers, and even Twitter.

---

[1] http://damiengwalter.com/

I call this the Joyce/Cheezburger position.

Books   Internet

Figure 8.4. Joyce vs Cheezburger

So quality of the words ("which are written, researched, edited, marketed" for books versus "ego noise" for the Internet) is one distinction between "books" and the "Internet," according to this view.

On the question of *quality* of words, though, it's clearly not the case that books, which are written, researched, edited, and marketed, can't be on the Internet. Indeed, one of the first ever web sites, Gutenberg.org[2]—started by Michael Hart in 1971—is dedicated to making public domain books freely available on the Internet.

Still, given that Gutneberg.org has been around for 40 years, it's worth asking why books on the Internet have not been particularly popular among the mass consumer market. I think the reason is simple, and it has little to do with quality of the words or cost. Until recently, most people didn't seem to want to read books on screens. I was one of those people. I read news and blog posts and Wikipedia articles and emails on a screen, but I just didn't like reading long-form text—even the great, free ebooks from Project Gutenberg—on a screen.

---

[2] http://gutenberg.com

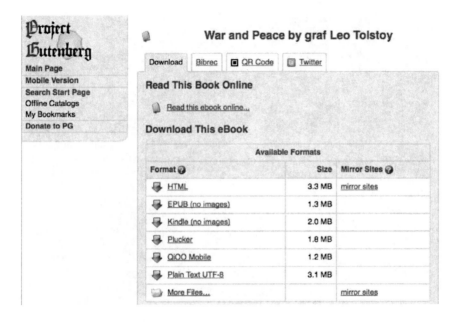

Figure 8.5. Free Ebooks from Project Gutenberg

So there was really not much incentive for publishers to make books into something that could be read on a screen, since very few people wanted to read books from screens. Instead people seemed happy to read books on paper and spend their time on the Internet making funny pictures of cats, blogging about their breakfast, and contributing to the world's largest encyclopedia.

Then came some new devices, with the full force of marketing giants behind them: Amazon's Kindle, the Nook, and for me, the revelation was the iPhone. If you can believe it, the first ebook I read was *War and Peace*, on my iPhone. I loved it. The experience was—for me—comfortable, convenient, pleasant, and revelatory. I was not a convert because of dogma, but rather because I just *liked* reading on this digital device, and my guess was that once other people experienced reading on this new breed of device, ebooks—with their myriad advantages—would win out.

And now, of course, ebooks have arrived, in force. In 2008—when I read *War and Peace* on my iPhone—about 1% of trade book sales in the US were ebooks. In 2011 the number was close to 20%. Many expect 50% of

Figure 8.6. Reading War and Peace on the iPhone

trade sales to be ebooks by 2015, if not sooner. Books may not yet be on the Internet in great numbers, but they sure are in people's Kindles, iBooks, Nooks, and Kobos.

How We Think about Ebooks

While we are in the process of seeing a massive shift in the technology used to read long-form content, to date we've actually seen very little real disruption in the structures (rather than mechanisms) by which people get their books to read. That is, the current structures of getting a book into a reader's hands (publisher -> seller -> reader) looks a lot like the print world. Instead of publishers producing a print book and shipping it to a book store that manages the sales to consumers, publishers now produce an EPUB and send it to an online retailer, which manages sales to consumers.

For all the main players (publishers, retailers, and readers), the ebook business sure looks a lot like the print book business.

And yet the stuff ebooks are made of is very different from what print books are made of.

Ebooks are, in fact, a lot more like websites than like print books. Or rather: they are almost *exactly* like websites. Ebooks are built in HTML, which is the programming language (or mark-up language, if you prefer) used to make websites. There really isn't that much difference between the stuff we use to build, say, an article about Britney Spears in the Huffington Post, and an EPUB of Don Quixote.

[Huffington Post Web HTML]

HTML from a
HuffPo article about
Britney Spears

```
<link rel="canonical" href="http://www.huffingtonpost.com/2011/03/30/britney-
spears-dolce-gabbana-femme-fatale_n_842399.html" />

    <meta name="keywords" content="britney, spears, dons, dolce, &amp;, gabbana,
in, 'femme, fatale', promo, pics, (photos), style" />
    <meta name="description" content="In case you haven&#39;t heard, Britney
Spears is back, better than ever, as they say, and dressed by Dolce &amp; Gabbana
in the promotional pics for her &quot;Femme Fatale&quot; album. But what&#39;s
more -- sounds like BritBrit has earned the designers&#39; praise." />
    <meta property="og:type" content="article" />
    <meta property="og:site_name" content="The Huffington Post"/>
    <meta property="og:title" content="Britney Spears Dons Dolce &amp; Gabbana In
'Femme Fatale' Promo Pics (PHOTOS)" />
    <meta property="fb:app_id" content="46744042133"/>
    <meta name="title" content="Britney Spears Dons Dolce &amp; Gabbana In 'Femme
Fatale' Promo Pics (PHOTOS)" />
    <meta name="category" content="Style" />
    <meta name="author" content="Hilary Moss" />

    <meta name="publish_date" content="Wed, 30 Mar 2011 08:03:11 EST" />
    <link rel="image_src" href="http://i.huffpost.com/gen/261732/thumbs/s-
BRITNEY-SPEARS-DOLCE-GABBANA-large.jpg" />
    <meta name="image" content="http://i.huffpost.com/gen/261732/thumbs/s-
BRITNEY-SPEARS-DOLCE-GABBANA-small.jpg" />
```

Figure 8.7. Huffington Post Web HTML

As we said before, books are just collections of words and media, with a certain structure—chapters, headings—and a bit of metadata—an author, a cover image, a title. If you are making a digital book, it makes sense that you would use the same programming language that you'd use to make a website, since that's pretty much what a website is.

But there is a catch: Publishers are afraid of websites and the Internet. And rightly so. The Internet gobbles up existing business models and spits out chaos. We've seen this with music and with newspapers and movies.

HTML from .epub of
Don Quioxte

```
<?xml version="1.0" encoding="utf-8"?>
<html xmlns="http://www.w3.org/1999/xhtml" xml:lang="en">
<head>
<meta name="generator" content=
"HTML Tidy for FreeBSD (vers 25 March 2009), see www.w3.org" />
<title>Don Quioxte</title>
<link rel="stylesheet" href="css/main.css" type="text/css" />
<meta http-equiv="Content-Type" content=
"application/xhtml+xml; charset=utf-8" />
</head>
<body>
<div class="body">
<div class="text">
<p><strong>TO THE DUKE OF BEJAR, MARQUIS OF GIBRALEON, COUNT OF
BENALCAZAR AND BANARES, VICECOUNT OF THE PUEBLA DE ALCOCER, MASTER
OF THE TOWNS OF CAPILLA, CURIEL AND BURGUILLOS</strong></p>
<p>In belief of the good reception and honours that Your Excellency
bestows on all sort of books, as prince so inclined to favor good
arts, chiefly those who by their nobleness do not submit to the
service and bribery of the vulgar, I have determined bringing to
light The Ingenious Gentleman Don Quixote of la Mancha, in shelter
of Your Excellency's glamorous name, to whom, with the obeisance I
owe to such grandeur, I pray to receive it agreeably under his
protection, so that in this shadow, though deprived of that
```

Figure 8.8. Don Quioxte EPUB HTML

Because the Internet could radically change the book publishing business, publishers are right to worry about it.

The solution to date, which addresses this legitimate fear, is to "constrain" ebooks. This means that a lot of the things we take for granted on most websites are just not possible with books. Copy/paste, sharing passages, and generally moving files from one place to another is much harder with ebooks than with other digital goods, because of a combination of constraints in the EPUB format, digital rights management, and device/platform lock-in.

ebooks may be built out of the same stuff as the Internet (that is, HTML), but to date we've managed to keep them relatively tame, compared to the wild and wooly world of the Web.

This is a good thing if you have an existing business model you wish to protect (and publishers and authors certainly do, rightly so).

But there is a cost to this protection, because in order to achieve this similarity with the past, we've intentionally *crippled* ebooks. We've constrained ebooks so they act more like print books and less like the Web.

Here are just some of the things we expect to be able to do with things on the Internet that we can't do with ebooks:

- copy/paste
- link to a specific chapter or page
- search for text on the Internet and land on the ebook
- leave a comment or feedback in a central place
- easily query an API about that ebook
- easily search and extract geographic data from an ebook
- etc!

Here is a question: if you can do certain things with a **print** book and other things with an **ebook**, and different kinds of things with a book on the **Web**, which of these options is more valuable to you as a reader?

Having just ebooks and print books? Or having ebooks, print books, and books on the Web? My answer is, from a pure mathematical view: print, ebook, and Web.

$$P + E < P + E + W$$

So what kinds of things might come about if books are connected to the Web? The truth is, we don't really know. And that is precisely why I believe books will end up on the Web.

Because when things are made accessible on the Web, smart people start to build exciting things. New things get born that we never would have imagined. We've seen this time and time again: think about what happened when we started sending correspondence through email, conversation through Twitter, when Google put maps on the Internet and made those maps available through an API. Making things available on the Web gives birth to new and exciting things we can't yet imagine.

The market economy and the innovative spirit of the Web are great at rewarding those who find ways to deliver more value to people. There will be immense commercial and creative incentive for new publishers to put books on the Web, because there is just more value for readers there. We don't know what the business models will look like. Subscription books? Advertising? Upselling other products? Serialized books? Something altogether different? We don't know yet, but eventually courageous new publishers will find out.

Old publishers will follow or perish.

And yet some people find the idea that books will be on the Web to be heretical. Because the Web is filled with lolcatz and ego noise.

But the question isn't what stupid things people have put on the Web in the past, but what great things we could do if books were connected on the Web in the future. That's what sets people who love books, and the Web, to dreaming.

Give the author feedback & add your comments about this chapter on the web: http://book.pressbooks.com/chapter/book-and-the-internet-hugh-mcguire

9. Web Literature: Publishing on the Social Web (Eli James)

Eli James launched `Novelr.com` *in 2006, and helped create the Web Fiction Guide in 2008. He has worked on the form and function of web-based books for the good part of 4 years, and is currently continuing that work at* `Pandamian`, *a company he helped create. You can find him on Twitter at:* `@shadowsun7`.

There is a belief today, particularly amongst Internet companies, that "everything is better with social." This belief is not unwarranted—as the rise of Facebook has shown us, social is central to all that is addictive and useful in the consumer Internet. One might argue, in fact, that "social" activities were the very thing that *created* the consumer Internet: the researchers that built ARPAnet intended it for collaborative research, but the social inventions on top of the Web—email, video chat, and Facebook—were what brought one's grandmother online.

Today, we have social apps for photography (Instagram, Flickr), social apps for bookmarking (del.icio.us, Findings), and—more recently—social apps for reading (Goodreads, Readmill). But what of publishing?

Social efforts tend to be as far removed from publishing as homegrown YouTube channels are from Hollywood. But unlike Hollywood—with its movie premiers and cinema-going experiences—the future of publishing cannot be separated from the distributive platform of the Web. It is only reasonable to say that publishers will soon need to roll their own digital platforms. It is also reasonable to argue that such efforts will eventually lead a publisher to consider incorporating social elements into their platforms. How might the social web fit into what a publisher does? Indeed, how has the Internet changed the way books are written?

In this essay, I explore the fringe edges of web-based social publishing: the writers, readers, and (mostly small) publishers currently experimenting with publishing on the Web. I hope that by examining what they've done, we will end up with a few ideas that may be used by other players in publishing. At the very least, we might have some indication as to the shape of the book future, a future that increasingly has to do with the Internet.

Fan Fiction

Let us begin our discussion with the elephant in the room: fan fiction. In a July 2011 *TIME* article, writer Lev Grossman described fan fiction as the dark matter of the publishing universe: invisible to the mainstream, but *unbelievably* massive. And it's true.

As of March 2011, fanfiction.net hosts 6,600,000 titles of the stuff, ranging in length from short stories to *Lord of the Rings*-style epics. This count does not take into consideration other archives, LiveJournal blogs, and still-active listservs, where minor communities are still actively posting, reading, and commenting on each other's work.

Fan fiction precedes the Web. In his article, Grossman tracked the origins of fan fiction to a 1964-'68 TV show *The Man From U.N.C.L.E.*, where the resulting fan fiction took the form of xeroxed fanzines, passed around by hand and word of mouth. This has changed, of course. Today's fan fiction is mostly Internet-based. Its practitioners moved to the Web in its infancy: first posting on antiquated bulletin board systems, then in mailing lists, and today on web-based digital archives such as the aforementioned non-profit fanfiction.net.

Fan fiction deserves some careful examination for the simple reason that its practitioners—out of necessity—have been publishing on the Web for far longer than anyone else has. The fanfic community has developed a number of interesting features, some of which are common to other web-based publishing efforts, as we shall soon see.

I would like to focus on three features in particular: the beta reader, works in progress, and reviews.

A **beta reader** is fan fiction terminology for a reader (or fellow writer) engaged in responsibilities similar to an editor for a more conventional author. Beta readers typically communicate through digital means and are responsible for the checking of grammatical, structural, and consistency errors in a fan fiction writer's work prior to public release. The relationship is sometimes reciprocal: writers who beta for other writers tend to receive the same services in return.

It is worth noting here that beta readers are not unique to fan fiction—in self-publishing, writers engage the help of one or two beta readers as part of the editing process. Zoe Winters, in her book *Smart Self-Publishing: Becoming an Indie Author*, admits that she has met all the beta readers she works with through social networking in some way.

Traditionally published authors also sometimes engage beta readers for help (traditionally called critique or writing partners). All the fiction authors I talked to at the SF Writer's Grotto either had reciprocal critique partners to work with or were actively looking for one. These writers also told me that most of their writer friends had such partners as well. But while these traditionally published authors met their critique partners in writing groups or at conventions, web-based writers, naturally, tend to find their beta readers through the Web.

The **work in progress** format of fan fiction makes it possible for readers to comment on chapters as soon as an author publishes to the site. This is nothing new when compared to the blogosphere, but it does result in a closer relationship between reader and writer that might not be otherwise possible. It also keeps fan fiction writers motivated. (These two observations are important for a number of reasons that we shall soon examine.)

Finally, **reviews** may be posted to the fanfiction.net[1] site at any time during a work's lifecycle, even while incomplete (in all cases, reviews are

---

[1] http://www.fanfiction.net/

marked with a chapter number, so readers may know which chapter in particular the reviewer is writing from). As with YouTube comments, these reviews tend to span a large spectrum of quality, from short one-liners (Please post another chapter! – 'Nick', 2011-12-12, on *Harry Potter and the Methods of Rationality*) to long, analytical pieces about the various ideas explored in the author's writing.

The majority of reviews on fanfiction.net tend to communicate directly with the author. Take, for example, the last paragraph of a review by "hobble" (2011-12-13, on *Harry Potter and the Methods of Rationality*):

> But all in all, fantastic work. Made me think, made all of us think. And all those bon mots—fantastic. Thank you for crafting this labour of love, and I hope you may keep honing your vast, varied talents. Reading through some of your well-deserved, glowing reviews, I have to agree. :) And as a former gifted child, thank you for creating a character I can identify with. (The loneliness and isolation, I mean, not the other stuff.)
>
> You have my gratitude, sir.

Fan fiction participants engage in what readers and writers have been engaged in for decades—readers communicating with their favorite authors, the communication giving equal pleasure to both. But where before such conversations happened through letter-writing, digital reader-author interaction takes place through the fast medium of the Web.

This speed of interaction is important for one other reason: it enables a participatory reading culture that—combined with comments in the blogosphere and on news sites—today's kids take for granted. This culture is not something to laugh at. A 2008 *New York Times* article titled *Literacy Debate: Online, R U Really Reading?* explored how the majority of teenagers prefer to read online. In one revealing passage, Nadia Konyk, a 15-year-old who writes and reads fan fiction (and prefers it to "book" fiction) says "No one's ever said you should read more books to get into college."

Konyk prefers fan fiction because "you could add your own character and twist it the way you want to be." Grossman's article profiles other fan fiction reader/writers, who participate because "it's a (fun) improvisation exercise" and it's "partially a political act" (e.g.: "MGM is too cowardly to put a gay man in one of their multimillion-dollar blockbusters...hrmm, let's fix that").

My point here isn't about the anti-intellectualism of the democratized marketplace (though perhaps a book may be written about that; see Jaron Lanier's *You Are Not a Gadget!*)—my point is that any publisher intending to move to the social Internet has to make peace with the participatory nature of the medium. On the Internet, readers and writers are often one and the same, and they *will* modify original work. While some see it as infringing copyright, the fans see it as a labour of love. It is better for a digital-first publisher to accept this and adapt.

We have not talked about the legality of fan fiction, because such a discussion is not necessary to this essay. It is obvious, however, that under current copyright law fan fiction will never be a serious publishing activity. But as we have now seen several basic features and habits that underpin web reading, let us turn to more publisher-friendly variants of the medium.

Web Fiction

Web fiction (also known as Web Literature, or WebLit) is original fiction written for and published to the Web. The format shares certain qualities with fan fiction, but we shall first examine the differences.

Unlike fan fiction, web fiction is published on blogs or blog-like websites. Web fiction writers have, typically, more serious aspirations than fan fiction ones: it is common for web fiction authors to write in arcs, publishing the arcs as ebooks whenever an arc is complete. But the defining feature for web fiction is that the largest, most successful web fiction sites have significant communities of readers clustered around them, and it's normal for these writers to attract lively discussions within minutes of posting a chapter.

Take, for instance, a discussion in the comment section of one such web fiction site, *The Legion Of Nothing*[2]:

> **SilasCova:**
> Nothing wrong with butch.

---

[2] http://www.legionofnothing.com

I somehow keep managing to forget Sam's description and having to back pages again to looksee. But she's cool

Another great monday read.

captain mystic:

unless the piece of plastic is like a broken transponder or something i dont know how sam plans to track them. and also i thought rod would be the one with mad tracking skills given as trolls are butch. lie that adjective.

MadNinja:

Sam is a magic user so she can use the broken piece of plastic from the car to scry for the kidnapers.

Thomas:

Totally Madninja, thaumaturgic law of similarity. I would have thought Captain MYSTIC would have spotted that one.

But yeah being called butch is not necessarily a compliment unless that's what you are going for.

Jim (author):

Captain Mystic/MadNinja/Thomas: That's more or less what I was going for.

Silas: Sam's got a couple descriptions–and one of them is closer to real than the other. Amusingly (I hope), we'll get a little more into that in a bit...

RogerWillcocks:

"Who where they" were?

Jim (author):

Thanks for that. I'm always amazed by how obvious some typos are once someone else sees them.

This element of community is addictive. It also makes good economic sense: if Jim Zoetewey decides to compile and publish the first arc of *LoN*, it's a safe bet to say that I and many others in his community of readers would purchase the book the instant it is released (*and* tell our friends about it).

There have been other experiments of interest in the field of web fiction. Writer Michael C. Milligan used to have a model he termed "Novel+," where a new chapter is released on his site every week, and impatient readers may pay to unlock full access to the story, in both web and PDF form. Writer M.C.A Hogarth has "sponsors" for her *Spots the Space Marine* serial, where readers will sponsor the writing of subsequent chapters (no new chapters are released until a sponsor steps up). This has worked well for both of them.

Unfortunately, such pricing experiments in web fiction are declining as ebooks have increased in popularity—many web fiction authors now follow the write-public-arc, build-community, release-ebook pattern of publication. It is also unclear if such experimental pricing models will suit publishers interested in moving to the Web. I would argue that such strategies—while profitable, cannot compare to the current explosion in ebook consumption taking place across the publishing industry. There is "easy" money in ebooks. It makes sense to do just that.

This begs an intriguing question: why do authors keep writing web fiction, in the open, when *it makes more economic sense to write privately and publish ebooks?*

Web Fiction: Interactivity

The answer is deceptively simple: interactivity. Interactivity is a *powerful* source of instant gratification. This isn't at all difficult to understand: if you are a writer, and you've just published a chapter, quick reader responses are extremely satisfying, rewarding writing effort not long after completion. Within hours you will have readers debating your characters' motivations, speculating about previous chapters or haranguing after you for another update.

If the community of readers is large enough, reader responses have sometimes supplanted a writer's desire to get published. I have had successful web fiction authors tell me that their web writing is fulfilling enough and engaging enough that they no longer pursue their publishing aspirations as aggressively as before. And—with self-publishing as a valid alternative, they see little reason to run the traditional gamut of submissions and rejections.

Internet startups have known for years that one way of engaging users is to bait them with social interaction. You repeatedly visit Facebook to check on what your friends are saying about (or to) you. You check Twitter or email most rapidly when a new reply notification appears on your computing device.

Fan fiction has shown us that it is possible to keep millions of people engaged in writing so long as there is feedback. Web fiction has shown us that it is possible to override a writer's desire for publication if the degree and quality of such feedback is ensured. These are not elements that are much discussed in today's shift to ebooks (in fact, most such arguments are economic), but it will be once we transition to web-first publishing. It is certainly a tool publishers need to understand.

Web Fiction: Discoverability

There are other problems that web fiction writers share with publishers. That web fiction writers are serious in growing their readership and "selling" their stories means that they have to deal with another common publishing problem: discoverability.

The web fiction community has dealt with this in several ways. Web fiction writers are ultimately responsible for building their own readerships (which I admit they do rather haphazardly). Efforts that have worked out in the past include: advertising on web-comic sites, word-of-mouth, and cross-promotion—be it through web fiction anthologies or via guest posts on other, topic-related blogs.

In fact, many of the strategies web fiction writers have looked into are the same ones site owners have commonly used to gain traffic for their websites. This makes sense: while potentially novels and books, web fiction is also—first and foremost—published as websites.

Along with Chris Poirier and a number of writers and editors from the web fiction community, in 2008 I helped create a filter for web fiction at webfictionguide.com.[3] The site includes a recommendations engine, an editorial reviewing system, and a forum to coordinate reviewing efforts. Its proposed benefit, I realize now, included the sort of network effects indie authors have accessed when selling on aggregated platforms like Amazon.

---

[3] http://webfictionguide.com/

It is possible to do a better job of providing this benefit, and we are currently rethinking certain elements as Chris embarks on a redesign. But publishers and writers who consider selling their products outside of Amazon's ecosystem will eventually need to evaluate the potential costs of losing networked recommendations. Building a platform of your own is a possibility, but it is difficult and potentially expensive. There is some hope, however: the marketing practices of indie authors may give us clues as to alternative coping strategies.

Indie Writers and the Social Web

Indie writers are self-published authors who write, edit, and publish their books without help from traditional publishing houses. Today's indie writers rely on Amazon's network effects in the following (generalized) way:

1. The writer uses his or her blog, Twitter, Goodreads, and Facebook accounts to channel readers to sign up for a mailing list.
2. This mailing list is used sparingly, for example when i) the author has a new book to announce or ii) the author has a promotion or contest or giveaway.
3. When the author has completed a new book, he or she sends an email announcement linking to the Amazon sales page.
4. The initial surge of purchases propels the book up Amazon's ebook rankings. If the author has done 1) well, his or her mailing list should be large enough for the book to hit an inflection point on Amazon's rankings. New readers now discover the ebook through these lists, perpetuating a virtuous cycle of purchases.

This is the ideal, of course. Not every writer manages to achieve this. But the successful writers use variants of this basic strategy—and the prolific ones reap extra benefits at stage 4, as a portion of satisfied new readers buy the author's other books.

It is important to note how much social media is used to achieve these sales. Indie authors do not publish their work publicly on the Web (unlike their web fiction counterparts), but most of them are active bloggers. Their blogs are the central gathering point for their readers.

The writers also give away free ebooks (or sell them at ridiculously low prices) to increase discoverability on Amazon. The smart ones, however, give away free ebooks as a reward for signing up to their mailing lists. This mailing list—coupled with their blog—is *everything* to the author's marketing strategy.

Seth Godin calls this technique "earning permission." He leveraged it for the duration of his publishing experiment, The Domino Project. Editor Mandy Brown argues something similar: that publishers need to foster and grow communities as a license to sell. Both operate on the same underlying principle: in the same way that I will buy Jim Zoetewey's book when he decides to release it, so readers who have signed up for an author's mailing list will be partial to purchasing the author's new ebook, and readers subscribed to a publisher's community will likely spend more than otherwise.

Publishers who build community would be able to decrease dependency on Amazon's networked recommendations. They have opt-in discoverability, if you will.

Lessons for Publishers

If the observations of the past few sections are distilled down to one core idea, what might that be?

Social interaction is addictive. It is fulfilling. Use it. This should, I think, be the biggest takeaway from this essay. We have seen how social interaction permeates every facet of today's web publishing: from beta readers in the writing process, to comments, reviews, and blog conversations for web fiction and indie publishing. We have seen how reader interaction has kept some web writers happy enough to delay the pursuit of traditional publishing. We have also seen how social interaction has kept millions of writers engaged in fan fiction. (Anecdotal evidence in both the web fiction and fan fiction communities suggests that fan fiction is often how some kids today *start learning to write fiction*.)

Closer to mainstream publishing, we know that self-published authors engage with their readers on their blogs, as well as their Facebook and Twitter accounts. This activity is no different from the fan mail that writers in previous decades received. But we also know that indie writers today use such social media to capture potential readers, as well as to market their books.

We have, however, seen little of this in "serious" publishing. I mentioned earlier that interactivity is not much discussed in today's transition to ebooks. This is understandable, as economic concerns weigh foremost on many publisher's minds. But while discussions on "ebookonomics" are important, it is inevitable for publishers to face the fact that, on the Internet, social interactions now make up the bulk of the Web's activity. We are also as a society shifting to a participatory digital culture. If publishers are to transition to digital outfits, they would eventually have to deal with this truth.

How might a publisher leverage the social web? The simplest possible way is for publishers to engage their customers on the Internet, adapting the marketing techniques indie writers have used to their advantage (this strategy is non-invasive, and is likely to be a no-brainer). Another–but harder–way is for publishers to provide their authors with better methods to interact with their readers. Technology permits it: if the author's books are available as a website (like web fiction, but perhaps behind a paywall), the publisher may provide for the author the same value and pleasure web writers derive from their writing–direct engagement with readers over a text.

This is a lot simpler than it sounds. The most basic version of this effort could be a publisher offering to build and maintain an authors's interactive presence: everything from blog to website to mailing list. The publisher may then build an audience for the author or redirect a portion of its existing audience to the author's sites.

There is an opportunity for publishers to provide conversation spaces for readers and writers on the Internet, especially when there's existing proof that millions of such conversations occur on the Web every day. The publisher-run tor.com,[4] for instance, is a good example of such a space. If anything, such spaces would "provide permission" for digital publishers, the same way indie authors get readers to subscribe to their mailing lists. And if that doesn't work out the way we intend, providing high levels

---

[4] http://tor.com/

of interaction is still a value proposition worth offering. If writers are motivated by reader reactions, what better way than to prove publisher relevance than to meet those expectations?

Regardless of whether you agree with this opportunity, there is no doubt that publishers, like the fans and writers before them, need to embrace the social web. The participatory culture of the Internet demands it. And this is a good thing–it affords publishers, their writers, and their writer's readers possibilities never before possible. It is something to be excited about.

Postscript: Other Experiments in Social Publishing

A few quick mentions of experiments that don't fit anywhere else in this essay:

1) We know today that collaborative crowd writing does not work. In 2007, Penguin and some new media specialists at De Montford University launched a wiki-based crowd writing project called *A Million Penguins*, which by all accounts failed (Alice Fordham, in a 2007 article for *The Times*, reported that "the project split into 'Novel A' and 'Novel B' and had links to alternative endings." She also spent a paragraph on the bizarre, recurring appearance of a writer intent on including bananas in as many places in the story as possible.)

2) That said, there are many other forms of social reading that we do not yet know will work. The Institute for the Future of The Book did an experiment called *The Golden Notebook Project*[5] in 2008. The project invited seven notable women to read Doris Lessing's *The Golden Notebook* in five to six weeks, commenting in the margins of the web-based book as they did so. This project was a success; if:book director Bob Stein says that the women who participated in the project loved it.

3) Web fiction author Michael C. Milligan has experimented in something he calls "livewriting": the act of writing a novel live on the Web in three days. His writing occurs on a JavaScript-powered frontend, where every character he types shows up live on a digital canvas. But that's not all: the audience interacts with him using Twitter, a chat box, and a live

---

[5] http://www.thegoldennotebook.org

video stream, which he turns on when writing. These channels are used to incorporate structured reader suggestions: every hour, before writing a chapter, he tweets a series of questions that one may answer, subtly changing the outcome of the story. And at the end of three days he edits the book and publishes it, sending it to members of the audience who have opted in and pre-purchased the book during the livewriting period.

While these projects may not have immediate economic value, they do highlight the variety of engagement opportunities web publishing has to offer. It is likely that ideas discovered in one of these experiments would be useful to the digital publisher of the future. As of today, they make known to us the adjacent possible in publishing.

Give the author feedback & add your comments about this chapter on the web: `http://book.pressbooks.com/chapter/web-literature-eli-james`

10. Making Books Out of Words (Erin McKean)

Erin McKean is the founder of Wordnik.com. *Previously, she was the editor in chief for American Dictionaries at Oxford University Press, and the editor of the New Oxford American Dictionary, 2E. You can find her on Twitter at:* @emckean.

Traditionally, the writer's reference toolkit has consisted of a dictionary and a thesaurus (sometimes augmented with books of quotations or allusions). These are books that are used to make other books, allowing writers (in principle) to check the strength and suitability of their words before committing them to sentences and paragraphs, before completing their explanations and narratives.

But just as some aerialists work without a net, many writers work without these tools, or are told that they ought to. Hemingway said "Actually if a writer needs a dictionary he should not write,"[1] and Simon Winchester (himself the author of two books about the Oxford English Dictionary) called the thesaurus "a tool for the lexically lazy"[2]). And the

---

[1] http://bit.ly/MkDNVm
[2] http://www.wordspy.com/waw/20031111115209.asp

lamentations over the shortcomings of the automatic spell-checker[3] have been loud and long.

It's no wonder that some have warned against the use of these tools: static paper (or static electronic) dictionaries and thesauruses (and books of quotations and allusions) are by their very nature inclined to be out-of-date, incomplete, and inadequate, because they have only been able to track the uses and meanings of words from a relatively small selection of previously published works. (Even the current online version of the *Oxford English Dictionary* includes only 3 million citations; the first edition of the *OED* cited only 4500 works.) The chain of events by which a new lexical creation is captured—a writer creates or changes the meaning of a word, publishes a work in which the new word is used, a dictionary editor sees it, a dictionary is published including it—is so long, and has so many points of breakage, that it's a wonder new words are ever found, or that new dictionaries are ever published.

Dictionaries and thesauruses, too, because they've long been creatures of print, are also necessarily over-compressed, reducing words to their broadest applications and their lowest common denominators. In a print-based dictionary, there's no way to include every possible word of English, much less to account for every possible context in which a word could be used, or for a printed thesaurus to give enough information around a word's possible synonyms and antonyms to be truly helpful to even the most conscientious writer.

But when all books are "truly digital, connected, ubiquitous," there won't be a need for the traditional (inadequate, static) dictionary or thesaurus: the collected sea of words will itself be "the dictionary" (with a little computational help). The dictionary will no longer be a separate thing (or two separate things, dictionary and thesaurus). The dictionary will be a ubiquitous metalayer on top of all digital text, matching content and context to answer questions of both production and comprehension (or mere curiosity).

A true dictionary metalayer would be instantaneously and continuously updated, near-infinite, multilayered, context-driven and context-rich, interactive, and, eventually, no longer a separate thing, but an intuitive part

---

[3] http://en.wikipedia.org/wiki/Cupertino_effect

of reading and writing. At some point it could even be a push rather than a pull technology, learning from readers' and writers' behavior, glossing unknown words and phrases or automatically and transparently suggesting alternatives to overused adjectives. Ideally, it would be accessible from every text, both atomic and interconnected, like the Internet itself.

For any word, the reader or writer could call up the "nearest" (or most relevant) information about that word. They could look for other examples of that word in the same book, by the same author (or by writers similar to the author), in the same genre, in books on the same or similar subjects or by the same publisher, or in texts published in the same year or in the same geographic area. Readers or writers could look for other examples where the word shares context: for instance, all the sentences where apples are golden and appear near the names of figures in Greek mythology.

This would be a two-way street, allowing readers and writers to comment, vote, recommend, and advocate for and against any particular usage, meaning, collocation, phrase, or quotation. This engagement would give every usage enthusiast (or "grammar Nazi") the chance to opine on the acceptability of "impact" as a verb or "funner" as a comparative adjective. Connections between words could be weighted by use (both frequency of being written and frequency of being read, annotated, commented upon, or looked up) and context (a thesaurus where distinctions between words could be visualized more concretely, making the process of selecting a synonym more accurate).

Instead of the insistently obdurate suggestions of current spellchecking programs (and "grammar check," both of which are sorely lacking in what can only be called "theory of mind"), we could have context-driven fuzzy matching, able to differentiate between "there" and "their" and equally capable of understanding proper names, novel combinations of morphemes (knowing "fallacious" and the prefix "omni-," it shouldn't choke on "omnifallacious"). Fuzzy matching techniques (such as the wonderfully-named "bursty n-grams"[4]) could help trace the development of ideas (or nab plagiarists). Techniques for identifying lexical and rhetorical patterns could automatically highlight and link sentences that are famous quotations (or that ought to be). Allusions (which could be thought of as lexicalized bits

---

[4] http://bit.ly/NPrX8A

of history) could be made explicit (or, of course, left opaque, to keep from spoiling the thrill of discovery).

This information layer would incorporate traditional sources, dictionaries, and thesauruses both generalized and specialized, but it would also treat every text as a source of lexical information: sentences where words are the subject of the writing, not the raw material for writing about things, are relatively abundant in the language (Wordnik.com explicitly searches for these sentences in text—we call them "free-range definitions"). Some are very didactic:

> "An aguantadora is someone who puts up with "it" and keeps going—"it" being whatever life throws our way."[5]

Others are more parenthetical:

> "The symposium will feature a new volume of 52 essays about association copies—books once owned or annotated by the authors—and ruminations about how they enhance the reading experience. Some include etymological information:[6] "Absorptive capacity," a term coined in the late twentieth century, refers to the general ability to recognize the value of new information, choose what to adopt, and apply it to innovation."[7]

[The one thing traditional dictionaries do that computational techniques find difficult is etymology: if you think of meaning as the demographic data around words, etymology is the genealogy of words, and requires specialized human investigation.]

It would also be possible to incorporate sentiment information, both explicit and implied: a search for "I love the word X," for example, turns up words like "burp," "curiosities," "douchebag," and "Shmorg"; "I hate the word X" turns up "retard," "abstinence," "hubby," "willpower," and "moist." (A similar technique is used by the site sucks-rocks.com.[8])

---

[5] http://bit.ly/OkQFeH
[6] http://www.nytimes.com/2011/02/21/books/21margin.html?_r=1&hp
[7] http://hbswk.hbs.edu/item/6702.html?wknews=05022011
[8] http://sucks-rocks.com/

Because dictionaries and encyclopedias differ mainly in scale (you can think of a dictionary as a specialist encyclopedia limited to words-as-things, instead of things-as-things), our sea of text could be mined to find encyclopedia-style facts, as well. (This is obviously akin to the semantic web.[9]) By looking for obviously factual statements (or factual statements about imaginary things, e.g. "Unicorns are beautiful creatures," "John Carter is a Civil War veteran who was transported to Mars," etc.) encyclopedia articles could be augmented with explicitly-sourced statements (or created automatically where human editors were not motivated to create them).

Discovery of related content, not just information about particular words, is a logical extension (and the original impetus behind most text digitization projects). Topical indexes and bibliographies would be bigger, more indexable, and more dynamic, although certainly more prone to problems of information-gluttony and the "just look at one more source" problem.

The traditional questions we have about words (what they mean, who uses them, and how) are not the only ones we can fish for answers for in the sea of words. Large-scale text analysis can be used to answer wider-scale questions about language and about culture. More than 5 million digitized books from Google Books have been released (in the form of n-gram counts[10]) for the express purpose of giving researchers (admittedly blunt and primitive) tools to investigate ideas as represented by words.

For instance, we can look at the relative trends in the use of –ess forms (like proprietress, ambassadress, etc.) as a proxy for the changing roles of women. A paper published in December 2010 in *Science* outlined this new field of "culturomics," which they defined as "the application of high-throughput data collection and analysis to the study of human culture." The authors also estimated that 52% of the English lexicon, "the majority of the words used in English books" were "lexical dark matter," not found in traditional reference books.

Treating all digital text as a single sea of words would allow for more

---

[9] http://semanticweb.org/wiki/Main_Page
[10] http://ngrams.googlelabs.com/

playfulness as well as more scholarship. Imagine navigating from one text to another via chains of connected words, going from:

> "To be sure they all sleep together in one apartment, but you have your own hammock, and cover yourself with your own blanket, and sleep in your own skin,"

in *Moby Dick*, to a sentence ending with the same phrase (your own skin) in *Uncle Tom's Cabin*:

> "When you've been here a month, you'll be done helping anybody; you'll find it hard enough to take care of your own skin!"

Games could be built around getting from one text to the next in the shortest number of steps with the longest phrases, or in finding the most unlikely connections between far-flung texts (by date or place published, or by topic, or by political sentiments of the authors). Imagine games where extra points could be awarded for playing words used by Nabokov or Shakespeare or Nora Roberts (or where prizes in games could be sponsored by publishers to increase discovery or awareness of their books and authors). The possibilities for Mad Libs, crossword puzzles, and word-search jumbles are endless.

Although one of the strengths of digital text is the possibility of human-driven annotation, bookmarking and sharing, the downside of human-driven data is the possibility of bias and limited attention span. In his accompanying essay, "Why Digitial Books Will Become Writable," Terry Jones asks:

> "Why bother with the complexities of semantics or natural language understanding when, if you simply let them, users will happily tell you what they're interested in and what web pages are about?"

But users often ignore "what everyone knows" and concentrate on the unusual. The *OED* faced this same problem early on. Readers focused on rare and learned words, ignoring the workhorses of English vocabulary. Editor James Murray complained that "Thus of *Abusion*, we found in the slips about 50 instances: of *Abuse* not five...."[11] By using statistical techniques, rather than pure crowdsourcing of items of interest, it's possible to see not only hotspots of attention, but gaps and lacunae in coverage. This use parallels what the Berkman Center for Internet & Society does with their Media Cloud[12] project, which tracks coverage of issues in the news.

This metalayer over the sea of words could drive all sorts of other tools: hotspot maps of texts and genres and topics, as well as instant visualizations of patterns of reading and writing and changes in ways of referring to things. (When does the whiz kid inventor turn into the captain of industry? When does being a locavore no longer need a parenthetical explanation?) There are certain opportunities (as well as certain problems) that only become apparent at scale. Will we find forgotten gems or drown in megabytes of irrelevance?

There are obviously technical issues involved in creating and navigating this sea of words–there will never be one single vat in which we store every text. But making every little bucket and cup able to share aggregate statistics and indexes and metadata across an information layer would go a long way towards creating the universal grasp of knowledge that readers and writers have longed for since Milton, apocryphally thought to be the last man in Europe who had–or could have–read everything there was to read.

Give the author feedback & add your comments about this chapter on the *web:*   `http://book.pressbooks.com/chapter/books-words-erin` `-mckean`

---

[11] `http://bit.ly/046yte`
[12] `http://www.mediacloud.org/dashboard/view/1?q1=64024`

11. Why Digital Books Will Become Writable (Terry Jones)

Terry Jones is founder and CTO at Fluidinfo, where he is building a distributed storage architecture for a new representation of information, and creating a variety of applications that will use the underlying architecture. You can find Terry on Twitter at: @terrycojones.

Historically, the ability for readers to contribute to published information has been sharply limited. Publication was considered, and very often still is, almost exclusively a one-way process in which a publisher produced information and readers consumed it. But readers have never been passive. While reading, they generate information of their own, storing it largely in their heads, marginalia or separate notes, and sharing it verbally. The subsequent publishing of reader-written letters to the editor, book reviews, errata and corrected editions, and the practice of putting laudatory quotes on the back of book covers are all examples of reader contributions to published information. The library cards in books borrowed from libraries sometimes carry annotations—occasionally social—left by other readers. Even the simple practice of inserting a bookmark into a book or dog-earring a page to remember where one is up to is a form of user contributed metadata.

The rise of digital systems—computers and networks—has allowed us to dream of and then implement systems that allow normal users to contribute and share information. This thinking can be charted over the last century via the landmark works of Paul Otlet,[1] Vannevar Bush,[2] Doug Engelbart,[3] Ted Nelson,[4] Tim Berners-Lee[5] and others. For an overview of this history, see Glut: Mastering Information Through The Ages.[6]

User-Generated Content

The rise of user-generated online social information systems, triggered by Delicious,[7] sparked a "there's gold in them thar hills"[8]-like recognition of potential value and numerous attempts have been made to monetize that value.

User-generated content, such as tags for URLs, is valuable in two main ways. First, allowing normal users to add their own information to things can provide for new and personal forms of search and organization. This value accrues to the user but also potentially to the publisher, supposing they have access to the data. Why bother with the complexities of semantics or natural-language understanding when, if you simply let them, users will happily tell you what they're interested in and what web pages are about? Second, if user-generated data can be shared, additional value is created as the data itself becomes, in a sense, social. Shared data creates value because it makes it possible to know what specific others (e.g., friends) are doing. It also allows non-specific discovery, creates network effects, and allows unanticipated combinations of independent heterogeneous information about the same things.

---

[1] http://en.wikipedia.org/wiki/Paul_Otlet
[2] http://en.wikipedia.org/wiki/Vannevar_Bush
[3] http://en.wikipedia.org/wiki/Doug_Engelbart
[4] http://en.wikipedia.org/wiki/Ted_Nelson
[5] http://en.wikipedia.org/wiki/Tim_Berners_Lee
[6] http://bit.ly/PEjwOp
[7] http://delicious.com
[8] http://en.wikipedia.org/wiki/Dahlonega,_Georgia

The recognition of this value—to end users, to content creators, to advertisers—is pushing technology towards giving users a voice. To date that has been done in specific vertical ways in the context of applications. Horizontally, we have the example of Wikipedia[9] which offers a writable web page for anything (modulo editorial control). While no attempt has (yet) been made to monetize Wikipedia, its value is immense. In my opinion, Wikipedia, including the computational infrastructure supporting it, is the most impressive of human artifacts.

Awareness of this value is also pushing publishers towards finding ways to let the audience, or more accurately "the former audience"[10] as Dan Gillmor[11] put it, have a voice.

When Does Publication Begin? Does It End?

Brian O'Leary[12] has written a compelling wake-up call[13] to publishers, warning that the traditional publishing model, driven primarily by content "containers"—both physical and, more recently, digital—is outdated. Brian urges a focus instead on "context" and argues that the form of the final information container should be merely a circumstantial by-product. He argues that publishers must focus on context, i.e., on the rich ball of information that surrounds the content that has traditionally been produced in the act of publishing. When focus is a priori placed on the container rather than the context, valuable information that doesn't fit the specific targeted container will necessarily wind up on the cutting room floor. From this point of view, the context—information surrounding and contemporaneous with the primary content should be considered a potential part of the eventual publication. The context might, for example, include metadata about a book that is created and disseminated before the traditional content.

Some questions: Given that readers are generating and accumulating information about published information, even if they are often forced to

---

[9] http://wikipedia.org

[10] http://oreilly.com/catalog/wemedia/book/index.csp

[11] http://www.oreillynet.com/pub/au/1201

[12] http://magellanmediapartners.com/

[13] http://bit.ly/etwb70

store it elsewhere (in their minds, in marginalia, in separate notebooks, etc.), might it also make sense to take the position that this activity is also a form of publication? If the information from readers is "about" the same thing, does it not conceptually form part of the same publication? If, with the rise of digital, the audience is increasingly able to contribute to the content, at what point can we consider that the act of publication is over, if ever?

These questions point to a change in how we look at the act of publishing. In the traditional model, a moment of publication was reached. Contextual information that did not fit the publishing container was left behind. "Read-only" content was delivered into the hands of the audience, who went away individually to consume it while publishers moved on to work on their next publications.

Contrast that model with one in the digital world. Free from the constraints of more rigid containers and with mechanisms that allow the audience to contribute content, it makes more sense to regard publication as something that starts much earlier and doesn't finish at the moment of initial dissemination. In fact I think it's defensible to argue that the act of publication never finishes—even after the last physical copy of a book goes out of existence. The memory of the book, the fact that it did exist, comments on the book, other metadata—in other words "context"—continue to exist, and also to accrue.

Book Publishing Goes Digital and Online

ebooks and ebook readers have taken the world by storm in the last several years. Amazon has announced[14] that they are now selling more ebooks than certain types of print ones. As extraordinary as this is, a more profound change will take place, because ebook readers are also online.

When an ebook device is online, it can make dynamic API calls across the network to send or receive information. The device and its content are not static. Additional content (context!) can be pulled from remote servers. For example, the Google ebook Web Reader supports several operations

---

[14] http://lat.ms/j4szQ5

on individual words.[15] New content (user-generated, or otherwise) can be uploaded.

This means that the online ebook device maps perfectly onto a broader definition of publishing—one that starts earlier and doesn't really stop. It means that the container in which content is delivered has in some sense become irrelevant. There are many ways to look at this, but the bottom line is that information is being communicated between the external networked world and the user by means of an infinitely flexible general-purpose computer. The form of the "container" that the top-level software ends up displaying to the user isn't particularly relevant (ignoring for now the controversial issues about which data formats are supported). If the device can pull arbitrary information from the network and assemble it as needed, to the extent that a container is even necessary, we arrive at a form of just-in-time container, where, as O'Leary puts it, the container is just "an output of digital workflows."

This situation has a close parallel in the world of modern web browsers. While HTML can be considered the traditional framing container, the reality today is that millions of popular websites are powered by client-side JavaScript that is in frequent communication with web servers. This takes place *while you are looking at a single* page, via asynchronous network calls whose results are used to update the structure and content of the Document Object Model[16] that underlies what you see on-screen. Indeed, in many cases it's most accurate to assert that essentially *there is no page*: the web server delivers a practically empty HTML document that contains a few basic tags and a bunch of JavaScript code. The code makes dynamic requests to begin determining and generating the content that should appear.

Just as browsing has to a large extent moved from delivery of static pre-built HTML containers to a model of looking at a page that is constructed and updated on demand, the ebook world can be expected to move from delivery of static pre-built ebook containers to something similarly dynamic. The ebook experience will degrade when network connectivity is lost, just as it does when browsing (perhaps falling back to

---

[15] http://bit.ly/kHOJPG
[16] http://en.wikipedia.org/wiki/Document_Object_Model

just showing the static non-interactive content). When the formal container shrinks to nothing more than a few HTML tags to hold the "content"—a program—then the container is more like a part of the handshaking protocol between device and server. What goes on computationally behind the user experience is pure application. It operates internally much more like a game than something with static discrete "pages," like a traditional website or book. Indeed, the intermediate step of the static ebook will in some cases be skipped entirely, as we will see below.

Openly Writable Storage

When we are given the chance, we choose to store information in places that make it most useful, and therefore most valuable. This is illustrated in many small everyday acts. Consider the name tags we unthinkingly put around our necks at conferences. We put bookmarks *into* books or dog-ear pages to recall where we stopped. We are adept at using Post-it notes,[17] putting them into places where the information they carry will be most useful. These are all examples of the same thing, of how we naturally tend to put information into context (there's that word again) when given the opportunity. In the digital world, Wikipedia gives people an always-writable location to store information about almost anything, possibly subject to the whims of Wikipedia editors.

Today, the digital default is that we can't always write. Most of the time we're in a read-only world, and when it is in theory possible to contribute information we can only do so in ways that have been anticipated, and if we have permission. It's a radically different environment for working with information. All too often when we have additional information about something we are forced to put it elsewhere, making that information less valuable. While Wikipedia works well for humans contributing shared information about things, it is not a suitable framework for applications to do a similar thing.

At Fluidinfo[18] we are building what we regard as a core piece of missing architecture—shared storage. Fluidinfo is a single shared online storage

---

[17] http://en.wikipedia.org/wiki/Post-it_note
[18] http://fluidinfo.com

platform. Like a wiki, Fluidinfo has a writable location for everything. Unlike a wiki, Fluidinfo has a permissions system that content owners can use to control read and write access for other users and applications. It also supports typed data and arbitrary data with a MIME type (image, audio, PDF, etc), and it has a query language for data retrieval.

The advantage of an openly writable storage platform like Fluidinfo is that it makes the world I described above possible. Given an openly writable object representing a book, a publisher has a place to store arbitrary information (context, metadata). Applications can use the identical place to store arbitrary user-generated information. All this information is stored in the place where it is most useful: with the thing it relates to. The Fluidinfo platform is built to provide flexible storage that allows applications and their users to work with information digitally in the same way they work with information in the non-computational world—by putting it into context, where it is most useful and valuable.

Economics

While some of these changes will be pushed by the value created by social user-generated data, as described above, there are additional economic incentives. Revenue models are a persistent problem in publishing static, monolithic chunks of information (as books, as HTML, in ebook formats). A move to a world in which devices run programs that pull small pieces of information from the network and assemble that information into a user experience provides not just richer and more dynamic content, but also a more viable and much more interesting revenue model.

For example, platforms like Fluidinfo make it possible to monetize the additional context information that a publisher holds but is forced to discard in a world of formal containers. Separating this context from the content it describes sharply limits what can be shown to users. If this information is stored in context, on the same objects that hold other metadata about the book, then so much the better. It is easy to imagine a publisher selling digital copies of Keith Richards'[19] book Life[20] and

---

[19] http://en.wikipedia.org/wiki/Keith_Richards
[20] http://en.wikipedia.org/wiki/Life_(book)

also making it possible to (later) pay a little more to have his footnotes or author's commentary embedded or provided alongside. This rich and valuable contextual information might take many forms.

Alternate models can also be tried. These include razor and blades freebie marketing,[21] giving away partial content and charging for the full version, or even wild-ass ideas like giving away the consonants and selling the vowels. Anything is possible.

The combination of atomized content, networked devices that can make API calls and a move away from static monolithic information formats takes us to a world of new revenue opportunities. If this model is backed by general underlying shared writable storage, it is also easy to imagine end users who are adding valuable information and charging for it. Reader contributions might be valuable to other readers in the form of reviews or annotations. Such annotations might be valuable to publishers in the form of errata, ratings, recommendations, and much more. Third-party contributions to the underlying data could also result in a richer experience and revenue to those third parties, as discussed below. In such a world, the distinction between writer and reader, between publisher and consumer, becomes extremely blurry.

An amusing and provocative demonstration of these kinds of ideas, was given during a talk entitled "Hacking THE book" at Book Hackday[22] in London. Nicholas Tollervey[23] demonstrated a small program that dynamically queried Fluidinfo to locate objects about verses in a given book of the King James Bible.[24] It retrieves tags on objects that hold information from the LOLCAT Bible[25] and The Brick Testament[26] (Warning: NSFW!), and automatically assembles the result into an EPUB[27] document that can be read on a wide range of ebook devices.

Although a version of the Bible written in LOLCAT dialect with illustrations from the Brick Testament is obviously not going to be of interest to a wide audience, it illustrates how customized and personalized

---

[21] http://en.wikipedia.org/wiki/Freebie_marketing
[22] http://www.pereramedia.com/perera-talk/book-hackday
[23] http://ntoll.org/
[24] http://en.wikipedia.org/wiki/Authorized_King_James_Version
[25] http://www.lolcatbible.com/index.php?title=Main_Page
[26] http://www.bricktestament.com/
[27] http://en.wikipedia.org/wiki/EPUB

these things can be. Such a program could easily request and display opinions, ratings, annotations and page numbers your friends are up to. It could provide definitions, translations, footnotes, extra images, links, and the like. Additional information can be independently tagged onto the same underlying objects by other applications, with the "book" being rebuilt or updated dynamically as needed.

Skipping an Intermediate Step

If static ebook containers represent an intermediate stage, a step on the way from paper books to "books" that are more like applications, it should be possible for that stage to be skipped in some cases. We are already beginning to see this. For example, the Pearson[28] subsidiary Dorling Kindersley[29] announced an API Developer Initiative[30] around their Eyewitness Travel[31] guides. "In the US, sales of international guidebooks fell 20 percent between 2007 and 2009" as described in this Sydney Morning Herald article.[32] The travel information is still valuable, but people are rapidly realizing that it is no longer necessary to travel with a book when you are already carrying a mobile phone that has the considerable added advantage of built-in GPS.[33]

While one reaction might be to modernize your valuable content by moving it to a digital ebook format, it likely makes more sense to instead jump straight to building travel "book" applications on a device that can make API calls when needed, in order to pull (or push) small pieces of individual content or to run searches. For example, "find all the moderately priced and nearby Indian restaurants that are already (or still) open." Dorling Kindersley has already done the work of collecting, creating, and curating all the necessary information and getting it into book form. The steps of extracting and atomizing it, making it available via an API and building a user interface are relatively cheap.

---

[28] http://www.pearson.com/

[29] http://dk.com/

[30] http://bit.ly/120aKt

[31] http://us.dk.com/static/cs/us/11/travel/intro.html

[32] http://bit.ly/g204um

[33] http://en.wikipedia.org/wiki/Global_Positioning_System

This approach makes good sense as a way to ensure published content is accessible in modern mobile contexts and hence retains or even increases its value. An API opens the possibility of licensed programmatic access to published content, making it possible for third-party developers to build applications. In many cases, the most cost-effective user interfaces will be mobile web browsers. This reality explains the strong interest in Books in Browsers,[34] sponsored by the Internet Archive.[35]

To take the example a step further and to link it back to shared underlying storage, consider the extraordinary careers of Bob Arno and Bambi Vincent.[36] They run a blog called Thiefhunters in Paradise.[37] They've spent decades visiting hundreds of cities, filming and interviewing criminals and collecting unique and valuable data on street crime. If some of that data were stored in the same location as Pearson information, a travel application could additionally license it from Bob and Bambi for display. Display could take the form of mundane additional textual content, but could also be presented in the form of augmented reality.[38] You could hold up your phone and "see" city crime contours, showing you dangerous neighborhoods. You might receive a vibrating alert if the phone detects that you're entering a bad part of town. The possibilities are endless. While this might seem like science fiction, it is not. Applications of this type are already in the marketplace.[39]

Tying These Threads Together

I've mentioned two areas in which valuable content around books is not being realized: contextual information that publishers accumulate but have nowhere to put, and user-generated content that appears following publication. The monolithic, read-only nature of books, including ebook formats, does not offer a natural place for this additional content to be stored, used, combined, augmented, and monetized.

---

[34] http://www.archive.org/details/booksinbrowsers

[35] http://www.archive.org/

[36] http://bobarno.com/

[37] http://bobarno.com/thiefhunters/

[38] http://en.wikipedia.org/wiki/Augmented_reality

[39] http://en.wikipedia.org/wiki/Augmented_reality#Applications

The natural world well illustrates how we very often make information more useful and valuable by storing related information together. So the first point is that publishing can be looked at as a process that is more spread out in time, beginning earlier and perhaps never ending. If we had a guaranteed openly writable information store, including a permissions system, we would always have a place to store and act on metadata around any digital book. The value in this additional data pushes the system in that direction, and away from static read-only content (containers).

If users and other applications are to be allowed to add information, there needs to be a mechanism for ebook devices to get at this information and to add to it. APIs and network calls provide that mechanism. Once information is present in APIs, devices will be able to pull it on demand and in small chunks. Given a permissions system that operates at the level of the pieces of information instead of on entire ebooks, there is a natural transition to a world in which access to that information is not free, in which application developers can license content and in turn charge for it by selling applications.

In that world, users or interested third parties can contribute and charge for additional metadata. When digital "book" readers are actually general-purpose networked applications, formal container formats such as EPUB will be de-emphasized, just as has happened with HTML. In fact, browsers, JavaScript, and the broad capabilities of HTML5 provide a natural way to move quickly and cheaply to that world. Content becomes more dynamic and personalized, readers are able to contribute their own information, and that information can be considered social, because it is shared. It is also heterogeneous, because it can come from a variety of applications. Heterogeneous information about the same thing offers the rich potential of being used in combinations that those who originally deposited it could not have imagined, creating more value and more opportunity.

In summary, I believe the digital book world, and the digital world in general, is on the verge of becoming a lot more interesting as we move inexorably towards a common aspect of the visions of Paul Otlet and his successors. We are moving towards a world of applications, including ebook readers, that are based in part on shared writable storage with its attendant benefits.

Give the author feedback & add your comments about this chapter on the web: http://book.pressbooks.com/chapter/books-databases -terry-jones

12. Above the Silos: Social Reading in the Age of Mechanical Barriers (Travis Alber & Aaron Miller)

Travis Alber is co-founder and president of ReadSocial *(a service that adds a social layer inside books and websites). Previously she founded* BookGlutton.com. *You can find her on Twitter at:* @screenkapture.

Aaron Miller is co-founder at ReadSocial and BookGlutton, Director of Technology, Chief Engineer at NetGalley, Senior Developer at Firebrand Technologies. You can find Aaron on Twitter at: @vaporbook.

Introduction

People have always connected through books. As books enter an era in which they too can become connected, we must ask new questions about the nature of reading. We must be free to experiment with the new changing forms of books, the ways that people connect through them, and new modes of interaction. Most importantly—in a many-to-many future, where everything will be connected to everything else—we must look at the ways readers identify with each other, and how they organize meaningfully across the arbitrary divisions created by market forces. Groups of readers and their preferences are, in many ways, more relevant than any single reader out there. Often a single reader is simply a consumer, a passive audience member, whereas a grouping of consumers can be something much more powerful: a community.

Networks of Readers

Where books go, reading follows—this will always be dependable wisdom in the publishing industry. Put books in hands, and the reading will take care of itself. Publishing is not an industry that contemplates the purpose or potential of acts of communication; it is a system of production, distribution, and promotion that attempts to capitalize on latent and unpredictable demands. At its very noblest, it is a tradition of providing the very best of human thought and creativity in distilled, bespoke form. But even then, the mandate is clear: get content, package it, get it in the hands of the people you want to read it. Get them to talk about it, hopefully in favorable terms, but in the end, sell the books, just sell them so they can be read.

It's a lofty publisher who tries to look above the bottom line to ask the question: but how *should* books be read? And not only to ask that question, but to understand that it's not merely a question of hardback or paperback, or Kindle vs. Nook. It's not merely about whether a book will be an app, or whether it will be available in foreign territories simultaneous with its U.S. release. It's not about Garamond vs. Bembo either, or the colophon or dedication, or who you can get to write the introduction. It's not an experiential question at all; it's entirely metaphysical, and it might even be better to start with the question: *why* do people read books?

We think there is a very simple but profound answer to that question: people read books to make connections. This can be considered at a cognitive level, through simple, repetitive pattern recognition, or at a conceptual, spiritual level. Either way, the basic work of the reader's mind is to make connections, and the basic mode of higher thought is to exist both in and out of the physical world for a bit, drawing lines between the two.

In any written work, there is a cognitive process of connection-making that makes up the act of reading itself: glyphs form letters, letters connect into words, words into phrases and sentences, sentences into paragraphs, paragraphs into a sense of semantic completion. As we read, we progress through linear rhythms of pattern recognition even as we gain higher understanding of an author's argument, a character's motivation, or an historical event. By connecting very small patterns together into larger ones, we connect concepts back to the real world around us, to real people and places.

The pattern-recognition part can be thought of as a linear progression, necessary grunt-work for the brain to get at the concepts. However, the tangential connections we make are the ones that matter to us—and they're the reward that is so hard to get to for those who have trouble with the mechanical work of processing the words and sentences. We may even make many unintended connections along the way, and sometimes it's those surprises that keep us going. From a description of a road on a summer day, we might recall a bike ride from our youth. From a listing of facts about milk, we might be startled by a sudden craving for ice cream. Perhaps during an introspective passage about spirituality, we look up from the page to see our future spouse for the first time.

A book and its patterns, and the place we sit reading it, and the person we fall in love with, can become forever tied together. It is at this level that reading interests and addicts us. We think of it as a solitary act, but it's often the connections we make back to the real world that make it so rewarding. These connections are sometimes even more interesting when made across larger gulfs. Fake worlds, or extinct ones, can interest us more than the one we live in. We're fascinated by fictional characters when they mimic or reflect real personalities. Even the most outlandish science fiction[1] can be interesting in this way, because of the allegory, or the grand sense

---

[1] http://en.wikipedia.org/wiki/Foundation_series

of scale that crisply dramatizes contemporary issues, or the parallels we can make between even the most alien worlds and our own. It's these very large, meaningful connections that are the ultimate goal of reading. It's the understanding we gain, or at least feel we gain, about the world we live in, and the people we share it with, that are the deepest connections we make when we read. In that sense, it is entirely social.

Understanding this, then, what does it mean to go back and consider the question: how *should* books be read? And not only that, but how should they be read, given the context they're moving into?

It's not simply that books have become "digital." We find ourselves reading in a new context that is not just about carrying our entire personal libraries with us or about realizing a dictionary just works better being part of *every* book. It's not just about the constellation of tweets, videos, podcasts, blog posts, discussion threads, and YouTube videos that now surround a publication, or about how we read our books in whatever situation we want—possibly on the same device that maps the nearest freeway entrance, possibly while texting each other about dinner.

It's about the context of a new medium, the Web, which is inheriting books. It's a medium, it seems, that better embodies the idea of making connections between things, places, people, and events than any other medium that has preceded it. In its meteoric growth, it seems to have captured our interest with this very quality. On the Web, we call connections *links*,[2] of course, but they are not much different conceptually from the kinds of links we make in our own minds while we read. What does it mean that books are moving into this medium, where connections are part of its very fabric?

Getting books along that path is the business of web designers and developers who are creating the next generation of books and book interfaces, and of the entrepreneurs who are building the next wave of distribution and communication channels for them. Perhaps books will always be called "books," but what they actually are might change, so that they could also be called "web bindings," a new kind of web page collection. In any case, they will all necessarily be linked to each other in various ways, just as most everything on the Web is.

But before that can happen, we have to solve a problem. When people

---

[2] http://www.wordnik.com/words/hyperlink

read digital books today, they are engaging in an activity that is all about connections, on a device that can potentially make those connections, but they're being prevented from making them. So again, instead of looking at the question of how people should be reading, we've so far only addressed the question of how to get books to them. Unfortunately, instead of delivering those books in silos of disconnected paper, we've delivered them in disconnected mechanical devices. Instead of going directly to the Web, we're taking a roundabout way, and the interests of readers, and the future of reading itself, suffer terribly.

That books are inherently social is not an undisputed point. In most cases when it's conceded, it's still argued that the act of reading them is still not in any way social. This line of argument claims first that reading is a solitary activity. It is done alone, has always been, and if the future holds something different, it is so far away that we should not distract ourselves with thinking about it.

This argument is reductive in three destructive ways: *books*, *social*, and *reading* are each oversimplifications of what we actually refer to with those words. They are dangerous to combine in any argument or theory. In fact, reading may be solitary, sometimes, but it's not *necessarily* solitary. When it's done in solitude, meaning without the help of others, or in physical and social isolation, it is often done so for the purpose of understanding or entertainment. To understand something, our brains must concentrate, and exclusion is necessary for that. And to enjoy something, we must allow it to captivate our imagination and senses, and this is a solipsistic activity. So in both of those cases, reading must be solitary.

But we all know, if we've ever learned to read with the help of a parent, or learned to analyze literature with a professor and group of peers, or discussed the latest Twilight book in a fan group, that much understanding and fun can occur around a book after we've had that first solitary connection to it. And in fact, the varieties of fun and understanding out there are far more diverse than the solitary ways in which we initially engage with our favorite books. Thus, much of the value in books lies in discovering that they are shared experiences, and seeing the spectrum of individual connections to them.

It's in that spectrum that the Web offers so much for the medium of the book. As a network of people and communities, it is also a network of voracious readers. As an extremely versatile and evolving visual medium for the consumption of content, it can nurture the solitary, experiential nature of reading. And as a network for other kinds of media, for social interaction, and for sharing, it can enhance the communal, educational, and analytical aspects of our experiences with books.

We Are All Book Gluttons

In 2005, despite the rise of social networking, digital books on the Web were limited to free editions of public domain works, loaded as a single, scrolling text file. The reading interface usually consisted of the browser's own scroll bars, the ability to share the URL of the book, and the customary contextual controls (right click for a menu of things you could do with the page or a range of text). As an experience, reading these books online was, in all cases, limited to what the browser itself offered.

There was no way to discuss the book in context, meaning as you looked at its pages. To us, it appeared as if all the people who cared about books online had casually flung them there in their rawest state. A few projects attempted to present them with sophistication, but by and large, it seemed none of the projects had put the kind of thought into creating those online forms that a web designer, developer, or information architect would have developed. And meanwhile, the rest of the Web, including other forms of older media like audio and video, was benefiting from the careful attention of a decade of thought about reflowable layout, digital typography, visual design, and user experience.

There were very few online reading options for books then, and those that existed weren't benefiting at all from being on the Web. To us, it seemed that the Web offered endless possibilities for a new kind of reading experience, something that was not possible offline, and not possible with printed books, but truly native to the way people already used the Web. An idea emerged, over the proverbial cocktail napkin and a round of bourbon, at a local spot in Champaign, Illinois. The basic concept was a web-based reading system that could connect people anywhere and let them discuss parts of a book as they looked at its pages together. It would preserve many things we loved about books, such as the importance of page layout, margins, readable type, but it would add what we liked about the Web: connections to other readers, a sense of communal experience, a window into other people's reactions, the chance to respond or add our own thoughts.

Being web developers, we did what web developers do when something doesn't exist and they have some time: we built it. In October of 2006, we began wireframing what would come to be called BookGlutton, a site that aggregated books and allowed unlimited consumption of them, with others, all in the browser. At the time, the social web that we know today was just taking hold. MySpace was the dominant social network, with Orkut and Friendster following. Facebook had opened to non-students[3] in September 2006, and Twitter had been founded just two months earlier, in July 2006.

In January of 2008, we launched the first public version of BookG-lutton.com.[4] At the time, no other website, service, or device combined access to book people with access to book content. Sites like LibraryThing, Goodreads, and Shelfari were focused squarely on giving people ways to share and discover book metadata, not book content. Each of these sites appealed to a different type of user: LibraryThing had a number of specific ways to track metadata, especially by edition; Goodreads was focused on short book reviews created by its users; and Shelfari, which was purchased by Amazon within six months of launching, was working towards a slick interface and a focus on finding other people who had read the same book. Many serious readers belonged to all three sites at some point (membership was free), but there was considerable overlap, and users generally picked one site that focused on a preferred trait. These sites had plenty of social components, but no content.

On the content side, Project Gutenberg, Manybooks, Feedbooks, and Amazon were all about downloading books to read offline. Gutenberg was the oldest way to get books and had always been free; Manybooks focused on providing as many formats as possible; while Feedbooks provided high-quality editions for the new mobile devices popping up everywhere. You could jump off from many of these sites to buy content, but much of what

---

[3] http://tcrn.ch/9n4WR8
[4] http://www.bookglutton.com

you could buy was still printed material. The ebook world was showing signs that powerful forces were about to make it grow fast, but it was still in its infancy in terms of what was available. The iPhone was the unexpected success in terms of providing a reading experience. An app called Stanza had managed to aggregate free books from the Web and allow users to flip through pages by swiping them back and forth; the high resolution of the screen made up for its small size, and the combined result was a very tactile, reflowable reading experience with plenty of content choices. On the dedicated device side, the first Kindle arrived in November 2007 and, along with the Sony Reader, set the standard for e-ink devices.

In the midst of the content distributors, the device makers, and the social book networks, BookGlutton sparked an interest in the notion of social reading: the act of reading while connected to other people, or the philosophy of reading as a connected activity, not an isolated one. It was a space that no product or service had entered yet, and it revealed something often overlooked or forgotten about books—that they have always been social objects. They have always provoked reaction, social change, conversation, dogma. They exist as educational tools, as propaganda, as centerpieces to entire religions. They are passed down in families, passed along as vehicles of knowledge, human history, scientific thought, and philosophy. They have provoked wars, helped broker peace, and been burned out of fear of their social influence. They contain our imaginations and our histories. They spark debates and influence law; they entertain audiences and inspire them to create new entertainments. Many books come down to us through long histories of oral tradition; others have been compiled meticulously over time through processes of committees and organizations. Books are vehicles for something much older than their containers, and that legacy is undeniably the larger society's record of its own interactions.

We think that an important shift is happening now, in the way that we think of books, which is to say that the Web is beginning to unlock some of the latent potential of them, potential that has been locked not just by their physical nature, but by their long history of commodification in physical form. The Web is quickly antiquating the notion that a book is a physical object you buy, read in solitude, and never think of again. A book is now an image on your profile, connecting you to anyone else with that image. It's an organizing topic for a virtual group or a badge on your blog, a vessel for topical conversation, a record of your education. It's now tweetable from a dozen different virtual places. Now, as books not only go digital, but move online, the natural dialog that already exists around them (and always has) can be amplified in ways we could never before imagine.

You can see evidence of this potential even in their commodification. The educational textbook market in the U.S. last year was $10 billion. That is a fair amount of trade happening on books that are intended for a shared, social context (classrooms and universities), with an explicit social ideal as a goal (furthering the knowledge of our young and preparing them to give back to society).

You can see it even when looking at the blockbuster titles from big publishing houses. Top sellers are often celebrities, politicians, or other individuals with strong social influence. The social network effects of such titles can be measured in terms of fan groups, website memberships and activity, Facebook likes, Twitter followers, etc. And it's not just that books have suddenly become social—they've always been social—it's that we're seeing a revolution in what the Web can do for anything that's already inherently social. The notion of gluttony—a concept that almost never has any positive social connotations—bears exception when it is applied to lovers of books, who proudly proclaim themselves avid devourers of these social viands. The Web itself is a glut of things, books included, and we are all social consumers of that abundance. Not only does it never end—it always grows in size. Even an infinity of gluttony won't consume it all. We are all destined to be book gluttons, in the most positive sense of the term.

Group Reading in a Browser

BookGlutton[5] is a destination, a reading system, a free catalog of books, and a community. It allows people to form groups and connections just as many social networks do. What distinguishes it is that books are read while on the site, right in the browser. Users create a group around a book, invite their friends, and comment on each paragraph. They can also see and respond to

---

[5] http://www.bookglutton.com

comments that have been left by others. The comments are asynchronous and grow over time, creating an additional layer of annotation content on top of the book. Readers can also join a chat room for the book, discussing it chapter by chapter.

We have always believed the web browser to be a better tool for reading digital text than any other application or device. This is a matter of heated debate, and is more or less defensible by degrees for different kinds of content, on different sites, at different times in recent history, but overall, we have believed in and encouraged the trend toward the browser eventually becoming the perfect reading environment for any digital content, on any platform. Recent advances have shown this trend to be accelerating, especially with the proliferation of tablets, where the browsing experience is more central. Traditional drawbacks to browser-based reading are all being addressed in rapid fashion on many fronts, faster than we've seen previously. The bigger historical complaints—poor typography, no offline capability, no paginated views and too many distractions—have been, or are being, addressed, via combinations of new standards and open source efforts, and most browsers now allow offline reading, third-party font support, and pagination. Services like Readability and Instapaper are aimed at reducing clutter, ads, and other distractions to reading content on the Web, and now there are many browser-based reading systems for books that focus on good typography and ease-of-use, whereas in 2006, there were none.

It would be easy to say now that it was a foregone conclusion that books would wind up in browsers. But at the time that BookGlutton was released, there was much skepticism around the idea, mainly for the historical complaints mentioned above. But it was not long before a viable path became clear, and that it was not only viable but probable. As Amazon's Kindle strategy[6] was revealed to be a multi-device, multi-platform strategy, and as Apple entered the race, not only with a tablet, but with a competing ebook application, and as Google released their own e-book store, built entirely around a browser-based reading system, and Amazon followed that with their own browser-based Kindle application, it became painfully evident for smaller players in the space that the browser would definitely

---

[6] http://www.teleread.com/uncategorized/amazons-long-play/

be playing a central role in our future consumption of digital books.[7] Furthering that, and perhaps stoking for an inferno, Amazon launched the Kindle Fire, a tablet clearly meant to rival the iPad more in its potential for media sales than its novelty as a device. Finally, as if to hammer home the idea of books becoming native web citizens, the International Digital Publishing Forum (IDPF[8]) in 2011 released their specification for EPUB 3, and by doing so confirmed a very close alignment with HTML 5,[9] the bleeding edge version of the markup language that makes up most documents on the Web.

Despite the stiff competition for readers, BookGlutton has gathered over 30,000 members and over 4,000 groups, of which some 300 are classrooms studying public domain classics. Anyone can add EPUB books to their group, and any book may be shared with any other user in the network. The core catalog, about 700 books at the outset, has since expanded to about 5,000. One of the draws is still the unique combination of virtual book groups with an in-browser reading experience. It is the living example of what has become known as "social reading."

Our goal in building a reading system was to address two modes of reading: the solitary mode, which required focus, concentration, and lack of distractions, and the social mode, in which interactions with the text and with other people are key requirements. In both, we wanted the book itself to be a central, dominant component. Initially we floated the social features on top of the page in a dialog that the user could drag around. This allowed for a narrower screen, but it also obscured the content (Figure 1). At the time it seemed unforgivable, but has since become an acceptable inconvenience on most mobile devices. By launch we had redesigned for a laptop screen and added two horizontal sliding bars that opened and closed, to hide and show social content (Figure 2).

BookGlutton's reading system tracks each user's location inside a book, relative to each other and the content points of the book, as a social map, the way you might want to know the locations of your friends at a party. The left side chat bar featured a "proximity factor" to provide a measure of

---

[7] http://bit.ly/MDncyL
[8] http://idpf.org/
[9] http://www.w3.org/TR/html5/" target="_blank

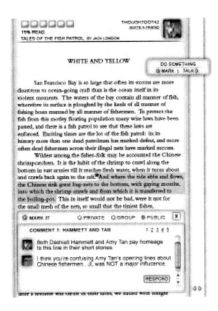

Figure 12.1. Original BookGlutton Unbound Reader

Figure 12.2. Current BookGlutton Reader

the relevance of each instant message to the current user's reading location: for context-specific conversations and for avoiding spoilers.

Figure 12.3. BookGlutton Chat Bar with Proximity

Although BookGlutton offers multiple types of communication, asynchronous is more popular. To attach comments to a paragraph, the user clicks on a paragraph to select it. The commenting bar slides open, and the user can type in a note. Comments may be public to the group or private. Some readers make private comments that are strictly word definitions, while others use the public comments to ask questions or react to passages. All comments also have a reply button. Responses are non-nested, for the sake of simplicity.

Reading a comment is easy—activity on a paragraph is denoted by a small red asterisk in the margin of the book.

Readers can manually slide open the Comment Bar and see where the comments in the book have been placed (clicking on one jumps users to that page of the book). There could be thousands of comments on a paragraph at any one time, but only those relevant to a particular group appear. Moreover, any paragraph can have multiple comments attached to it, with multiple replies to each one, which can lead to a lot of data living on top of a book.

One of the salient truths that has arisen from operating and studying

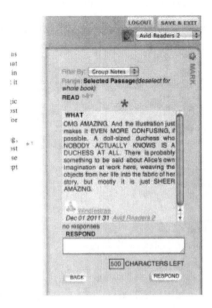

Figure 12.4. BookGlutton Annotations Bar

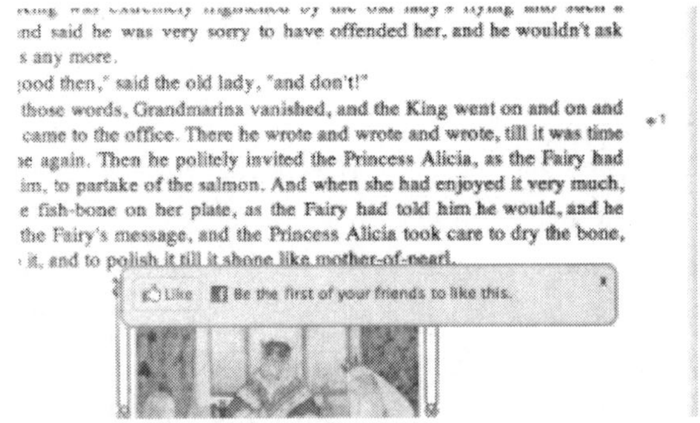

Figure 12.5. BookGlutton Highlight with Asterisk

BookGlutton as a website and community is one that seems to be gaining importance all across the social web: the importance of groups in fostering social interaction, especially groups that have real-world grounding.

Groups form all the time on social websites, of course, but they can be divided into two key types. The first is an assortment of strangers who simply gather around something—a topic, a meme, a product, a celebrity, a favorite food, a news article. The bond between these people is usually weak. When one invites another to take some action, the likelihood of that action happening is fairly slim.

The second type of group is a group of people who know each other in real life. The likelihood of one member inciting another to take some action is fairly high. In the early days of the BookGlutton site, when a member of a group invited another to join the group, it was usually because they knew them in some physical setting, and the conversion rate was nearly 80 percent for those kinds of invitations. The stronger the real-world bonds across virtual groups, the better the interaction and engagement will be.

It would seem to be self-evident, when stated this way, but early efforts at social networking online largely ignored the importance of groups. The exception was the network with the most velocity on its growth rates. The initial viral growth of Facebook owed a lot to the method of deployment: one college campus at a time. Since every student on a campus could be verified by virtue of owning an email address with that institution's .edu domain, there was a strong parity between the real world bonds and the virtual ones. This created extremely high conversion rates, and high-velocity growth.

Reading, as a social activity, is no different from any other social activity in this regard. The interactions between readers of a book, the engagement with the book itself, and the bond among group members are all significantly enhanced by some grounding in a real-world group unit, whether it's a classroom, a college, a family, or a church.

With BookGlutton, we did not initially realize that the expectations for a book-related site were geared powerfully toward searching for a title, finding it, downloading it, and reading it somewhere else. Those users quickly became disappointed, because that was not the system that we had built. We had built a group reading system, meant for shared experiences of a text, group annotation, and a sense of community around the act of reading and annotation. It was ideal for people who knew that learning about a book is best done in a group setting, or for people long distances from each other who wanted to let reading the same book draw them closer together. We realized that we were not emphasizing the group aspect of it enough. We were seeing many users come and stay, and invariably they were the users who had come seeking that group experience around a book.

Now, when a user registers on BookGlutton, a group is automatically created for him or her. Each group has an associated reading list. It is then up to the user to invite friends to the group or add more content to the reading list. Users can have many groups, the core of which are personal connections. Many are still based around a book or a concept, although we still see the most successful groups having a corollary offline.

Figure 12.6. BookGlutton Group Page

The center of group activity is the Group Page. Users can jump into the current book from this page, message all users in the group, or leave a message on the group wall. Any user can also change the current book for the group's reading list. Multiple methods of communication meet different needs.

Content on BookGlutton comes from a variety of sources: free public domain titles, free books from Feedbooks and Girlebooks, excerpts from

Random House and McGraw-Hill, original publications by BookGlutton, and for-sale books from O'Reilly and Holarts Books. BookGlutton also offers an HTML to EPUB converter for writers who need to get their content into the EPUB format for discussion on BookGlutton.

Figure 12.7. BookGlutton Catalog

Much activity on BookGlutton centered around excerpts, lower-cost and free content. Major authors added comments to some of their book excerpts, and readers responded. New fiction writers uploaded their work and got feedback. English as a Second Language (ESL) groups used it to learn context and vocabulary. Around three-hundred school systems and universities began to use it as an online component of their classrooms.

These uses taught us some valuable information about how groups interact and how offline and online associations influenced each other. At one time 79% of all group invites were accepted, and 20% of new users started their own additional group. We were seeing things we hadn't expected and would have never predicted. But the biggest realization came after a full year of having a book store. We were running three separate businesses: distributing content, promoting content, and making content social. It was this last business that interested us. No one seemed to think it was even a business, and we weren't sure yet either, but we did know it would be a big aspect of what books became.

The Read Social Mantra

By observing BookGlutton over a four-year period and experimenting with other, smaller proof-of-concepts, we came to several realizations about how we should try to move things forward. The first was that the content network, the reading platform, and the social layer are three distinct businesses. Each of the three specializations requires its own technical considerations, strategy, and business development plan. A small company or group of people cannot handle all of the challenges of each of those businesses combined. Even large companies falter when they attempt to reach outside their realm of expertise in one of those domains.

Secondly, the social layer, which we call the group layer, is new, and as such it requires dedicated thought, experimentation, and collaboration. To create experiences that "just work," every user interface consideration makes a difference: from the steps involved in posting a public comment, to how groups are defined, to how comments are managed long term. Moreover, as the user base becomes more comfortable with social networking and how it's integrated into systems, expectations change. It is extremely difficult to get it right the first time. Iteration is key. This is especially difficult for large companies with a close eye on profitability, as it might take several iterations to increase conversion rates.

Another thing we noticed: while many people might be casually interested in browsing a stranger's comments on a book, very few will want to engage with those comments. In a group, on the other hand, there is often some top-down structure, or an assignment or other group goal. This makes interaction important and connections trusted. Trusted connections facilitate more open communication and engagement with the book.

We learned that for books, asynchronous is better than synchronous. This was contrary to what we expected. The Web has become more "real time," and we had assumed people would want to announce each time they've opened a book. In fact, we used Twitter to allow people to do just that, but it wasn't what they really wanted. Instead we found that while a rapid-fire, real time discussion is occasionally valuable, books are different. Most books are a longer-term commitment than other media and are consumed at a slower pace. People dip in and out of them. They are grazed on, ruminated on. Some require great study and thought before their messages are clear to us. They are, in many ways, asynchronous. As a result, it's rare that readers will meet at the same point at the same time. Our conclusion: the 24 hour, global nature of the Internet makes asynchronous communication the preferred mode for long form media.

Based on these realizations, we built a new system, ReadSocial, which focuses exclusively on how to connect people across reading systems. Instead of offering a destination (like a website), with content (like an ebook), ReadSocial offers all content owners a way to add group-based, asynchronous commenting to what they've already built. From ReadSocial.net any content owner (blog owners, small ebook publishers, iPad magazine apps, ebook reading systems) can choose a usage tier and get a bit of code that ties into the ReadSocial system. This will allow their users to create groups, attach comments, images, and links, and respond to comments by others.

Figure 12.8. How Readsocial Works

ReadSocial uses open groups, tracked via hashtags (for example #janeaustin or #peoria_readers or #mrs_james_hour2). Anyone can read posts to any group (if they know the group tag). Users are identified via OAuth, which is the mechanism used by Twitter and many other social networks. It's not a perfect solution, but it's one widely used solution to the problem of accurately identifying users across systems. It encourages the use of aliases—the same user might be able to OAuth themselves from a different network each time, but the network they use is seen as an authority on who they are. In this way, other users can at least have some

Figure 12.9. How Readsocial Works

reassurance that the joe_schmoe they know on Twitter is really validated by Twitter, even though he's posting on ReadSocial.

They may also see a joe_schmoe from Wordnik and know that it's the same Joe Schmoe they know, but if they see a joe_schmoe from evilnet.unknowndomain.com, they can steer clear. It's not the solution everyone is looking for, but it's working for many services now, and it solves one problem that ReadSocial must solve: how to ensure that offline bonds are driving online interaction. Offline users might not all know each other from Twitter, and that's fine for ReadSocial. Likewise, they might not all buy books from Amazon and read them on Kindles, and that's fine too. A person can read and post with the same group tag on any system that uses ReadSocial, with any content, using any OAuthority as their identity network.

Using open groups and group tags, an individual can read the same paragraph or article and "group surf," getting different commentary with every change in group context. Moreover, any reading system can pull in new and changing content immediately. For example, the #ows group wants to comment on news. Members can go to any site, iPad app, blog, or other content channel with ReadSocial installed. If the same article is syndicated across all of these places, then #ows comments will appear in the margin. A user may read or respond to a comment or post their own.

Anyone can build a client interface for the ReadSocial service. If a

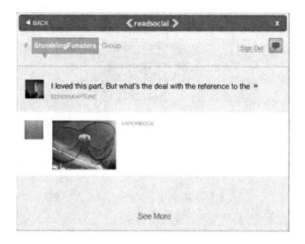

Figure 12.10. ReadSocial Web Client

Figure 12.11. ReadSocial Inside an iPad App

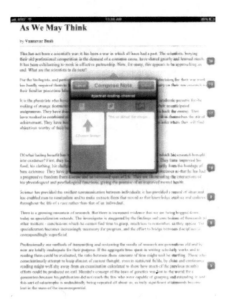

Figure 12.12. Attaching a ReadSocial Comment on the iPad

company wants a completely branded experience with additional features (such as recommended groups or book recommendations), it can build on top of the API. For companies that just want to get going right out of the box there are the open source client libraries for web and iPad (which include the visual components for the interface that that users need to create groups and manage comments).

Conclusion

We're now at least six years into a new age of social reading. Community interaction is a natural extension of the Web, and we will continue to see more sophisticated integration of features that have their roots in the Internet. The Web will be our guide. In working through the design and development of BookGlutton and ReadSocial, we made some key discoveries about social reading:

- Groups are not necessarily groups of people, but topical filters for conversation. It's not necessary to think about a group made up of people accepting invitations; it can also be made up of concepts and ideas. A group can use a topic as an organizing force. We see hash tags used this way on Twitter.

- Groups are often related to real-world communities, events, and networks. The more off-line interaction a group has, the stronger the ties; offline user groups transcend siloed technology purchases. The strongest web-based products have a connection to the real world. ReadSocial respects *those* bonds, not the ones between vendor and consumer, by enabling open notes that cross silos.

- People are used to commenting publicly on things that are public, moreover some things are inherently public (i.e., an untweeted tweet is not a tweet at all). As long as the user is aware of the context, an open system works. Closed systems and systems with complex levels of authentication and privileges are desirable too, but at this point in time, it may be better to start in earnest on solving the problems that we're ready to solve.

- Location/passage identification is going to be up to reading systems, standards groups, and content publishers.

- Interfaces and systems for storage, sorting, searching, and grouping of shared items will be the expertise of the social layer. To create trust with your users, it is important to be straightforward and clear about who owns comments, where they go, and who can see them. Like web search, entire businesses will be built around these simple concepts of filtering and interfacing with social reading data.

- Getting network effects is a dedicated task (a.k.a. building good social networks is really hard). ReadSocial doesn't invent its own network, it builds on top of existing ones.

- The conversation layer is where publishers and providers of reading systems tend to get lost, as it's often at cross-purposes for them. Specializing in the overlay interface creates distinct value.

Even in Web-based systems there will be many approaches. One would be to offer a fully integrated solution of reading system, book, and community from a single source. BookGlutton gives us insight into benefits and drawbacks of this type of system. If a company owns the content and has the technical savvy to run the reading system and group management, it can be a powerful experience. It is more in-line with traditional group invites (users invite others via email), and the level of control of the group and reading system can offer a heavily personalized experience. Systems like this are great for gaining metrics, and they offer a wide-range of possibilities for customized activities. Of course, drawbacks stem from the same level of control. Successfully managing a system is more complex—and the focus on community is often lost in the quest for a flexible reading system and adequate content.

ReadSocial offers a different approach—the API. It offers the ability to quickly add a social interface and share content with other systems. The ability for networks to pull in content from other networks (and push it out) can be powerful. The system works best with the greatest network effects; like most social systems it gains value the more it is used. The open group tag allows for content-based groups as well as people-based groups, and it works easily with an offline component, which we've found is a major driving force.

We know that some of this is guesswork. OK, *a lot* of it is guesswork. But the important thing is not to dismiss what's actually going on right *now*. People are reading differently already. It's the readers who are determining the future, not the large corporations we think are dictating the way people read. Give them tools to read the way they want to, and watch how they do it, and learn from what you observe. Iterate on that. And keep it simple while you do. If a system looks too hard to use or seems too hard to understand, no one will try, and you won't learn anything. The most exciting part of what's happening now is that there are a thousand possibilities. We might not have a fraction of the time to do them all, but there are millions of other people out there getting interested in this future. Let's share ideas and make the future happen sooner.

Give the author feedback & add your comments about this chapter on the web: `http://book.pressbooks.com/chapter/above-the-silos -travis-alber-aaron-miller`

13. User Experience, Reader Experience (Brett Sandusky)

Brett Sandusky is Product Manager at Macmillan New Ventures where he oversees agile user experience design, development of new digital products, eCommerce, research and data analysis, and mobile applications. Formerly Director of Product Innovation for Kaplan Publishing, Brett's expertise also includes digital strategy, product usability, content integration cross-platforms, and digital marketing. He lives in Brooklyn, NY and can be found on Twitter at: @bsandusky.

Let's start with a hypothesis: ebooks, as we know them today, are an artificial and interim step in digital development by publishers. As such, they will go away.

In any discussion of the current and future states of ebook development, in particular with regards to User Experience (UX), it is inevitable to begin with this pronouncement. As we delve into UX principles and how they affect digital product development, usability and reception, we begin to see that the ebook for what it is, and how it will evolve.

There are many definitions for User Experience. In fact, it is a discipline that covers many areas of concern. While some practitioners limit their scope to only issues related to usability, contextual inquiry or design, UX does, in reality, encompass all of these issues and extends further to encompass a holistic approach to product design and implementation.

This means that the actual scope of UX covers everything from the first sparks of ideation, guiding product development teams in their endeavors, to marketing practice, through post-launch development, customer service and how end users interact with a company. In short, UX covers a broad range of internal and external curated interactions that collectively have the objective of producing and maintaining a usable product for end users.

Through these various means, the ultimate goal of the UX practitioner is to present data-informed options, so that product teams can make informed decisions about their products. Creating a product is a process of significant give and take and compromise; it is impossible to create a product that does everything for everyone. The aim of the various disciplines that make up UX is to elucidate the various paths and compromises that one could take, present data showing the impact of each of these paths, and allow for proper decision making to take place. This holds true for all facets of UX from design to usability to interactions with users.

For the purposes of this chapter, we are going to focus on the areas of contextual inquiry and usability in product development. We will see how each of these are affected and enhanced by UX practice. Ultimately, we will be looking at and evaluating the ebook, as it currently exists, from a UX standpoint.

Contextual inquiry

Every usable product should begin with some form of contextual inquiry. Contextual inquiry is a process involving several types of activities that collect data from users to help build a product they need. The process related to contextual inquiry should be part of the initial phase of product development; it is meant to inform product ideation.

It is important to note here that the aim of contextual inquiry is to determine what features and functions a user needs. *Need*, here, is opposed to *want*. In product development. self-reported wants from users is the wrong approach to building usable products. First off, users are rarely able to express their latent needs for a product and translate those needs into specific feature sets or pieces of functionality. More important, however, is that users may be completely unaware of the capabilities and limitations of a device or file format.

Consider these two examples:

As a product developer, I am highly involved in following customer service inquiries, user-generated analytics, product reviews and social media chatter about the products that I put out into the world. One major complaint that we hear time and time again is that ebook products do not work on PCs or laptops. This issue is much more complex than just making the file available. The user may be completely unaware of the implications of what it actually means to have proper e-reading software on a computer in order for them to read an ebook on that device. To the user, device support and availability is simply a decision made by the publisher. While there may be valid business reasons to exclude certain devices or outlets from distribution, most publishers are not actively trying to limit their audience by making it difficult or impossible to purchase and access their content.

The flip side of this is another example of availability. Quite often, I see inquiries from customers asking why certain products don't work on specific devices. So far, this is the same thing we were just talking about. However, in this case, the product is available on the device they name. At least 50% of the inquiries about device support and availability relate to customers who are simply unaware that the product they want to use is already available on the device they want to use. Users just don't know where.

A simple remedy to this is marketing, but that still does not capture the whole story. What is important to see, here, is that our customers are not always in sync with our products. And if we cannot expect them to know everything about our product offerings, including simple information (to us!) about device support, how will they know how to suggest a coherent strategy for the future?

This is where contextual inquiry comes in. To develop a product based on contextual inquiry, the product developer spends time observing end users and capturing information that will lead to developing a coherent list of features and functionality pieces. The tools of contextual inquiry include, but are not limited to:

- behavior observation
- user surveys
- affinity diagramming
- creating user personas, and
- ethnography.

By using these tools and watching a user do the tasks they need to accomplish with a tool, the UX practitioner will begin to take note of all the deficiencies and product requirements for based on observed user behavior.

This user behavior data become one of many data snippets that are compiled when considering a project.

For publishers to apply contextual inquiry techniques in evaluating user needs for ebooks, we are presented with two very crucial challenges:

1. The current limitations of the EPUB format and e-reader device support produce a negative impact on the user experience we are able to offer to our customers; and
2. Users are uninterested in the reasons behind publishers' inability to offer better products.

Compounding these challenges is the fact that one of the principles of contextual inquiry is to delay decision making (in this case, let's use decisions related to format, for example) until data analysis is complete. The output of contextual inquiry should inform product development teams of required and non-necessary (nice-to-have) components for feature sets, functionality and design. This can easily lead to the conclusion that, to offer the best user experience, publishers should not be building ebooks at all. Rather, there is an entire gamut of digital products that live both on- and offline that can offer more supported features to include.

Usability

We'll come back to the idea of the UX of ebooks. But first we are going to look at usability and how this fits into our decision-making process.

If contextual inquiry is concerned with product ideation and inception, the domain of usability is product testing and improvement, followed by user acceptance. Whereas contextual inquiry begins with no or very little knowledge about the product to come, usability tests the product that is. Usability is less concerned about adding feature sets, as it is about evaluating feature sets and making sure they perform properly.

As with contextual inquiry, usability relies upon observation as a source of information used to steer decisions. However, there is also the added benefit of having an existing product to evaluate. In an ideal situation, the product itself would yield data, usage analytics, to product teams. These analytics can then be combined with observational data to create a detailed picture of a product's performance.

When we look at usability of ebooks, we are looking at the usability of the device and of the specific software used to render the EPUB file on that device. Publishers are dependent on device manufacturers and retailers for the large majority of decisions made related to reading experience. Differentiation is a de-facto function of device and not currently being driven by publishers who are making the products.

This notion is particularly important as we begin working with the newly accepted EPUB 3.0 specification. The main obstacle to implementing the next wave of enhancements to ebooks lies not in a publisher's ability to develop these new products, but rather with adoption and support of the new capabilities by device manufacturers.

The overwhelming majority of the EPUB 3.0 spec is based on HMTL, CSS, and the optional support of Javascript libraries. Every one of the elements new to EPUB is already supported on the web. While e-readers support web browsers and e-reader software universally finds its code base in web browsers, a large number of web capabilities and features are 'turned off' in the ereader environment. The decisions pertaining to which features are supported, when, and how they are implemented are made by the device manufacturers. This leaves publishers with very few options, mostly involving design and layout, with which to create a differentiated experience from their competitors in the digital space.

For print products, publisher can and do make many decisions related to user experience. These decisions affect paper quality, printing styles, cover design, layout, fonts, typesetting and the like. With digital products, few options remain in the hands of the publisher. Devices can override stylesheets, fonts can be unsupported and color may not be an option.

The crux of the problem is this: in the digital space, user experience is the primary differentiator between companies which create and provide content. How is it, then, that publishing has allowed the primary source of market differentiation to be outsourced to device manufacturers?

The reality of the situation is that publishers have for too long not thought of their practices in terms of user experience, and many are not creating digital products as anything more than an offshoot of their printed materials.

I would offer this: readers are less interested in a parity experience of print when purchasing digital materials. They want the full benefits of the digital reading experience. They want the benefits of the technology. They want the convenience offered by digital books.

Conclusion

Coming back to the original premise, then: given this landscape, what does the future of ebooks look like?

Let's begin by getting one thing out of the way: ebooks are webpages. The code base is exactly the same; the functionality and interactivity of the web is possible within the EPUB wrapper.

As publishers begin to pay attention to their digital workflow, they will see that things like contextual inquiry and usability become essential to success for digital products. It is my hope that the absolute necessity of user experience practice becomes a leading principle for digital product development.

In a world where publishers focus on user experience, we will begin to see that ebooks represent a single file format with certain benefits and limitations. This is the case for many other formats. The decision to offer a product digitally should not default to one format or another, but should be an organic part of the product development cycle.

As it currently stands, we are in the infancy of offering a wide variety of digital products, ebooks, websites, native apps, web apps, and many combinations of these things. Publishers are just starting to see that the reader experience, long their concern, is now also the user experience.

———————————

Give the author feedback & add your comments about this chapter on the web: http://book.pressbooks.com/chapter/user-experience -reader-experience-brett-sandusky

14. App, Meet Book (Ron Martinez)

Ron Martinez is the founder of Aerbook, *and its parent company,* Invention Arts. *He's a prolific inventor, with close to a hundred and fifty issued patents or patent applications currently in flight. Prior to his current work at Invention Arts, Ron worked for a number of years as Vice President, Intellectual Property Innovation for Yahoo! You can find Ron on Twitter at:* @ronmartinez.

When considering the evolution of the book, it's useful to look at the dynamics in other forms of media. We have enough history now with computers as an expressive medium to see that some dynamics are repeated so reliably that they may as well be considered laws. Take, for example:

The Laws of Surprise and Demand

- The first iteration of a platform delivers enough to establish that platform.
- Platform capabilities evolve faster than does the content.
- Content innovators surprise the marketplace with delightful new experiences made possible by the evolved platform.

- People demand these and other delightful new experiences.

In the technical medium, the act of surprising people with cool new experiences leads to demand for those experiences. It may seem shallow, but it's not, really. It's kind of the story of human expression in all forms of media, if you think about it.

Recent market experience illustrates this invariable progression. Take computer games, for instance, and the continual stair-stepping of fast-evolving platforms. They have to evolve first, because you can't make content for a non-existent machine, and they are soon followed by the games that take full advantage of the new capabilities. From Pong up through graphic adventures, role-playing games, flight simulators, massively multiplayer games, and now social and mobile games, each new set of cool platform capabilities is followed by cool new games that use the new capabilities.

So, what does this have to do with publishing books? For text-based, immersive narrative of one kind or another, it turns out, not a whole lot. There's not much a graphics card, geo-locator, or sprawling social graph can do to improve upon a great novel. In fact, it's pretty clear that attempting to inject any new platform capability into the existing form and expecting a good outcome is a misunderstanding of the laws. The resulting experience must also be delightful. *Pride and Prejudice* interrupted by a video clip is not delightful.

But the potential for other forms is real, nonetheless. Entire classes of books, those I'm interested in, like illustrated non-fiction, children's books, culinary titles, how-to, and special interest books, have until recently had to sit out the revolution. The first-generation, text-centric, reflowable ebook platform has been incapable of delivering even the baseline capabilities these books require.

And so, books like these have had to go outside the ebook format to try another that offers more capabilities: the app. There are marvelous apps available in every category I mentioned. For publishing, the dynamic has played out like this:

- The first iteration of a platform delivers enough to establish that platform. (Think Kindle/genre fiction.)

- Platform capabilities evolve faster than does the content. (Think iPad.)
- Content innovators surprise the marketplace with delightful new experiences made possible by the evolved platform. (Think app makers.)
- People demand these and other delightful new experiences. (Think apps.)

More specifically, think of the aforementioned children's book apps, as well as culinary, popularized science, travel, and how-to apps. "Revolutionary new book platforms" like PushPopPress once aspired to redefine the ebook itself–as an app.

Well, what is it that the app does that the ebook cannot?

Until recently, things as basic as ensuring that an illustration and the related text appear together as intended was something only apps could do. But there's more. Apps can provide motion graphics or animated characters that instruct and mesmerize, synced sound and touchable components that reveal illuminating information. They may support non-linear navigation when useful, integrate with social networks, and gain from location awareness. Apps can deliver physics engines that enable graphics to capture the dynamism of the real world. The solutions delight, yes, but they also solve design problems in new ways, the sine qua non of meaningful functionality.

The eBook Platform Evolves: App Capabilities Migrate into Books

Now it's the ebook's turn to get advanced capabilities, and if the laws hold, books designed from the outset to take advantage of evolved capabilities to deliver delightful new experiences will flourish.

At the moment, Apple's iBooks is the most technologically capable ebook platform, though each certainly has its strengths. Apple was first to market with the fixed layout EPUB format, reliably pairing illustrations and text. It is built atop Webkit, the advanced browser technology behind Apple's Safari and Google's Chrome web browsers, with many of the same

HTML5, CSS3, and JavaScript capabilities powering the most advanced web apps.

It's truly remarkable what can be done in the current version of iBooks. Design labs like Aerbook and others, notably Liza Daly and Threepress Consulting (now part of Safari Books, which is partly owned by O'Reilly Media, publisher of this book), have demonstrated the potential of this platform.

Lately, Apple has taken the lead in migrating experiences that have been successful in native apps into the ebook reader itself, making it standard equipment. For example, the "read to me" feature, the word-by-word highlighting that entire children's book app companies have been built upon, is now standard in iBooks. It's possible to add soundtracks to books that span multiple pages. This deceptively simple capability alone opens up a range of new possibilities for graphic novels, dramatic performance paired with source texts, music-based books, and narrative, illustrated non-fiction.

Given past experience in other media, we know that other ebook platform makers will soon enough deliver these kinds of things and a lot more. The EPUB 3 standard provides a way to script all kinds of interactivity and to communicate with servers, further broadening the expressive palette of books. It's clear that numerous books, perhaps most books, will have no use for any of this. But there are thousands of existing books and currently unforeseen titles that will inevitably be imagined and brought to market. This time they will come as ebooks, not as apps.

How Will "The Rest of Us" Contend with Yet Another Set of New Technologies?

In the early days following a platform's generational evolution, only wizards, those with seemingly arcane knowledge ("eye of newt, attribute of div") can actually make anything. It's one reason that app developers get to charge such impressive rates. But this changes as platforms mature, and moreover, we live in an extraordinary time of makers and toolmakers, freely or inexpensively contributing what they know and what they have made to anyone who's interested.

There are plug-and-play software components composed of intricate clockwork mechanisms that require little more of the creator than an ability to drag-and-drop. There are APIs (application programming interfaces) granting simplified access to vast networks of information and social graphs, again, with the requirement that the creator know only how to point-and-click.

A perfect example of this is WordPress. At the turn of the century, building a media-rich, customizable content management system-backed website like today's typical WordPress site was an extraordinarily expensive and complex undertaking. Today, it is drag-and-drop, point-and-click. Maybe you can't do everything that the most adept web designers can accomplish, but you can do a great deal. You can do more than enough.

It's inevitable that app-like presentation and interactivity will become available to ebook makers, much like WordPress plug-ins, ready to be configured, styled, and lit up within one of a wide range of highly configurable templates. Tool makers are working on these things now, and Apple's iBooks Author software is a first strong step in this direction. It takes little more than an inquisitive spirit to sign up as an Apple developer and see examples of the ebook platform's advanced capabilities, in many cases already available. The ease with which they can be implemented is only growing.

Of course, none of this matters without something meaningful to publish, any more than having the fanciest maple box of water colors will enable you to paint great paintings. The perennially good news is that talent, passion, and the courage to create will never be drag-and-drop. But if you have these, it's also nice to have that big box of paints. Especially if it's practically free.

Give the author feedback & add your comments about this chapter on the web: http://book.pressbooks.com/chapter/app-meet-book-ron-martinez

15. The Curation of Obscurity
(Peter Brantley)

Peter Brantley is the Director of the Bookserver Project at the Internet Archive, a San Francisco-based not-for-profit library. He was previously the Director of the Digital Library Federation, a non-profit association of research and national libraries. He has worked in senior information technology management roles at the University of California; the New York University Libraries and Press; Rapt, a startup firm focusing on advertising optimization, acquired by Microsoft; and the mass market division of Random House. You can find Peter on Twitter at: @naypinya.

The problem with reading, when you are trying to think about books, is that you wind up abstracting the act of reading and what is read–the cognition, the understanding of character, story, or explication, and the dreamworld of immersion. This does horrible things for our comprehension.

As we encounter the book's future, we also face the challenge of not knowing the true state of the thing it is we want to talk about. To be droll, it has not changed but is in the act of changing, and may yet soon be the thing it will become while preserving certain aspects of what it is. It is as if Schrodinger's Cat is made real; the book exists in a superposition of forms, paper and virtual; yet when we pause to consider it, we must perceive it in the light of one, casting only a vague and translucent shadow on the other, lest it appear as an enigmatic muddle.

Books on the Web

I make the assumption that as books increasingly become digital, they will be presented on the Web. The browser—or more specifically, the browser's rendering engine, e.g., webkit—has been the dominant rendering mechanism for digital content ever since the advent of the Web. The Internet offers a low-barrier distribution mechanism for information, and the browser provides an interaction container for a relatively coherent set of standards over content presentation and behavior. As the Web becomes more ubiquitous, HTML's cluster of more or less open standards is ever-growing in sophistication, adding support for sensor data and geo-locational awareness as well as more transparent media inclusion and user feedback.

What the Internet does not provide is a sense of boundedness. When books become unbound experiences on the Web, there is no package to download and preserve, nothing encapsulated to protect. As a librarian, one of the most glaring and problematic ramifications of the networked book is the deleterious impact on cultural preservation. Networked books are inherently less substantial than containerized digital books, much less so than print ones. To preserve a library, or a publisher's backlist, will increasingly require preservation of the Web.

Web-based culture is at tremendous risk of loss, because we have few standardized means of recording it. Even the Internet Archive's Wayback Machine[1] can provide no assurance of permanence. Nor does it provide any assurance of completeness. There is nothing today that says of a book on the Web: "I am a book and worth preserving." Our only recourse is determined planning and the sagacity to ensure that our culture is recorded as many times as possible, in as many ways as possible, and should one

---

[1] http://waybackmachine.org/

website blank out, it be redirected to a place that still responds to a HTTP GET.

Web-based content also demonstrates the "Show me the money!" conundrum. It is hard to generate revenue from individual pieces of content on the Web, yet atomic (unit) pricing has been the dominant model for book markets. We can expect subscription or site-based access models, but they will only be compelling to the extent that books self-organize or are aggregated by publishers and retailers into online communities. An aggregation might be content neutral, such as an expansion of Amazon's store into a more fully web native environment, or it might be a topic-focused, curated site for specific areas of interest.

There are technical areas of uncertainty as well. The dominant ebook standard, EPUB 3, is essentially a self-contained website in a file that incorporates a manifest and a specified set of included content. There is no assurance that publishing will seek a future EPUB 4 that would support a *manifest* of links; in other words, to pose it as a question, will restrictions on application behavior be attractive enough to warrant the production costs and barriers of standards compliance? That is not clear. Already, browser rendering engines are beginning to support EPUB parsing and rendering. It is conceivable that they could extend that support to defined, bounded parameters governing permissible content, interactions, scripting, and privacy. It is also possible that the EPUB development process may become so interwoven with HTML standards that the distinction between book and web will eventually fade entirely.

Beyond the question of what gets published, there's the question of who publishes. Publishers fulfilled the task of content preparation for a physical supply chain and generated accompanying uniform pricing control and revenue mechanisms. By dint of a fairly stable set of organizations working in the same industrial process over the course of decades, the historical publishing business harmonized our concept of the book to an easily manufactured and shipped product using an expected set of industrial partners. Although a coffee-table high art book exhibits significant differences from a mass market "pulp" romance, they are both easily recognizable as different species of the same genus. That is not likely to be as true in the future.

Publishing has also impacted who writes, and how. A system of advances for creative output to be executed for delivery at a future date and well-worn machinery around author-agent-publisher relations and contracts have meant that individual production roles were well established and widely considered normative. These relationships were critical when the authors of a book could not readily be an integral part of the distribution and sales process.

Writing books for the Web will require a different set of relationships. The widespread availability and robustness of blogging software has moderated the most difficult aspects of crafting web-compliant code. Although web standards are arguably growing more complex as they accommodate a wider range of browser behaviors, the software ecosystem around blogging will inevitably match this pace. With push-of-a-button distribution, many of the traditional publishing activities are obviated. The ability to incrementally publish and solicit community feedback marries well with community-sourced funding services such as Kickstarter. Community-centric design and funding is likely to create a different kind of literature than author advance-led publishing.

It seems inevitable that these changes in how publishing is executed will touch with a heavy hand the product of the creative process. Books and their successors may have a fungibility that we do not presently encounter outside of the academy's scholarly communication practice, where any number of pre-prints or a post-print might easily substitute for the worth of the formally published piece. More critically, when one can revise and link to external content trivially, the boundaries of any work become more porous. What evolves out of this process as the dominant social form for cultural education and entertainment may not be something that we refer to as a book, or if the term persists, its meaning may slowly but subtly shift as reader expectations change.

Books as Text

Despite the felicity of media-agnostic machine-mediated information creation and access, text remains an attractive format for idea production and consumption. Via literacy, it offers a low threshold for cognitive processing and conceptual understanding. Although often punctuated with illuminations, such as graphics, pictures, maps, and the placement of text on the virtual or physical page as a canvas, text as a base layer is easily converted into mental imagery and learning. It is an efficient way of telling stories and providing narratives, whether fictional or not. It is also, fortunately, one of the most parsimonious vehicles for cultural preservation possible.

All books that have been migrated to the network present the availability of enrichment: linking out to resource articles, online interactive maps, multi-user environments that add new layers of engagement. Yet a simple textual, and often linear, narrative offers something even simpler: the ability to not fully elucidate, to not share extra layers of detail and information, and create shadow through parsimony.

Part of story-telling is about choosing artifice. The curation of a certain amount of obscurity enlists our minds in the drafting of a story, a mood, and a dream—all in concert with the work of the author. Great literature is made in the interweaving of self and story.

I am increasingly convinced that a great deal of human story-sharing must persist at the simplest level available. We are not very intelligent creatures; we poison our world, craft intricate designs of power that do violence to hopes and dreams, and treat each other with willful, artful cruelty. These are not necessarily the hallmarks of a long-lived species. I suspect our ability to use the full level of technical tools at our disposal to assist our storytelling has been superseded by the potential complexity of the stories those tools can tell. It is our storytelling singularity, and one we have yet to master.

We are just beginning to grapple with how we learn from and use complex media. Creative arts will have to acquire an understanding of when and how we can take advantage of presentation technologies now emerging. When should their affordances be made visible, and when should they collapse into transparency? Most importantly, we need to ensure the reader can retain control of the experience they increasingly help to craft, always permitting them to choose when they suspend disbelief. Stories will increasingly become ours at an explicit level through choice and act, rather than simply through our implicit imaginings. Augmented reality and haptics will influence the manner in which we expect information to be presented, but they will not replace narrative.

It is true that we are surrounded by books that, by their nature, should always have been digital and never books at all. We froze them into a physical form because that was all we could do with tabular data and rich information. Atlases made rigid as oversized picture books, compendia of various facts and speculations printed as so many beautifully designed encyclopedias. Cookbooks and phonebooks presented as a series of manually navigable facets: soups, vegetables, meats, and desserts on one hand; an alpha-sort order listing by name, and type-of-business on the other.

It is intriguing to consider how punch cards, and the Hollerith language in which they became uniformly coded, allowed us to manipulate the simplest of otherwise frozen facts; first one way and then another. Sort by name, street address, or zip code. Examine one response cross-tabulated by another. These were the beginnings of databases made fluid in a digital form, through query. They offered a target for a curiosity more nimble than the scrutiny afforded by older finding aids: tables of contents and indices. Unlike the printed book, computer card decks were inflexible in the formats of information they could capture: text and numbers. Computers were hardly residential: the requisite analytical equipment was impractical to acquire for the home environment. One could not compare black-eyed pea recipes in one's cookbooks by throwing a deck of cards into an analytical engine.

Living in Obscura

The world occupied by the book both grows and shrinks. The genesis of Wikipedia was transformative in the lay understanding of how data could be presented and interacted with online, with the broadest level of access. To conceive of a book on birds, seashore shells, or the plants of Hawai'i without the framing of Wikipedia is impossible. We see a growing use of linked data concepts to embed metadata within online data repositories, allowing them to be interlinked easily, to tell new kinds of stories. User queries against the growing assemblage of information deepen our understanding of the world, and make for it a more mutable framing.

Yet in a fashion, this interlinkage of experience begins to redefine our lives. Role and ritual seem plastic in all but the most fundamental binary aspects of parent/child, awake/asleep. The tools we use subtly interweave business and family, entertainment and education, work and play. Reading is a world-of-its-own activity, but the book as an object was merely a harbinger of the combined real-world isolation and digital integration we craft more generously for ourselves with mobile computers, tablets, and phones. We must not cling to the firmament of the object as it becomes virtualized by a growing permeability of real and virtual life. We tell each other stories, but we tell them in a digital shadow of ourselves. For us those stories become real, when we touch and join our stories together.

One of the last winnowing spheres of our separateness is the privacy we previously were able to enrobe ourselves in by being in a specific place, and not any other. As books take residence on the Web, our browsing, acquisition, and reading experiences are intrinsically uplifted to machines for processing, mining, and re-presentation in recommendations and other marketing. Who we are, seen through the lens of what we experience, becomes commoditized. For the reader, as a user, it will be important to fight for the ability to control the distribution of our information and to provide mechanisms for people to exercise control of how information is shared, and with whom.

It is a difficult design task for the Web to simultaneously deliver privacy education with empowerment, but it is something that we must engineer into the fabric of our virtualized existence, even as we begin to embody it ever closer to ourselves. It is not something to ask of the book; rather, it is something to demand of our technology and our tools. Business prerogatives are independent of the fundamental respect for individual rights; to consider privacy as something that we must manage communally will require the creation of both legal and software codes. Rights are not policies or practices.

Story-telling is a nexus of our technology, intuition, and empathy. We can embrace and celebrate its future as long as we preserve one for ourselves.

Give the author feedback & add your comments about this chapter on

the　*web:*　http://book.pressbooks.com/chapter/curation-of
-obscurity-peter-brantley

16. A Reader's Bill of Rights (Kassia Krozser)

Kassia Krozser, publisher of Booksquare.com, *covers the intersection of technology and publishing. Kassia has worked in web and digital publishing for over ten years, focusing primarily on content development and management. As co-owner of Oxford Media Works, she consults with clients and develops digital publishing initiatives. You can find Kassia on Twitter at:* @booksquare.

Every revolution has to start somewhere, and the digital books revolution started with readers. Oh sure, Amazon and Sony helped with their reading devices, but it was the people who created and sustained a demand for ebooks even as publishers considered them too small a market to worry about.

And it is the reader who is bearing the brunt of the rapid, sometimes erratic, sometimes brilliant transition of traditional publishers into publishers of the future. We—the readers—have experienced windowing schemes, formatting disasters, and, of course, Digital Rights Management (DRM) machinations that restrict our access to the books we've purchased.

To this day, I still cannot extract certain books I purchased directly from a publisher from the stranglehold of Adobe Digital Editions. In fact, every time I open ADE, it becomes an exercise in absurdity. My rule? If you, the publisher, make me use ADE, then I, the reader, will take my business elsewhere.

Yet I stick with digital books because they give me the best reading option for my lifestyle. I find I will suffer a lot to read books. Which reminds me of an awful summer day, an overly long walk to the library, and, oh yes, a sunburn. But hey, I came home with new books to read!

Publishers write manifestos. Publishers compile bullet-pointed lists detailing their value. Publishers assert their legal rights, their moral rights, their evolving copyright rights.

Maybe it's time that readers did the same. We are, after all, the ones who shell out our hard-earned money to purchase books. We serve as the greatest unpaid marketing team ever assembled in the history of the world. We play by the rules, and we should demand a voice when someone decides those rules should change.

Yet, too often, when publishers talk about readers, they mean devices, not humans.

A Reader Bill of Rights

Thus, it is time for a Reader Bill of Rights. A Bill of Rights seems a uniquely American thing, shorthand for the first ten amendments to the United States Constitution, but such listings of express rights go back to 1689, when the British laid out rights and liberties after King James the Second did some bad, bad stuff. Then, of course, there was the Magna Carta, which was an early Bill of Rights. Heck, one could argue that the Code of Hammurabi was our first attempt to wrap some legalese around rights.

Demanding—and obtaining—rights is something our species does. Before we get too deep into the ebook rabbit hole, it is essential that readers lay out their demands and associated reasoning. It is also incumbent on publishers to acknowledge and respond to these demands. Thus, a dialogue will be born. On the reader side, we won't get everything we want. Publishers, if they don't want us to exercise our Right to Walk Away, will accede certain points. Both sides will come away better understanding each other.

Because—and this is really, really, really, important—readers *want* to pay money for books. They want to read books. They want to talk about books. They want to force beloved books into the hands of innocent bystanders in the hope that those bystanders will love those books just as much as that first reader did.

Readers are the most important part of the publishing food chain, after, of course, authors. Hmm, let me take that back. Without the formal publishing structure, authors will still find a way to reach readers. Readers will still find a way to discover authors. So, let me declare it so: readers are the most important part of the (traditional) publishing food chain.

So, what rights do readers demand?

The Right to Read

What we want, when we want, how we want.

Sounds so simple, doesn't it? Books haven't really worked this way, of course. For some books, windowing has been part of their lifecycle. First comes the hardcover, then (maybe) the trade paperback, and finally, the little mass market paperback comes trotting along, a long time after that marketing push that creates consumer awareness. Windowing makes a certain sort of sense in the world of print—hardcover books make some good money for publishers.

Windowing makes *absolutely no sense* in the world of digital books. This is a world where an ebook can appear before the print book is, well, printed (this would normally lead me on a detour involving better internal controls and suggestions that anti-piracy zealots should not cast stones and all that). This is a world where the conversation about the book, or, shall I say, awareness of the book, happens instantaneously. I am sorry to report that same awareness evaporates when the next shiny object appears on the horizon. For so many books, the moment to capture a reader's attention is fleeting.

It is incumbent upon publishers to make sure the book is available in the format readers want during that moment.

This extends beyond the U.S. market. The world of publishing is no longer insulated. It is no longer segregated by territory. In some ways, it is no longer segregated by language. The way readers, publishers, and everyone else in the food chain communicate is instantaneous and global. What sense can one make of staggering international release dates?

What sense can one make of a world where rights sit on the table while pirates make sure local readers are well-served?

I am sure there was a good time for publishing to practice business as usual when it comes to ebooks—I cannot think of one, but will assume this to be true—but right now, it is essential that the part of the publishing ecosystem that makes sure readers get the books they want, when they want them, how they want them gets its act together right now.

The Right to Read Freely

With print books, readers can do many things. They can purchase them in various formats (hard cover, trade paperback, mass market paperback) from various retailers—there are no differences in the books sold by Barnes & Noble and your local independent bookseller. They borrow that exact same book from the library, though some may have special "library binding" to make them last longer. They can donate the finished book to Goodwill, take it to a used bookstore for cash or trade, toss it in the trash (oh, no, don't!). They can even press the book into the hands of family or friends, knowing a shared book is a book that will be shared again.

With ebooks, not so much. Through their insistence on DRM, publishers have ensured that readers cannot get the same format from every retailer, much less the local library. We cannot share our ebooks easily with friends, much less family. Donating an ebook so another reader can discover a great author and read? Forget about it! And what happens when we reach the arbitrary "device limit" set by publishers for our books? We must go through contortions to get to the content we pay good money for.

In fact, the only thing we can easily do with our ebooks is trash them.

There is something seriously wrong with the business model of ebooks.

We, the readers, demand the ability to read freely, to be freed of the chains that lock us into a single retailer or device. We demand smarter ways to share—if not the whole book, enough to entice our victim. We demand fewer device restrictions. Let us, at least, have the ability to port our books freely as we buy new devices.

The Right of First Sale

For as long as people have been buying books, they have been purchasing the right to do whatever they want with them. For some, this meant sharing with family and friends. For others, this meant cutting a hidey hole into the page and secreting away valuables. We've sold our books for money or traded them for more books. We've transformed our books into works of art. If you ask a reader, you will discover he or she has done things with books that can only be mentioned in whispers.

However, we did not technically own our books, what with the authors owning the underlying intellectual property. This prevented us from doing stuff like copying the words and selling them as our own. We were fine with this limitation because we owned the physical object, and short of the aforementioned copyright infringement, we could do whatever we damned well pleased with those books.

And we did.

Then came ebooks and a whole new set of rules. Suddenly, our books were subject to DRM. Ain't no reader who loves DRM, but I can guarantee there are major retailers out there who give praise to the DRM gods every day. DRM restricts the reader's former rights under the First Sale Doctrine. The First Sale Doctrine, if I may paraphrase, essentially allows the consumer all those lovely rights mentioned in the first paragraph of this section.

With digital books, the rights we enjoyed—though, I will admit it is unlikely anyone will cut a hidey hole in an ebook—have evaporated. We cannot resell an ebook. We cannot (easily) share an ebook. We cannot donate an ebook to charity. In fact, exercising the very rights book buyers have enjoyed since the beginning of book buying time could lead to charges of copyright infringement.

It could lead to otherwise upright citizens being labeled, oh this is hard to type, *pirates.*

Yeah, in the digital world, you are a criminal when you try to exercise the same rights you enjoy in the print world.

This is wrong. Don't misunderstand me. I fully understand how easy it is for someone to steal a work. It's happened to me. But losing my First Sale rights means I am getting less "book" for the money I pay. And that changes my perspective on the value of what I am purchas... er, licensing.

Oh, yes, we will be getting back to this idea.

The Right to Valued Content

Publishers often talk about this or that new thing "devaluing" books, but I am here to say it is the publishers who are doing their own product the most harm. Every time a publisher allows a print book or ebook to be released with poor editing, poor proofreading, and poor quality, the value of books in general diminishes in the mind of readers.

We deserve better.

If publishers want us to value their content, then publishers need to lead by example by producing content that shows how much they value both their authors and their customers. This means putting and end to things like consistently substituting the character "1" for "I". No more bizarre line breaks mid-paragraph. No out-of-order content (seriously, how does this stuff get past quality assurance?). No missing content. Remember, when reading a book, traditional quotation marks make far more sense than the HTML code for said quotation marks. And so on.

The sad fact of the matter is these types of errors appear in just about every ebook I read, from publishers great and small.

Listing the common conversion errors I see in ebooks could take hours, and that is just plain wrong. When I start a book, I shouldn't have to worry about errors, but there is always that niggling doubt in my mind: *What if this is a disaster?*

Sometimes, the problem is so egregious I return the book. Sometimes, I carry on, only to scream in frustration when a massive error destroys the author's carefully wrought prose, ripping me out of the story. Really, there is nothing more frustrating than preventable screw-ups ruining a climactic scene. No. Thing.

Consistent, persistent, across-the-catalog errors are the fastest way to devalue content I know, and the fault lies directly with each and every publisher who allows bad books to be sold to readers. I no longer trust publishers to do right by their books, and, by extension, me.

We deserve better.

The Right to the Whole Book (with a Shout-Out to the Right to Good Metadata)

This seems obvious, doesn't it? I mean, shouldn't a book be whole from the get-go? So what is a whole book? I, after multiple decades of reading, have a fairly good idea of what this means. In addition to the words that, strung together, comprise the story (or stories) being told, there is stuff like the name of the author, front matter, back matter. Oh, and cover art.

If a publisher is convinced these elements are important enough for the print edition, surely they are important enough for the digital edition? Sure, the cover art may not be as pretty when viewed in the grayscale of e-Ink, but, hey, that cover is part of what I pay for (in all honesty, sometimes those shades of gray really make artwork pop).

Or that front and back matter. Stuff like teasers and descriptions of the book. The author bio. The author photo. These are, according to publishers, important to the book package. Oh sure, not as important as the actual words that comprise the meat of the book package, but important nonetheless.

Funny, I cannot remember ever seeing an author photo in an ebook, but maybe I just haven't looked hard enough.

Yes, ebooks are different, so, yes, some creative rethinking of traditional elements needs to be employed by publishers to ensure this type of content makes sense to readers. There is nothing, I tell you, nothing more disconcerting to be suddenly dropped into (unmarked) teaser content, only to have the next page filled with entirely different time, place, and characters. This is fixable, and it matters. (See "The Right to Valued Content".)

When publishers talk about the value of a book—and, more importantly, how certain initiatives devalue the book—they are very righteous on this point. I think offering a less-than-complete version of any book to consumers shows that the publisher doesn't value that content. It also says the publisher doesn't value the consumer purchasing the content.

Is that the message publishers want to send in this day and age?

And with ebooks (and, let's be honest, print books), there needs to special attention to the information about the book. This is known as metadata. The topic has been covered previously in this book, and it doesn't hurt to say more. Getting the metadata right leads to better discovery. It leads to better cataloguing. It leads to better reading experiences. At no time should a book go out with metadata that indicates the author is the publisher's marketing director (unless this is, in fact, a true statement).

We, the readers, have a right to get the whole book and nothing but the whole book.

The Right to a Reasonably Priced Book

I know the monetary value of a book is in the eye of a beholder, but ebooks, frankly, cost too much money. This is particularly true given that the quality of the digital book is sometimes orders of magnitude below the quality of the print edition. And, of course, what I get in digital is nowhere near the same as what I get in print.

As I mentioned previously, as an ebook purchaser (or, more accurately, licensor), I am losing a whole host of rights I enjoy (note: present tense) with print books. As mentioned in my Right to the Whole Book, often I am getting less book than my print purchase counterparts. And I noted that my Right to Valued Content is seriously compromised by the ebook production process.

(This final point, I sincerely hope will be rectified immediately, or traditional publishers will surely lose market share to new entities that place a premium on offering quality digital content to their customers.)

I am willing to accept some trade-offs, like, oh, my Right of First Sale, if the price I pay for my books reflects this concession. I am willing to overlook the fact that my ebook isn't quite as full-figured as its print counterpart, if the price I pay for my books reflects this concession. I am willing to buy lots and lots of books, if the price I pay for my books reflects a serious consideration of what I get, what I lose, and what publishers can sell that book for while making money.

I am not naive about the underlying costs of publishing (this stuff, I do every day). I am not naive about the marginal costs of ebooks (this stuff, I do every day). I know the margins for digital, and, because I want the publishing industry to flourish, am thrilled they are as high as they are. If I were to be very generous to publishers, I'd say they were making 75% margins, after the retailer split. If I were to be more realistic, I'd put those margins in the high 90% bracket. Noting, in both instances, that the costs of editorial, production, marketing, and overhead remain largely the same in digital as they do in print.

And these costs must necessarily be factored into the overall cost of the book.

Knowing this, ebooks are priced too high, mostly because their prices are reflective of a print model. I get that publishers are still trying to work out the kinks of how to price ebooks, but those kinks are more like major bends. While publishers navigate them, they face serious competition from the self-published author, the digital start-up, and pirates, not to mention competition from other media.

Yeah, yeah, yeah, I get it. Books are special. I wouldn't be writing this if I didn't think so. But books are part of the entertainment media mix—please, don't get distraught, this is merely a factual statement!—and books have to be competitive with other media.

And, I will say it again, ebooks cost too damn much!

The Right to Excellent Customer Service

With the Big Six shift from the so-called Wholesale Model to the Agency Model for ebooks, publishers are now, essentially, selling books to consumers. The retailers act as service providers for the publishers, generally fulfilling the order, facilitating the financial transaction, and, oh, bearing the brunt of consumer frustration. Ever try to contact a publisher about an issue with an ebook?

I have, and I am here to say the whole process went about as well as you'd expect.

Which is to say, there was no communication back, no easy method to make contact, and, of course, no resolution to my problem. Seriously, when a customer contacts you to say, "Hey, this ebook you published was nearly unreadable because your conversion process was not followed up with a halfway decent proofreading process," don't you at least give that consumer the courtesy of a response? A thank you for doing the publisher's job? A "we are very sorry, and we are going to do everything in our power to make this right for you right now."

If you are going to sell me books, then you must treat me like a valued customer. Amazon, Barnes & Noble, All Romance ebooks, Kobo, Books on Board...these are conduits between you and the consumer. You, dear publisher, are the seller of the book. Act like it.

The Right to Innovation

Some famous dude once said that people don't know what they want until someone gives it to them. I'd say this is half true. Consumers are smarter and more technologically savvy than, I worry, publishers realize. We know how the Internet works, and we don't understand why (certain) books don't work like the Internet. We don't understand why bookish content, in this day and age, feels so...print-ish.

Right now, readers are like explorers, seeing the boundaries of books, realizing the potential of content, and wondering what's on the horizon. We don't necessarily know what we want. We don't necessarily know what can be done (though we certainly have opinions). We just know that some books can be more.

This means we are expecting publishers to, well, tell us what we want. Give us lots of options, some of which we will embrace, many of which we will reject because innovation means there will be a lot of stupid stuff. Remember, we don't necessarily know what we want.

But we want publishers to be innovators, to give us options. In some ways, this may be a thankless task, but, I suspect, in many ways, this will be the path to a wild, crazy, amazing future. Don't wait for us to ask.

The Right to Privacy and Security

This may not seem like a big issue, but as publishers (hopefully) develop direct contact with consumers and readers, it will become important, particularly as publishers move into direct-to-consumer ventures such as the multi-publisher sales and discovery venture called Bookish. While developing the (presumably) cool features and algorithms, publishers need to be developing strong, effective privacy policies and controls.

Likewise, as publishers enter into joint ventures and partnerships with third parties—app developers, book-related ventures—the privacy and security of customers must remain paramount to publishers. It's the little things...like protecting names (real and not-so-real), credit card information, and personal information such as addresses.

We have a right to have our privacy and security guarded zealously, as zealously by publishers as this information is guarded by librarians. That is the standard I hold publishers to.

The Right to Walk Away

If a publisher doesn't give us what we want, we can take our money elsewhere. And we will. Hmm, that sounds awfully threatening.

Here's the deal. If the quality of ebooks from major publishers remains low while the prices remain high, then other reading options looking increasingly attractive to readers. Here is an example. I purchased a publisher-produced reprint of a favorite book, and it was riddled with conversion errors. There were so many that I wrote the publisher to complain (and, of course, received no response). The price was $7.99.

I purchased an author-produced reprint of a favorite book. It, too, was riddled with errors. However, I only paid $2.99 for the second book, and, to be honest, the overall number of errors was smaller.

So, why would I ever again trust the publisher of the $7.99 book? Why would I risk my money and waste my time? Since there are so many other reading options available to me, I choose to walk away from books produced by this particular publisher. I am not unique.

I find I do a lot of walking away. That is what happens when you break trust with your best customers. They shop elsewhere. And right now, with the competition for reading growing exponentially—every time a funny picture of a cat appears on the Internet, it cuts into someone's reading time—publishers cannot afford for readers to walk away.

For most of my reading life, I've asked very little of publishers. Good books, mostly. I think it is because I was able to take so many of my rights as a reader for granted. I never had to worry about the First Sale Doctrine. Never had to think about getting the whole book. Never really worried about quality control (though I did sometimes wonder what some editors were smoking when they published books that my cat could write with more clarity and development of story).

It is only with the digital transition that I realize what I am losing.

And I demand that my rights be honored.

Give the author feedback & add your comments about this chapter on the web: http://book.pressbooks.com/chapter/a-readers-bill-of -rights-kassia-krozser part three.

The Things We Can Do with Books: Projects from the Bleeding Edge

17. Communities of Writers (Jürgen Fauth, Fictionaut)

Jürgen Fauth is the co-founder of Fictionaut. His debut novel Kino *is out now from Atticus Books. You can follow him on Twitter at @muckster. Fictionaut is an innovative literary community that combines elements of a social network with a self-selecting literary magazine. Follow @fictionaut for news and @fictionautrx for recommended stories.*

Introduction: "Chronologie"

In 2008, Carson Baker and I launched Fictionaut, a literary community that combines elements of a social network with a crowdsourced literary magazine. The site's genesis, however, started much earlier. By 1996, it was becoming clear to me that the Internet would profoundly change publishing. At the time, I was a graduate student at the University of Southern Mississippi and worked with Frederick Barthelme on moving the *Mississippi Review* online, making it the first traditional literary magazine to take to the Internet. Fascinated with the possibilities, I started my own online German-language magazine, *Der Brennende Busch.*

Anyone who knows German will agree that *Der Brennende Busch* is a terrible name for a magazine. One of the first sites of its kind in German (or any language), it had a good run anyway. This was the era of screeching modems and AOL discs clogging mailboxes, but from the very beginning, I wrestled with fundamental questions of how to translate a print magazine into a more fluid online incarnation.

What did it mean, for instance, to have issues on the Internet? Did it still make sense to collect work I had accepted for publication into distinct packages, or should it be put up as soon as it was ready? I really began to understand the possibilities on a trip to Ireland, where I found myself formatting essays a contributor had sent from Japan to be posted on a server located in the US for a German-speaking audience—all at no cost.

The answer I came up with for *Der Brennende Busch* was a section called "Chronologie." I waited for enough material for a new "issue" to post to the front, but I immediately linked newly accepted stories on a "chronology" page that listed material in reverse-chronological order. "Chronologie" was what we now call a blog. In the 1990s, nobody had heard that word, and my half-hearted embrace of the idea made sure that it went nowhere. *Der Brennende Busch* had its moments, but eventually I gave up on it as I focused on my doctorate.

I'm telling you about "Chronologie" not to claim that I invented the blog, but because it taught me something crucial: I would never again let my attachment to old metaphors ("issues") keep me from embracing the possibilities of a new medium. Moving forward, I was going to follow the technology wherever it would lead and try out whatever was possible. This is a principle I have since internalized: don't attempt to force a new medium to conform to your habitual ways of doing things. If it's difficult to code, set up, or implement, chances are you're doing it wrong. Instead, you should have faith in the technology and follow the path of least resistance—let the medium itself show you the way forward. This became the founding principle of Fictionaut.

Literary Magazine 2.0

Around the turn of the century, I tinkered with Zoetrope's online writing community and continued to select fiction for *Mississippi Review*, but I felt that the growing world of online literary magazines—outlets for short fiction and poetry—hadn't quite adapted to the Internet as well as they could have. The cost of bandwidth and storage space was falling, and anyone could post fiction on a personal site with ever-increasing ease. I couldn't help wondering what it meant to be selected for publication by this magazine or that. Surely, there had to be a more native way to publish fiction on the Internet that transcended not just the metaphor of "issues" but of the "magazine" itself.

I suspected that the answer had something to do with turning the crowd of readers into editors, but things didn't quite click until the arrival of the social web. Twitter, Facebook, and especially Flickr changed all that. I was particularly taken with Flickr's "interestingness" algorithm, which automatically selected the most appealing uploaded photos depending on user response. In 2006, I thought that it was only a matter of time until someone launched a site devoted to posting fiction similar to Flickr's photosharing service. I sketched ideas for this fiction community, quickly realized that I didn't have the programming skills to make it a reality, and put it aside.

Two years later, the social web was exploding, but there still wasn't a sign of a site that put what we then called the web 2.0 at the service of writers and readers in the way I had imagined. I was working on what would become my debut novel, *Kino*, and I was about to become a father. Yet I felt that there was a real opportunity—in fact, a need—for the site that I had begun to call Fictionaut.

I'd long harbored a sense that the ecosystem of online and print literary magazines wasn't adequately serving writers, readers, or editors. Too many writers submitted to magazines without having bothered to read them. Readers were confronted with a bewildering array of choices, while editors were overwhelmed with submissions. I had experienced this system firsthand from all angles, and I was hoping that Fictionaut, using a variation of Flickr's "interestingness" algorithm, might be able to provide an alternative.

A Radical Experiment

In Carson Baker, I found an enormously talented and enthusiastic collaborator with great business and design skills. Neither one of us had ever held a job in the publishing industry; even my novel is being published by up-and-coming independent press Atticus Books. While many industry insiders cannot conceive of a new model in which they have no place, our outsider status gave us the freedom to try anything.

Together we began custom-building Fictionaut from scratch. Our principles were clear from the start: we'd keep the site as open, simple, and versatile as possible; we would trust the technology to lead the way; and we would grow the community with care.

Fictionaut started as an experiment; we had only our time to lose. The idea was to radically rebuild publishing from the bottom up. We tried to assume nothing. In fact, our working hypothesis was that the only two people absolutely necessary for publishing are the reader and the writer (aided by our recommendation algorithm). We resolved to add other functions only as we re-established that they were necessary.

The logic was this: from a purely technical standpoint, the problem of "publishing" had been solved. Anyone can now start a Tumblr blog or upload a Word file to Amazon and be published within minutes. The problem, then, was no longer technical but editorial.

It was always crucial that Fictionaut would attract not only writers but also readers. The site had to become a destination, an automated magazine where one could easily find interesting work. To this end, we developed our own version of Flickr's "interestingness" algorithm, a simple recommendation engine that picked the currently most viewed, "favorited," and commented-on stories and poems and presented them on the front page, via Twitter, and in our newsletter.

Would we really be able to run an online magazine that allowed anyone to post? We weren't sure, but we were going to try —after all, on the Internet, if something is possible, somebody is going to do it sooner or later, so why not us? Before we launched, there were serious doubts that the vaunted tradition of editing a literary magazine could simply be crowdsourced, and we weren't so sure ourselves. But the Internet had already given anyone the opportunity to publish on their own blogs, and the only way forward was to find out if technology had an answer to the flood it had created.

Giving Up Control: Surprises

We decided to proceed cautiously, balancing our principle of openness with the desire for quality. We had seen too many Internet boards swamped and drowned by abusive or selfish participants. We took guidance from the community blog Metafilter, which evolved through careful self-policing and periodically opening and closing signups. To attract readers and fulfill its goals as a magazine, Fictionaut would have to maintain a certain level of civility and literary quality.

To this end, we started the site in a very small beta test, hidden from the eyes of the public. With the help of a board of advisors that included authors, publishers, agents, publicists, and social media experts, we slowly extended invitations to talented writers of our acquaintance and then asked them to invite their most talented friends in turn.

We patiently grew the site and fine-tuned it for a year before we made it visible to the public. During that time, we attracted a wide range of forward-thinking writers of all levels of accomplishment as well as literary magazines, who began using the "groups" function as a way to showcase work and attract new readers.

From the time that we sent out the initial batch of invitations, Fictionaut has been full of surprises—the first of which was that the recommendation engine actually worked (with an asterisk or two—more on this in a minute). Not every worthy story is necessarily picked up by the algorithm, but the stories listed in the recommendations are reliably interesting and of high quality.

The good manners of our users provided another surprise. Anyone who has ever attended a writing workshop or witnessed an all-out Internet flame war could expect a writing site to exhibit the worst of both worlds. Somehow, though, the opposite happened: if anything, the comments and feedback on Fictionaut are too nice and supportive, if there is such a thing. Hard-hitting criticism is reserved for special workshop groups such as "The Woodshed." Fictionaut is a supportive and safe place to post fiction without fear of being attacked or ridiculed. Whenever the rare troll has reared its ugly head, we intervened and found a solution quickly.

Running a site as open as Fictionaut, we have found that when you give up control, good things happen. Instead of strictly defining how Fictionaut is supposed to be used, our goal has always been to give users maximum flexibility on how to interact with the site. In turn, a couple of distinct ways of using Fictionaut have crystallized, some of them well beyond what we had imagined.

There is no right or wrong way to use Fictionaut. Private and professional readers comb the site to discover fresh voices, and there have been many cases where editors have picked up stories first published on Fictionaut for publication in a traditional literary magazine. Some writers have published books and signed agents after posting on Fictionaut.

Others wouldn't dream of sharing their work publicly. Instead, they get together in closed or private groups to discuss unpublished and sometimes unfinished work and get feedback on drafts without ever making them publicly available at all. Since Fictionaut allows users to take down or edit work at any time, writers have maximum flexibility to leave their writing up only until they want to improve it or, perhaps, submit it elsewhere for publication.

Still others use the site to republish work that has appeared elsewhere but might be out-of-print or hard to find. Once the rights revert to them, authors are free to put them anywhere, and Fictionaut can give older stories or poems that are languishing in back issues an elegant online home.

The heaviest users of Fictionaut tend to be writers trying to build a larger audience for their work. For those looking for online notoriety, perhaps of the kind that will eventually translate into a book contract, the site rewards frequent participation, intensive commenting, and posting work that is polished and usually short. The rise of flash fiction has gone hand-in-hand with fiction published online, and it's easy to see why: it is quick to produce, quick to consume, and allows writers to build up an impressive portfolio of work published in many venues in comparatively little time.

Which brings me to one of the qualifications I mentioned earlier when I said that by and large, the recommendation engine is working very well: in an online environment, it can be difficult for longer stories to get read and noticed. As is the case almost everywhere else on the Web, the work that gets the most attention on Fictionaut tends to be shorter. But with the rise of ereaders and tablets, the pendulum may well be swinging back to what Twitter calls #longreads. Of course, there are Fictionaut groups dedicated to longer stories as well as novel excerpts.

Another surprise has been the rise of the Fictionaut blog. Originally intended as a simple news blog that would announce changes to the site, it has grown into a full-fledged literary destination, with regular columns by half a dozen contributors. Content includes in-depth chats with our writers about their work, regular roundups of publications by Fictionauts, and the "Fictionaut Five" series of interviews with writers as diverse as Mona Simpson and Robert Olen Butler, frequently focusing on matters of craft. We also publish reviews and portraits of Fictionaut groups. We just started a series in which guest editors pick their favorite stories, a hand-selected layer that highlights work that might have been overlooked by the automated recommendation engine.

The State of the Fictionaut

At this point, Fictionaut has over 5,000 members who have published over 20,000 stories, including work by Amy Hempel, Marcy Dermansky, Mary Gaitskill, Charles Baxter, and Ann Beattie.

Our problems since the launch have been, I assume, the problems of any startup: dealing with a lack of resources to keep pace with the social evolution and growth of the site. Because of limitations of the current design, we haven't been able to open signups just yet, and there is a long list of requests for invitations that we'd love to fill. Plans for the future include an overhaul of the front page to have it offer new views of recently posted stories and recommended stories. We also plan to foreground the groups. These changes will allow us to handle more users posting more frequently while maintaining our goal of displaying the best work at any given time.

Finally, we are looking into making stories available in more formats, and for a price. So far, Fictionaut is financed through advertising provided by the LitBreaker network, which specializes in ads relevant to our audience. But with over 20,000 stories, many of them outstanding work by highly talented writers, we're also exploring ways to use our brand and our community to sell these stories. We plan to offer an opt-in system that allows our writers to either continue using the site as they do now or to join the publishing arm of Fictionaut, while sharing the revenue, of course.

We're also considering subscription models that would regularly deliver the most highly recommended stories to your ereader or mobile device as well as a system that allows us to easily collect stories selected by editors or users into anthologies.

Conclusion

Fictionaut has been an incredibly thrilling, frustrating, surprising, time-consuming, and eye-opening experience. It has led me to some of the most satisfying professional relationships of my life, and it has opened my eyes to the transformative power of simply starting something. If it's a worthy idea that solves a problem, people will offer their help, and the results will be much greater than anticipated. Fictionaut hasn't made anybody rich yet, but the human and artistic relationships the site has enabled over the years are a great reward in their own right. Our tagline calls Fictionaut a site for "adventurous readers & writers." Ours is a vessel of discovery launched as an experiment during a particularly tempestuous time in publishing. The journey so far hasn't been without difficulty, but we've made a wealth of discoveries along the way already. On to new shores!

Give the author feedback & add your comments about this chapter on the web: http://book.pressbooks.com/chapter/fictionaut-jurgen -fauth

18. On the Therapist's Couch: Books as Apps, Really? (Neal Hoskins, WingedChariot)

Neal Hoskins is the founder of wingedchariot. Outdoors and onscreen it's all about the obvious. You can follow him on twitter at @utzy. WingedChariot makes beautiful multilingual applications for many screens. Their work sits at the intersection of quality print and digital production. Follow @storiestotouch for news.

I begin with a personal story. By the time these crisp chapters come out, three years will have passed since WingedChariot made its first app. In terms of app development, this is long ago, but in practice it is really only 36 months.

That first app was an 18-slide picture book that was designed to be read on a 3.5 inch screen. Readers swiped to move the page and saw a total of six animations of a sheep on a motorbike. At the time, many people laughed at this effort. "What is it?" they asked. "Really? A children's book on such a small screen?"

Then, in 2010, larger-form tablets arrived, and boy, we were off, as in "Vroooooooooooooooooooooooom."

But track back a little to 2008 when the first app stores were opening. At the time, we were inspired by innovators like Scrollmotion and Enhanced Editions. These and other firms were pioneers, ones that saw apps as a way to provide books with pictures, sounds, and interactivity in a much more friendly and hands-on way than publishers ever achieved on formats like the CD-ROM or floppy disk.

Hardware met software met digital storefront and combined to provide the conditions for the widespread acceptance and growth of apps. Looking back, it seems obvious that the convergence was going to happen. But with the new tools came the equally obvious human confusion: "What about the browser? What about HTML and its layout cousins? What about the internet?"

As tablets moved from mythical to magical in 2010, we soon started to ask, "Does it really matter where all of this is going?"

When it comes to the potential for enhanced ebooks, there were—and remain—plenty of doubters. Underscoring these reservations, a presentation by Evan Schnittman (late of Oxford and Bloomsbury, now with Hachette in the United States) famously included a tombstone that read "ENHANCED EBOOKS AND BOOK APPS 2009–2011". Language like "enhanced what," infamously presented by a large publisher not so long ago in London, gave proof that we are indeed struggling to win the hearts and minds of established publishers.

Are we all washed up before we even get into the world of interactive app making? Do we fear the publisher as media producer? And if we do fear that, why? Is it a lingering legacy of how we think we sucked at making CD-ROMS?

I suppose at this point I could present hundreds of definitions and well-honed quotes on what a book is, how we define them, associate with them, what we love or hate about them. There are too many clever ones, but very few wise ones.

To answer the question "How can we get out of this maelstrom created by our own ingenuity?", let's turn to a LinkedIn discussion group that took place in May 2011:

Creating App or EPUB will be a question of delivery. If I want to sell my content in a bookstore like iBooks I create an EPUB. If I want it in a "department store" like the App Store I create an App. Since more and more Apps are made via frameworks which also work with HTML5, CSS, and JavaScript ("web app" is a keyword), App and ePub are only different containers of the same content, book or however you want to label them. (Uwe Matrish)

Matrish provides the answer to the publishing dilemma. There are formats emerging that may lead to making apps for all platforms. There may be new nuts-and-bolts tools (they are certainly NOT there yet) that will allow us to read through the browser. But it is really for publishers to decide whether they want to make packages and core code bases for some sorts of content, or not. There is no single answer.

Naturally, there are the arguments of cost and scale, but through experimentation those who really care about being publishers will define themselves in the new way and understand it for themselves.

Instead of panicking, take a deep breath and be resourceful. Study the flotsam of the moment and grab onto something solid. (William Powers, Hamlet's Blackberry)

In short, for me, the real "e" in enhanced ebooks has always been "education." One has only to look at some of the best learning content to see why we make apps. Look at the amazing work of Nosy Crow, Touchpress, or PushPopPress. Consider the fascinating visual archiving of apps like Bilbion and the New York Public Library.

In these, you see why this new medium works: a complete match of content machine and educational exploration that pushes out new forms of visual learning and entertainment.

Compare this with chapter books and text. To my mind, a black-and-white text display screen provides the quiet, contemplative reading experience that many of us are seeking. That is to say, the Kindle, the Nook, the Sony ereader, and a Kobo device are the right choices when it comes to just text and reading. Despite the arguments made elsewhere, I couldn't see for a very long time any useful changes to the text-based book, not until the writer comes with her or his own idea to exploit this new medium. In that regard, we best ask Bob Stein[1] or Chris Meade[2] those questions.

Different Flavors

Back in 2008, there was only one app store. Now, you have a veritable ice cream parlor of them. Examples include:

- The HP webOS app catalogue[3]
- The Android marketplace[4] (which actually has an ice cream sand-wich metaphor[5] come next year)
- The Blackberry store[6], from RIM
- Symbian (the Ovi Store[7]), now thrown in with Microsoft
- The Windows phone[8]

and last but not least

- The Apple app store[9]

For a great and free summary developers' guide, just go here[10] for a wonderful 8th edition handbook.

Everything in the Mix

At the end of this short chapter we come back to the beginning. The more I think about the creativity of apps, the more I realize that there are so many ideas of what stories can do and how information can be displayed.

It helps to understand where all this came from. I have a number of friends who were working in London during the 1990s when the first

---

[1] http://www.futureofthebook.org/
[2] http://futureofthebook.org.uk/
[3] http://bit.ly/mgYBjt
[4] https://market.android.com/
[5] http://bit.ly/hObEm3
[6] http://us.blackberry.com/apps-software/appworld/
[7] http://store.ovi.com/
[8] http://www.microsoft.com/windowsphone/en-us/apps/default.aspx
[9] http://www.apple.com/ipad/from-the-app-store/
[10] http://bit.ly/1ySOZD--PDF

attempt at mobile software and information on portable devices were being made. Apple smugly called this "baby software" (hello, Newton?).

Yes, it was clunky, and yes, it was sometimes hard to use. But we had to go through those years and all that development to get to where we are now. Publishers who want to see their content on modern screens are blessed with new and easy tools and a number of emerging standards.

Where we are now is a long way from the early versions. While there are different things in the mix today, the early icon screens are not that far away from what we have now. In one of the best roundups of what went on before in ebook publishing, Ars Technica[11] provided a look at all the failed machines. Sobering, yes, but these were the real brave hearts. The era of PDAs sowed the seeds of the modern smartphones and ultimately ebooks, apps, and the like.

It is endlessly fascinating and sometimes laughable how much the future of the book is put into discussion by publishers. This path was never followed by the record or film industry. When the digital juggernaut arrived on their doorsteps, they simply called up their lawyers. As noted in a tweet by Hugh McGuire:

> The future of books in the digital age is apparently writing books on the future of books in the digital age.

Print book apps, EPUB3, HTML5, and CSS3 will all remain on the scene in one shape or form. They will combine, morph, mix, and fall in and out of love with each other. There will be new writers and new publishers who arrive and flourish and some large household names that disappear and are remembered and archived in other books.

Perhaps we need our own massive, interactive app that explains from the time of Saint Augustine what books and reading went through. Mr. Gutenberg "was a businessman and technologist" like some of us writing here. In the future we will carry a library in our old leather bags that will simply be the thickness of a page, offering text or even color, and then it will show us sound or pictures or whatever we decide we want from it; in the end it is us who will choose how we want our stories told.

---

[11] http://bit.ly/ud9A

So it is with every new thing. In the words of Henry Ford, "Progress happens when all the factors that make for it are ready,[12] and then it is inevitable."

Epilogue

It's a cold February day in 2012. A survey of publishers released at one of the recent digital conferences found that fewer feel apps are the right way to go. In fact, publishers have anxiety over the tablet as a platform in general (really!).

In retrospect, this doesn't seem too hard. Choose your form, publish your work, pick your stores. With many larger publishers, I am convinced that apps are being shunned because they are reluctant to retool their staff.

In the time since I wrote the first version of this chapter, publishers have lost webOS, no longer supported by HP. This leaves publishers with three main contenders for app development:

- Apple iOS
- Android
- Windows Phone 7 and Windows 8 (forthcoming) for tablets

At the time of this writing, Apple and Android cover more than 80% of the new mobile sales, but those shares have shifted significantly over the last few years. In all likelihood, we will continue to live in a multiplatform world for some time to come.

Multiplatform life is hard, but it is life as we know it now. Publishers need to choose their platforms, publish on them, market their products, learn from their work, and ultimately publish again. In the end, we should have heart. As noted by Mike Kruzeniski, I think good app work will always take a cue from fine print work.[13]

Although the decision a publisher makes about web, hybrid, or native app development will vary on a case-by-case basis, in the end I think that Peter O'Shaughnessy shows the way in saying "web first, hybrid second, native third."[14]

---

[12] http://www.youtube.com/watch?v=g7_mOdi3O5E
[13] http://bit.ly/rafTLt
[14] http://www.peteroshaughnessy.com/day/2012/01/17

With respect to interactivity, an interview with Theodore Gray from Touch Press[15] provides valuable perspective. Touch Press basically makes the best bookish super apps. There are all sorts of tools out there, but for the newest, most creative and content-driven uses, native software development kit (SDK) may be the likely winner.

For WingedChariot, we have a good set of five apps. Though a smaller publisher, that leaves us with almost as many apps as larger players like Penguin. We have spent a year in research and seen a lot of our future avenues in schools delivering excellent content on any screen (via the browser in these cases). Some of the research included:

1. Children's views on paper books versus electronic devices[16]

2. Children exploring Stories to Touch[17] from WingedChariot on portable devices

3. Children's reactions to Scruffy Kitty,[18] a WingedChariot multilingual app

4. Teaching languages[19] with Stories to Touch

5. Classroom activity[20] using digital Stories to Touch

6. Thoughts on the future of the book[21]

7. Electronic devices in the classroom—languages and literacy[22]

You can hear about that and more in a 2012 inteview[23] I did with Joe Wikert, publisher at O'Reilly Media.

Since 2009, I've learned that *all* of the best apps are informational games at heart, whatever the genre. Books are fascinating sets of data and streams of information.

At WingedChariot, our pillars of "languages, learning, and play" sit well with that. We'll continue on our jolly path welcoming successive generations of tablets and other devices. I dare say that we will also embrace two-

---

[15] http://oreil.ly/zjz5ev

[16] http://youtu.be/plX5o6pN99U

[17] http://youtu.be/6FGMe4-zguM

[18] http://youtu.be/3RL6rrBxGSA

[19] http://youtu.be/t4HLf5ipRO4

[20] http://youtu.be/aHIkxHVStiY

[21] http://youtu.be/9aI4eK7WSFU

[22] http://youtu.be/afwrM4KDCKI

[23] http://oreil.ly/yC1S7q

way educational TV, where your apps and television character programs interact. Now there's something to think about....

Give the author feedback & add your comments about this chapter on the web: http://book.pressbooks.com/chapter/wingedchariot-neal-hoskins

19. The Engagement Economy (Bobby Gruenewald, YouVersion)

Bobby Gruenewald serves as Pastor, Innovation Leader at `LifeChurch.tv` and as the co-founder of the YouVersion Bible App. Bobby has been featured in the Washington Post, TechCrunch, CNN, CBS, NPR, and was listed by Fast Company as one of the 100 Most Creative People in Business in 2011. You can find him on Twitter at `@bobbygwald`. YouVersion and the Bible App were created by LifeChurch.tv. They have been installed on tens of millions of devices, and the YouVersion community has spent tens of billions of minutes engaging in Scripture, in more than 100 different languages.

Content isn't king anymore. It has been dethroned by engagement.

Whether it's a quarter-life crisis, a mid-life crisis, or an end-of-life crisis, the publishing world is struggling to find itself. For hundreds of years, it was enough to offer the best content: masterfully written text, helpful or beautiful illustrations, compelling titles, and eye-catching covers.

But then the world moved online. New channels for content emerged, and the global community began not only consuming it, but also contributing to it. It wasn't enough to hear what others had to say or see what they produced. We wanted to interact with it, adding our unique voice.

Meanwhile, printed matter continued to follow the well-worn path of its predecessors. Once the sale was made, there was little thought given to influencing how much or how often people engaged with the content. It seemed to exist on a parallel plane with online content. Of course we bought books online and read about their launch there, but we couldn't become part of the story.

The Bible has not been protected from this cultural shift. For many decades, well-meaning publishers spent significant time, energy, and money distributing Bibles in hopes of bringing God's Word to people around the world. And yet, with all of the resources that were invested in delivering the text, there was little focus on whether it was being read or how to increase engagement.

The collision of the print and online worlds brought about the concept for YouVersion.com. In 2006, blogs were ubiquitous, YouTube was a household name, Facebook was made available to non-college students, and Twitter was in its infancy. We had entered an era in which everyone had access to a digital printing press. What could it mean for publishing, and furthermore, for the Bible?

Much as the technical innovation of the printing press revolutionized the availability of the Bible, we wondered if this new environment could transform the distribution and interaction of the world's most popular and most published book.

The idea was to offer an online Bible where people could not only read Scripture, but could also associate and annotate any web media (photos, blog posts, video clips, journaled thoughts, etc.) to a verse or series of verses. Today, the concept of user annotations and user-contributed media doesn't seem unusual, but the early days of YouVersion predated Google Books, the Kindle, and its analogues. There weren't examples of people taking literary works and allowing users to annotate them with media and contribute content.

In the months that followed, we embarked on a journey of making YouVersion a reality. Our first challenge revealed just how little we knew about what we were getting into. It didn't occur to us that modern Bible texts are all copyrighted works that publishers have invested millions of dollars in developing. This wasn't freely available content; it required licensing.

The second obstacle we encountered was the reluctance of publishers to allow user-annotated contributions to their content. While they could see the changes happening in the online world, they didn't see where the technology was going to lead. It was alarming to some, but others were curious. Throughout that first year, we worked on building those relationships, developing trust, and getting permission to use texts. At the same time, we had a team working on developing the site.

In September 2007, we launched YouVersion.com. The results were good, but not great. People were interested in using the tool, but it was clearly an early-adopter crowd who connected with it. The growth of YouVersion wasn't viral and didn't seem to carry a lot of momentum in terms of growth.

With only 20,000 people using it, it didn't appear this concept was catching on. Were we too early? Did we not execute the idea well? Did it just need more time to catch on? While the answers were elusive, it was clear that it hadn't changed how the Bible was being consumed and distributed.

There was one more thing we wanted to try before scrapping the concept. We launched a mobile version and quickly noticed that the nearness of the content increased the amount we engaged with it personally. We also noticed increased traffic on the site. It was as if we discovered something on accident—proximity directly affected engagement.

At the same time, the birth of smartphones gave us an opportunity to re-evaluate our strategy. We had stumbled into the mobile revolution.

After Apple offered developers the opportunity to create apps for the iTunes app store, we started to work on the Bible App. We wanted to see if what we sensed about mobile was accurate. As we worked on the app, we hoped that we might see as many as 100,000 downloads in a year.

What happened far exceeded any of our expectations. Three days after launching, more than 80,000 people installed the Bible App.

These people weren't just installing the Bible to have it sit on a hidden screen (or whatever might be the mobile equivalent of a dusty shelf). They were opening it frequently and spending a significant amount of time engaging. Having asked ourselves how technology might affect distribution of the Bible, this app became the turning point we were looking for.

Fueled by the new-found momentum, we worked on licensing additional languages and versions of the Bible. We also ramped up our development efforts, looking for further ways to help people to have daily and ongoing engagement with this Book.

What we saw over the next few years blew the doors off our too-small dreams and plans. The smartphone and app markets exploded. It was clear that changing the format to digital distribution with social engagement was a new paradigm for Bible publishing. Since then, the Bible App has been installed on tens of millions of devices and users have spent billions of minutes using it to interact with God's Word.

This new paradigm doesn't apply to just religious content. The shift that's taking place in publishing is moving away from monetizing content to monetizing engagement. Though YouVersion is not something we are trying to monetize, we are intensely focused on engagement.

Seven Factors that Drive Engagement

In working to understand how users interact with our app, we've identified seven factors that drive engagement. These factors include: social interaction; personalization; multiple devices and formats; gamification; community contribution; multiple languages; and personal investment.

1) Social interaction

From the very beginning of YouVersion, we have integrated social tools into our offerings. Now, tens of thousands of people are sharing content every day, reaching millions of people via SMS, Twitter, and Facebook. This is part of the new paradigm. People aren't just consuming content, they're engaging in conversation about it with their community—something many book publishers hadn't contemplated even five years ago.

2) Personalization

It's not unusual for people to carry a beat-up Bible that's bulging with bits of paper, filled with notes in the margins and covered in multi-color highlights throughout the text. We have extended that personalization to help users add their highlights, notes, and bookmarks to the app. This metadata is easily accessible on multiple devices, but it no longer clutters the reading experience. Users can also customize their experience by adjusting fonts, sizes, and backgrounds as well as the display of various layers of metadata like translation notes or cross references. The more that app users invest in personalization, the more likely they are to continue engaging with it.

3) Multi-device, multi-format offers

If we want to take part in content regularly, it needs to be present in our lives and literally meet us where we are. While, traditionally, most publishers have tried to target a specific format (hardcover, paperback, audiobook, etc.) to specific buyers, we've learned that a multi-device, multi-format, cloud-enabled consumption experience dramatically increases engagement. Instead of limiting themselves, users can access the content at any time in nearly any environment.

4) Gamification

While the Bible isn't a game, the concept of rewarding achievement and offering encouragement is very helpful in building a higher level of consistency in how people engage. We focus on daily engagement by using structured reading plans that track progress, give badges, and leverage smart communication all in an effort to help people achieve goals. We found this approach has created a way for the printed text to take on a dynamic daily freshness. Publishers that provide and reward systematic engagement will drive much more loyalty.

5) Community contribution

Through public notes in the app, the Bible becomes user-annotated. The community at large makes interesting contributions that highlight meaning and bring insight. (The community generally polices itself and reports inappropriate content.) These contributions bring additional value as the community grows. With these features, an unchanging Book is better able to reflect the constant change present in our culture.

6) Multiple languages

The Bible App is available in hundreds of versions and more than 100 languages, allowing people to carry the equivalent of stacks of Bibles with them on their mobile device. Because we have integrated an API into the app, it can fluidly accommodate new versions and new languages. This format means a large collection of works can be accessed through one platform. Digital tools give publishers a ways to offer content in many more languages than were economically feasible in the past.

7) Personal investment

When the YouVersion community saw new languages being offered, they began to ask if we would offer the Bible App in their native language. Our answer? We can if you help us. Motivated teams of volunteers emerged to help us localize the Bible App as well as our user communication, support tickets, blog posts, and more. But these teams weren't just helping translate. Because they are personally invested in the app, they are passionate advocates and help spread the word about the Bible App to their sphere of influence, in countries and languages where we didn't have a substantial presence previously. When we bring a significant contribution to a community, we want to see it succeed.

Published content used to operate in exclusivity. Publishers and large organizations acted as the gatekeepers to determine whose work had the opportunity to make its way to a larger audience. Now every person with an Internet connection can not only publish, but also build a platform and earn a viable income completely outside of traditional means. It's naïve to think that publishers can corner the market on content anymore—that's no longer the opportunity for monetization. When we shift attention to people's behavior and how they interact with the content, engagement becomes the real product.

Give the author feedback & add your comments about this chapter on the web: http://book.pressbooks.com/chapter/youversion-bobby-gruenewald

20. How Do Books Get Discovered? (Patrick Brown, Kyusik Chung, and Otis Chandler, Goodreads)

Otis Chandler (@otown) is the co-founder and CEO of Goodreads.com; Kyusik Chung is Vice President, Business Development at Goodreads, and is the co-founder of Discovereads, which was acquired by Goodreads in 2011. Patrick Brown is the Community Manager at Goodreads. Goodreads is the world's largest site for readers and book recommendations. Follow @Goodreads for latest news and updates.

We've all fallen under the spell of a truly great book. But where did we originally hear about it? How did we come to choose that particular book from among the literally millions of books in the world? Did a friend hand it to us and say, "You have to read this!" Or did we hear about it on NPR's "Fresh Air"? Or was it a Goodreads Recommendation that convinced us to give it a try?

From the publisher's perspective, discovery has always been shrouded in mystery, a sort of alchemical process through which readers find books they love. With a community of more than 7.5 million people and 280 million books shelved, Goodreads is uniquely equipped to shed some light on this eternal question. In early 2012, our CEO Otis Chandler gave a talk at the Tools of Change[1] conference in New York City presenting some data that helps get at one of the most pressing questions facing the publishing industry today—how do readers discover books?

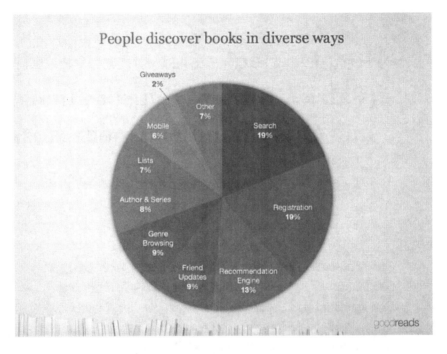

Figure 20.1. People discover books in diverse ways

What we found is that readers discover books in several different ways. While this may not seem surprising, it should serve as a reminder to authors and publishers that no one promotion or marketing technique is enough. To successfully promote a book, you have to reach out to readers in a variety of ways.

We compiled a summary of the various methods Goodreads members use to find books on the site. One of the biggest things we learned—or should we say confirmed—is the power of word of mouth. Searching for

[1] http://www.toccon.com/toc2012

titles on Goodreads is the top way people find books for their to-read shelves. That means they first heard of it elsewhere—likely from friends or the media. Search represented the method of discovery with the widest distribution of titles, from the very popular to the very obscure.

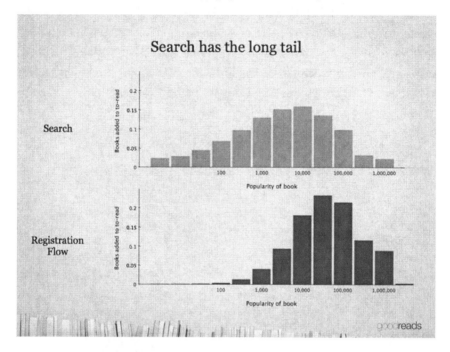

Figure 20.2. Search has the long tail

Some of the methods for finding books, such as the registration process for Goodreads, favor very popular books. We want to make sure you see something familiar when signing up, so we show books that many readers have liked. But other methods of discovery, such as updates from your friends and searching for specific books and authors, are better for finding more obscure books.

Since we launched it in September 2011, our Goodreads Recommendation Engine[2] has been incredibly successful. It was designed to show you interesting mid-list books (books that are neither bestsellers nor completely unknown titles) that you may not have heard of. As shown

---

[2] http://www.goodreads.com/recommendations

in the graph below, we succeeded. This makes sense, as nobody needs an algorithm to tell them about a bestseller. It's also worth pointing out that on the lower end, our recommendation engine has a minimum threshold of several hundred ratings so we know enough about a book to be statistically comfortable recommending it. So authors, if you know of a strong comparable title to your book and you are able to market your book to those readers—and they respond by adding your book to their Goodreads account—our recommendation engine will notice this correlation and be even more likely to suggest your book to the right readers.

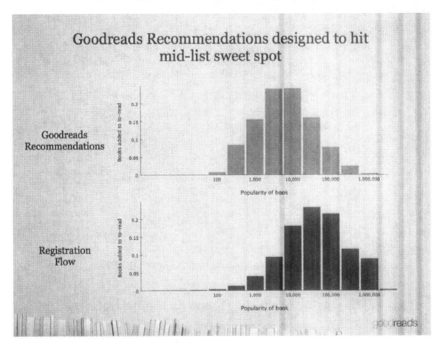

Figure 20.3. Goodreads recommendations

To find out more about where people initially hear about the books they read, we ran a survey of more than 3,200 Goodreads members, asking them how they discovered books. The results were somewhat surprising.

As you can see, most Goodreads members get book recommendations from their friends, either on Goodreads or off. Conversely, very few Goodreads members rely on Twitter and Facebook to hear about new books.

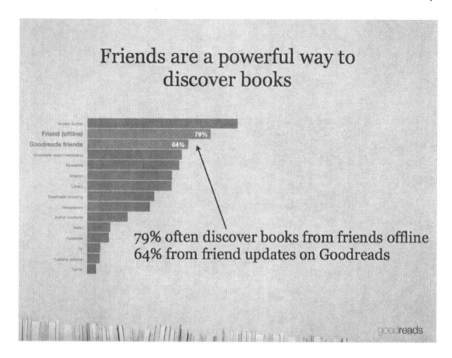

Figure 20.4. Friends are a powerful way to discover books

And, as we've shown previously,[3] an appearance on a popular NPR program or *The Daily Show* can give any book a "pop" on Goodreads. It's worth noting, though, that maintaining that level of interest in the book relies on word of mouth. (In the graph below, the blue line shows the number of times *A Slave in the White House*[4] was added after a member searched for it, and the brown curve shows the number of times the book was added because a member had seen a mention of the book in a friend's update.)

Discovery happens in a multitude of ways, and a successful marketing campaign should take that into account. But there are a few strategies that seem to work well.

Our best advice, both for authors and for publishers, is to work hard to establish your core fan base. The more momentum you get, the more it will build. Encourage readers to rate and review your books. This will not

---

[3] http://bit.ly/nzvFFS
[4] http://bit.ly/PbGACR

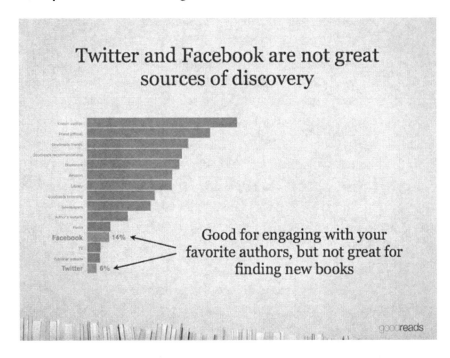

Figure 20.5. Twitter and Facebook are not great sources of discovery

only help generate word-of-mouth buzz, which is essential for a sustained promotion, but it also helps get your books onto the appropriate book lists[5] and onto places like the Goodreads Recommendation engine. Our Listopia[6] lists are a great source of discovery for our members, including lots of mid-list titles. They tend to be specific, such as World War II Fiction or Pacific Northwest Books, so having your book on the right list can make a huge difference.

If you're an author who already has a following, be sure to promote your book heavily to your existing fans and fans of similar authors. Add a Goodreads badge[7] or widget[8] to your website or blog and encourage your readers to add your books and become your fan. If you're just starting out,

---

[5] http://www.goodreads.com/list

[6] http://www.goodreads.com/list

[7] http://www.goodreads.com/api#logo_and_images

[8] http://www.goodreads.com/api#atmb_widget

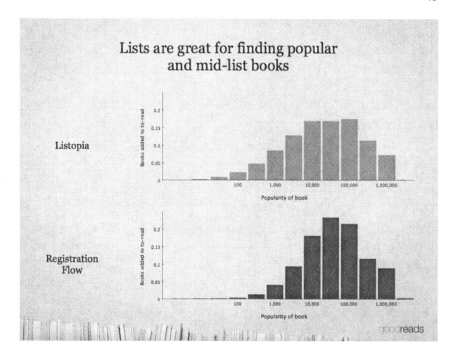

Figure 20.7. Lists are great for finding books

reach the right readers with an advance giveaway.[9]

Figure 20.6. Appearing on the Daily Show

We've collected a range of interesting data on how readers discover their books, much of which is included in a slideshow whose link appears below. As Goodreads continues to grow, we will bring the book publishing community still more of this kind of in-depth information.

Give the authors feedback & add your comments about this chapter on the web: http://book.pressbooks.com /chapter/goodreads-otis-chandler

---

[9] http://www.goodreads.com/giveaway

21. The Surprising Power of "Little Data" (Peter Collingridge, Bookseer)

Peter Collingridge (@gunzalis) is co-founder of Enhanced Editions *and MD of* Apt Studio. *He recently joined* Safari Books Online.

IT'S ALL IN THE DATA...

At least, that's what we realized a year into our first startup. It was in early 2010 when we looked into the analytics from our enhanced ebook apps, and recognized we had stumbled upon a goldmine—a voyeuristic peek into the habits of when and how a reader reads.

In 2008, I had co-founded a company called Enhanced Editions, with the humble goal of making the ebook that the iPhone deserved. By mid 2010, it was clear that we weren't going to make it as a business, and we changed course, *hard,* to capturing as much data about readers as possible. It wasn't a random pivot, but a change of direction absolutely informed by our failure to sell enough apps.

Our first app (*Bunny Munro*, by Nick Cave) had succeeded in capturing the imagination of readers, publishers, authors, and journalists around the world. It earned us enough downloads, sales, and column-inches to make us actually believe that we had invented the first truly digital book.

However, try as hard as we might, this initial hubris gradually wore off as we conclusively failed to convert our initial success into a sustainable business.

Bunny reimagined the ebook as a multimedia experience: we synchronized the audiobook (read by its rock-star author) to the ebook, which was itself designed with the utmost typographical care that the iPhone allowed. We included 13 videos of Nick Cave reading, carefully filmed against projected backdrops. We produced a live news feed of exclusive material, and the audiobook included a soundtrack written and performed by Nick, timed to key points in the narrative.

Possibly my favorite piece of coverage described the app as "the moment digital publishing came of age." Unfortunately, we realized (too late) that one of the major drawbacks of the business was that it didn't solve a burning problem for our customers. This is something any VC (and at least some MBAs) will tell you is vital to a startup's success.

In fact, it was unclear to us who our customers were—publishers, authors, or readers. We aimed first at readers. Unfortunately, none of them was waking up screaming in the middle of the night, "I need audiobooks synchronized to text and the ability to watch videos of my favorite author alongside beautiful typography."

Any technical or user experience achievements we had made were in stark contrast to our commercial achievements, which were in turn out of sync with what our multiple data points were telling us.

Our failure to sell enough of the apps didn't line up with what our analytics were telling us from within the apps. People spent a huge amount of time reading and listening. The audio sync was by far our most popular feature (with video surprisingly low on people's priorities), and people were using the app between 50 and 200 times per month, for around an hour each time.

So if the apps weren't in themselves lame, this suggested a failure elsewhere—in marketing and promotion. And as we dug deeper *it became clear that connecting digital products to their target audiences required a whole new set of capabilities that publishers simply don't have.*

Here was a real problem: what does good, successful promotion look like as publishing changes from print to digital and from B2B to B2C? This seemed like a real problem that we could sink our teeth into. It also had a steady supply of very well-defined customers (publishers! agents-turned-publishers! authors! self-published authors!).

Now that anyone can create and distribute a book to a global audience of millions in a matter of seconds, successful marketing is the single activity that will define institutional publishing. Indeed, it will provide the differentiation publishers need to justify their place in the food chain in the 21st century.

However, book marketing is broken. It is not evolving at the rapid speed of other parts of the industry. Shockingly, many campaigns look identical to those planned ten or more years ago, relying on PR and big-budget poster campaigns.

Why do campaigns stick so rigidly to this formula? There is not—nor has there ever been—any empirical understanding of which combination of marketing strategy and tactics works. Currently, publishers might spend between 5 and 10 percent of their revenues on merely hopeful marketing, with little idea of what works and what doesn't. There is very little after-the-fact analysis.

> "It's difficult to determine what marketing strategies helped, hurt or were just a waste of time." –*WIRED* author David Wolman, quoted in *Nieman Report Winter 2011*, on promoting his Kindle Single.

At Enhanced Editions, we firmly believe the answer to this problem lies in what we call "little data"—the methodical analysis of campaigns, in combination with more agile marketing techniques. By focusing on "little data," publishing can dramatically improve its return on marketing investment.

> "When it comes to the really important decisions, data trumps intuition every time." –Jeff Bezos, CEO Amazon

Publishing houses still make their marketing decisions based largely on gut feel rather than on data. New entrants to the publishing ecosystem— Amazon, Apple, and Google among them—all employ data-driven decision-making approaches. In the same way that you wouldn't consider launching a website without analytics, the same should be true of a digital book: ebooks are, in effect, just websites.

Making a significant change in how publishers make marketing decisions will not be easy. The data that is currently available to publishers is becoming increasingly irrelevant to an ever more digital marketplace.

In the United Kingdom, where Enhanced Editions is based, Nielsen sales data is provided weekly, and gives no insight into ebook sales. It does not break down sales by day or by hour or by location. The absence of specific data on sales makes it impossible to separate the impact of one activity from another in the course of the week's sales.

At the same time, Amazon rankings have become an industry standard proxy for performance. When we researched the market, we heard many stories of publishers obsessively refreshing their product page during a day to help drive telling variations in sales rank. Telling into *what* was less clear. The ranking itself was seen as a goal, rather than one measured against a particular activity or tactic.

So we started with a belief that a data-driven understanding of consumer behavior is fundamental to the future of the publishing industry. After researching how publishers were quantifying the new world (answer: barely more than the refresh button on a browser), we decided to stop making apps, focusing instead on building Bookseer, a market-intelligence service for books.

Bookseer currently captures the "little data" that are a by-product of other activities. The real-time data "exhaust" of the Web, combined with details of promotional activities provided by the publisher, lets Bookseer build a systematic picture of the variations in performance across thousands of titles.

Bookseer collects as much information as possible about these books. The data it captures can include:

- price on Amazon
- hourly sales rank

- print and ebook sales data (uploaded by the publisher)
- what is being said about a book or an author in the media, across social media and on the wider Web
- marketing promotions
- the makeup of bestseller charts and so on

We collect this data in a variety of ways, and we do it all in real-time. As long as we can identify significant events—media coverage, a tweet, a price change, a review—at a specific moment in time, we can measure the effect of that event on sales. In doing this, we can clearly show the individual activities that are directly influencing sales, and of course, the ones that are not.

To share a couple of examples: The first is a big-budget marketing campaign from the UK.

Case Study 1: Aggregated
Amazon Sales Rank: All 7 (Redacted) Titles

The campaign had little impact on the other author titles: the books in the campaign did not have significantly higher sales than those not featured

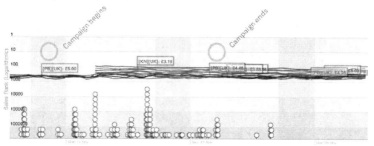

Note: Yellow circles demonstrate social media activity (see next page)

Figure 21.1. Case Study 1: Amazon Sales Rank—All 7 Titles

We tracked all even titles written by a well-known author, in digital and print format, in advance of a nationwide poster campaign (with a social media component) that promoted three of the seven titles. The remaining four titles were tracked as a "control" to measure baseline performance on the non-promoted titles. We also tracked mentions of the author name and the social media keyword promoted on the posters. Given their prime locations, these posters probably cost between of £75–£100,000.

We tried to close many of the open loops in publishing data. As well as tracking Amazon sales rank, price changes, and social media activity, we included Nielsen sales so we could see how closely Amazon sales rank and actual sales are correlated. This approach helped frame all the activity in hard commercial numbers.

Case Study 1: (Redacted)
Amazon Sales Rank: Kindle (red); paperback (blue); Sales (columns)

(Redacted) was released in July, while the campaign was between November 12 and 22 between Points 1 and 2 below.

The campaign appeared to do little to stem the decline in the sales and sales rank since July - though there does appear to be a slight increase in sales of 150 units in the first week of the campaign

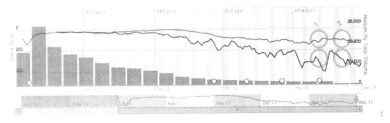

Figure 21.2. Case Study 1: Amazon Sales Rank—Kindle vs Paperback

On the above chart, the navy blue lines at the top represent the hourly sales rank of the paperback. Because it is incrementally harder to get higher up the chart, the scale is logarithmic, with the top section reflecting the rankings between 1 and 10. Kindle and print charts have their own rankings. The blue bars are the actual paperback sales through Nielsen, and the red lines are the Kindle sales rank.

The first circle (1) shows when the campaign started, and the second circle (2) shows when it ended. The poster campaign made very little impact on sales, which were already declining. If one was generous, one could attribute a slight increase in actual Nielsen sales (of around 150 copies), and a slight stemming of the downward trend of Amazon sales rank during the campaign, but the impact isn't exactly jumping off the chart.

Case Study 1: Aggregated
Facebook Likes (blue), Facebook mentions (purple) & Twitter mentions (orange)

The campaign (between Points 1 and 2 below) also failed to stimulate much social media buzz, particularly when compared to the social media activity after publication in July

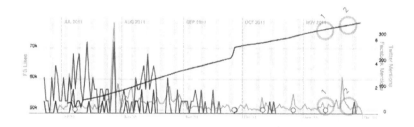

Figure 21.3. Case Study 1: Facebook Likes vs. Twitter Mentions

This second chart shows the social media metrics. Here, the blue line is the number of Facebook "fans" for the author, which is steadily climbing, but which remains unaffected by the campaign, again shown between point 1 and point 2. There *is* a spike in the instances of the Twitter hashtag promoted on the posters, although the total number of tweets generated was 37. You can make up your own mind as to whether this poster campaign was worth the spend.

A second case study also highlights the risks of big-budget print marketing as a vehicle to drive book sales. This data collected for a "chick-lit" title published in the UK, with a heavily digital launch spend focus. Ads were placed on YouTube, and a high-traffic community website (with a strong demographic crossover with the book) was targeted. All advertising space on the website was bought, pointing to the Amazon product page.

Furthermore, an author livechat and two direct emails to site subscribers—over 350,000 of them—were secured. Estimates are that this required an investment between £30,000 and £50,000.

On Bookseer we can see when:

1. Advertising goes live on site
2. Live chat takes place
3. The author appeared on BBC Breakfast TV and was interviewed in the Evening Standard
4. Two emails were sent to groups of 175,000 subscribers

Case Study 2
Amazon sales rank: paperback (blue) and Kindle (red)

The homepage takeover (i), advertising (i / ii), and email shots (iv) had very little effect. Instead, the main driver was (free) coverage in the Evening Standard and BBC (iii)

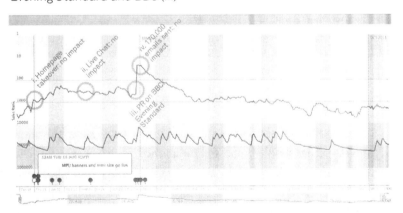

Figure 21.4. Case Study 2: Amazon Sales Rank—Kindle vs. Paperback

This next chart zooms in on the data on an hourly basis to show exactly when the emails were sent (1) and (2), and when the BBC and *Evening Standard* pieces went live. While the BBC had much more effect than the *Standard*, in combination they both delivered great returns—much greater than the emails.

Case Study 2
Amazon sales rank: zoom-in

Zooming in further (which Bookseer can do to an hourly basis), it is even clearer that the emails had no effect, but the BBC impact was most significant

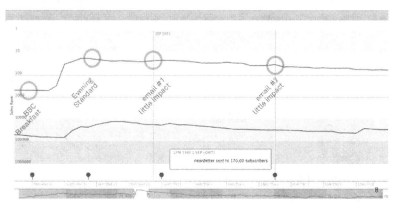

Figure 21.5. Case Study 2: Amazon Sales Rank—Zoom-in

As to effectiveness, you can make up your own minds. We have other case studies that we think overwhelmingly demonstrate the need for an entirely new approach to book marketing. The question we want people to ask is, "With this data, would I spend my money in the same way again? How would my campaign differ?"

Such an approach is one that (obviously) captures and analyzes data. More fundamentally, it is more agile in response to the data. Avinash Kaushik, analytics evangelist at Google, describes modern marketing as a "portfolio" approach planned and executed in tandem with real-time tracking and optimization. Kaushik also says that businesses should spend at least 10 percent of their marketing spend on (measured) experimentation. At Enhanced Editions, we couldn't agree more.

Smart marketing spreads its bets wisely rather than believing that expensive media space booked months in advance is the best marketing tool. Smart marketing monitors and hones multiple activities on a daily basis to find the right mix of PR, social media advertising, search engine advertising, and direct mail. It looks at broad ranges of data in real time to see which activities work, and it tweaks and refines through split A/B testing and audience segmentation. After each campaign, it adopts its learnings into future marketing efforts, rather than repeating the same campaigns over and over again.

By being hands-on (as opposed to just throwing money at the problem) publishers can monitor and turn a failing campaign into one that sells more books and delivers a much improved return on investment (ROI).

Bookseer is designed to demonstrate the impact of any digital or print marketing approach, and to quantify it against the most tangible metrics in publishing: sales. Given the massive amount of time spent on social media, we also display Twitter and Facebook "buzz" in comparison to the other activities, so publishers can measure the ROI for this as well. Unfortunately, it's not simple as just looking at some graphs...publishers need to change the core ways they think of marketing.

> "We need to develop new skills in data analytics, listen to our readers, and understand what they want and what they will pay for." –John Makinson, CEO Penguin

Simply measuring isn't enough. This new marketing approach undoubtedly calls for significant training and investment in skills, skills that publishing does not currently have, yet which are fundamental to delivering the consumer-centric vision of the major houses around the world.

> "[Random House must...] change from being a B2B company to being a B2C company." –Markus Dohle, CEO Random House

In the short term, a data-centric approach allows publishers to be much more reactive to an individual campaign. They can tailor their activity to the bits that are working and stop those that aren't. It allows them to compare the impact of PR against marketing spend and measure the outcome of a price change. They can see what worked on a competitor's title, and they can learn from it for their own.

But, more excitingly, in the medium- to long-term, one can build up an incredibly large corpus of data that can then be mined algorithmically to run predictive scenarios for books you will publish, using data from those that have already been published.

We believe that this "big data" approach can inform future publishing strategies, answering questions like: what is the optimum price, format, and time of year to publish? Who will be the most successful retailer for a given title? Who are the top five journalists or reviewers who have the best track record of driving sales in this genre? Who are the most influential social media people to reach out to? What will the sales be, and therefore, what is the right advance to pay?

These questions have always been fundamental to bringing books to market, and it is time that real-world data played its part in answering them.

Give the author feedback & add your comments about this chapter on the web: `http://book.pressbooks.com/chapter/bookseer-peter -collingridge`

22. Exaggerations and Perversions (Valla Vakili, Small Demons)

Valla is the CEO and co-founder of Small Demons. Prior to Small Demons he held several positions at Yahoo!, most recently VP Product with the Entertainment Group. Valla is a graduate of Georgetown University's School of Foreign Service and on leave from doctoral studies at St. Antony's College, Oxford. Small Demons connects all the details of books, identifying and cataloging all the people, places, and things in book to offer readers an unparalleled ability to go deeper into the stories they know and love.

Publishing. As I've come to know this space over the last couple of years, I've found two themes that dominate the discussion around change and "the future." They are so dominant, they're somewhat tyrannical. Since there are two of them, I like to think of them as the Twin Tyrants of Change.

They are, first, format, and second, reading. With format, it's a variation of "print to digital," "professionally published versus self-published," "the end of the book and the death of publishing." Sometimes it becomes "books as apps," "enhanced books," "chunked books," or "never-ending and always updating books."

Then there's reading, with questions like, "What does reading look like in a digital world?" "Is it enough to 'just read' or does reading itself need to be more interactive?" "Do we have enough readers?" "Why don't we have enough readers?" And of course, "Where do we get more readers?"

There are many dollars being invested and many technologies being built around format and reading, so much so that this seems like the natural way forward. And the conversation, the prevailing wisdom, only helps to cement this notion that the future lies in the change in format from print to digital and the different reading experience that format change brings.

Every time I hear this prevailing wisdom, I'm reminded of two things. The first is Ted Levitt's classic essay, *Marketing Myopia*, in which he argues that an overemphasis on a current product distracts us from the needs of future customers. One of the things that makes classics *classic* is that their message retains its relevancy over time. It's hard not to think of format and reading as blinders when you're wearing Ted Levitt glasses.

The second thing that comes to mind is William James's *The Varieties of Religious Experience*. I read this book as a freshman at Georgetown, and it has permanently affected how I look at scoping phenomena and identifying opportunity. Although he was born and lived his life six decades before Levitt, James provides a simple approach for avoiding marketing myopia and creating new value. It is the approach we used in developing Small Demons.

So, William James: he was interested in understanding the religious life. And he chose to study it by looking at extreme, or what he called pathological, individual experiences, instead of those you might find at organized institutions. Describing his method in 1902, James wrote, "It always leads to a better understanding of a thing's significance to consider its exaggerations and perversions, its equivalents and substitutes and nearest relatives elsewhere."

This led me to ask what happens when we look at publishing through the lens of exaggerations and perversions? Can we find a way out of the Marketing Myopia induced by our focus on the Twin Tyrants of Change: format and reading?

Absolutely. We just have to shift our gaze.

Instead of formats and reading, let's narrow our focus, as James did. In this chapter, I'm going to focus on one type of book—the story—and break it down to some of its basic elements—like characters, settings, and spells. Then I will look at what happens when we focus on individual experiences with characters, settings, and spells in an exaggerated way.

Meaning we'll forget about format; we'll forget about reading; and we'll ask, "Is there something big to be learned from characters, from settings, from spells? What can we gain by understanding the people who obsess about these?"

Let me show you three examples, and then I'll explain how these exact examples led to Small Demons.

First, characters. I've always loved stories, in large part because I loved the characters. Robin Hood, Michael Connelly's Harry Bosch, Al Pacino in the *Godfather*, Max Frisch's Stiller, Batman, Rocky... It's a long list. So sure, we know characters attract. But let's look at how some of the rest of the world, outside of format and reading in publishing, looks at character.

Cosplay[1]—a big phenomena in Asia, but in no way limited to Asia—involves dressing up as characters out of games, down to the last detail. This gives a real-world presence and life to fictional beings. It blurs the boundaries between the lived and imagined.

Acting. Let's consider Christian Bale in *The Machinist*. He lost 63 pounds, or 36 percent of his body weight, to play this role. To get into character, he transformed every aspect of his real body[2] to conform with the needs of a fictional body. This is just one example, of course, as the list of actors who undergo extraordinary measures to bring characters to life is well known.

In cosplay and in acting, the incredibly accurate portrayal of characters is valued so much that its practitioners routinely compete for prizes. There are multiple competitive festivals for cosplay, while the Oscars and similar awards are given annually to actors.

Back in the world of books, stories are *full* of characters. Our contact with them is usually limited to the time when we're reading. You read *Robin*

---

[1] http://www.cosplay.com/
[2] http://bit.ly/Nt8LPs

Hood, and you see the lead character in your mind. You read Katherine Dunn's *Geek Love*, and you're in the middle of the weirdest family dynamic you've ever seen. Then the time comes when you stop reading and move on to something else.

Except there are loads of people who do stop reading and don't move on to something else. They routinely, even always, in an exaggerated fashion, *get into character*. So maybe there's something about characters, then, that is worth exploring.

Next, let's consider settings, or what I'll call today "worlds."

I've been reading comic books for as long as I can remember. As a kid, some of my closest friends were found on the pages of DC Comics. I know every detail about these characters and their worlds, and I'm not alone.

You see, comic book fans, we are a pretty big niche. And we're perversely drawn, in an exaggerated way, to uphold the "rules" of comic book worlds. In comic speak this is known as continuity, but it basically means, these characters, they live in a world that is real and has its rules. Batman has a history. Spider Man has a history. Their history is real, and if a later writer reinterprets or changes aspects of it, everyone is up in arms.

In fact, the obsessiveness with continuity is so strong, so exaggerated, that people who read DC and Marvel Comics refer to the settings for these stories as distinct Universes. The DC Universe, The Marvel Universe. These aren't abstract ideas. They are fully fleshed out and chronicled by fans and publishers. For decades, Marvel and DC have published various versions of a "Handbook" or "Who's Who" to their universes. In these guides, you'll find the height, weight, hair and eye color, powers, marital status, family status, business relationships, group affiliations, place of residence, and history of every major and minor character in the DC and Marvel Universes.

The setting for DC and Marvel characters, where Batman and Spider Man swing across rooftops and the city skies, is not just imagined. It's chronicled with an obsession matching real-world mapping.

Now back to books. So many books take place in shared universes—some purposely, some accidentally. Some books are so detailed in their settings they have their own self-contained worlds, whether fully real or fully imagined. We see these places in our mind as we read, and typically we leave them behind once we put the book down. We put them away when the reading stops.

Like characters, maybe there's something about setting that's worth a closer look. Comic book fans and their exaggerations and perversions seem to think so.

OK, one last example, and then I'll tie this all together. Let's talk about spells.

A great story casts a spell. We hear "Once Upon a Time," and we're conditioned to receive—it's storytime. We hope the story is so good it takes us somewhere, captures us, becomes something we can lose ourselves in.

If you have a favorite story, you've probably experienced this. But if you've experienced it, then it makes it a common experience.

But here, we're interested in exaggerations. Perversions.

So, here's someone who looks at this differently: Grant Morrison, one of today's most successful comic-book writers. One of Morrison's most well-known series is the cult classic, *The Invisibles*. (It's mind-blowing, by the way, if you haven't read it.) In an interview[3] I read years ago and have never stopped thinking about, Morrison talked about writing the *The Invisibles*:

> "Right at the beginning—when I started writing *The Invisibles*—I sat down and tried to cast it as a spell. I even did a bungee jump to try and empower the spell. Now it has taken on a life of its own. Things I have put into the comic have actually happened—to the point where I can put things into the comic and MAKE them happen."

OK, so now we have someone who takes spells and the magic of storytelling a lot more seriously. You and I, we get lost in the world of a story. Someone like Grant Morrison thinks his stories shape the world.

And you know, he's not the only writer who feels this way. I've read variations of this in many other author interviews, too.

So what does this tell us? That he's crazy, perhaps? Or that there's something about the power of a fantastic story that resists compartmentalization? That seeps through from one world to the other? That the world

---

[3] http://www.barbelith.com/cgi-bin/articles/00000033.shtml

about us may be more fictional than we realize, and that the fictional world more real?

What if you took that seriously? What if you took this all seriously:

- that characters live beyond the page,
- that settings are worlds worth exploring,
- that spells can break through from one medium to another.

Welcome to the Storyverse.

That's what we did, and are doing, at Small Demons. We treat the stories—specifically the people, places, and things inside them—as a connected world of their own. We take seriously the idea that people want to get closer to characters, that they want to travel through the streets, cities, and regions of a novel or a work of history. We believe that a story can cast a spell beyond the page and into your everyday life and broader cultural experiences.

Practically, this starts with data gathering. You can't get at stories as their own world until you start mapping what that world looks like. For us this means indexing stories—fiction and nonfiction narrative—for references to the people, places, and things within them. This leads us to generate an index per book of all these interesting topics, each worthy of further exploration.

The second step is connecting: relating the details of one story to all the other stories that share those same details. This allows us to say, first, in *High Fidelity* there's a lot of music by Bob Dylan, and then, if you follow the trail of Dylan's music, you'll find all these other books that share it.

As we start to do this for many books, first tens, then hundreds, then thousands, what emerges is a shared space of storytelling. The details of books gathered up so the story can continue on into the future, in whatever fashion the reader sees fit. Maybe this means reading *High Fidelity*, then listening to all the music in it. Maybe it means visiting the *Spook Country* setting, Mr. Sippee's in Los Angeles, for broasted potatoes—really, it could be anything.

At the heart of it all is the conviction that the "future" of the book isn't about its format or how you read it. The future of the book is about extending each individual reader's connection with the story. We no longer need to say that the experience of a book needs to stop on the page, or in the mind.

When looking to do something new in publishing, to create new products for new markets, it helps to begin by looking elsewhere. Step away from conventional wisdom and journey to wherever there's intense, crazy, fervent passion—the core of something new. The beauty of much of this industry is that it is created by and consumed by people who share this crazy passion, these exaggerations and perversions. Why not listen to them?

Give the author feedback & add your comments about this chapter on the web: http://book.pressbooks.com/chapter/small-demons-valla -vakili

23. **Pain and Its Alleviation (John Oakes, OR Books)**

John Oakes is the co-publisher of OR Books, *a publishing company that "embraces progressive change in politics, culture and the way we do business."*

(In which the publishing industry is compared to a dead Norwegian Blue parrot, and evolutionary theory is briefly discussed.)

At the most elemental level, pain serves a purpose. It teaches those of us who survive the experience. If we don't learn, we go on suffering—or we vanish from the earth.

In discussing contemporary publishing, there's really only one mystery. Why does a collection of sophisticated, intellectually curious adults, many of them with substantial financial resources at their disposal, perpetuate a system that has failed? To quote John Cleese whilst attempting to return his deceased Norwegian Blue, publishing is "stone-dead," an ex-parrot nailed to its perch, as it were, by sporadic bestseller and backlist sales. It hinges on guesswork and cronyism, on antiquated, environmentally and fiscally disastrous supply and production systems. The persistence of this system would be understandable if there were no alternative. But there is, and it's not even based on proprietary technology. It's primarily a matter of attitude, of being willing to try a new direction.

Not too long ago, I was reading about the "Red Queen Theory of Evolution." A concept first put forth by the American evolutionary biologist Leigh Van Valen in the 1970s, it was named after the bloody-minded chess piece in Lewis Carroll's *Through the Looking Glass*. In the relevant passage, the Red Queen says to Alice, "It takes all the running you can do to keep in the same place." Van Valen applied this metaphor to evolution, suggesting that species are in a constant race for survival and continually must evolve new ways of defending themselves throughout time. It seems to me this metaphor is exactly what we need to keep in mind when considering book publishing today. There are a million different paths to stability, if not success—but there's one sure route to disaster, and that's staying in place.

I've worked with medium-sized independent publishing houses, with start-up houses that could barely pay the rent, and those that were more concerned with interior decoration than the bottom line, with those for which the editorial direction was more the scattershot, anarchic approach of "throw everything at the wall, and see if something sticks," and those that cultivated books over a period of time and believed in focused, careful editorial curating. All companies, large and small, shared the horrific experience of the sales conference, of justifying in a few minutes why the little world represented by a particular book was to enter the publishing universe. The motivation of the sales force was not the issue: whether glassy-eyed, stunned into somnolence by the hundreds of titles they'd have to represent that season, or energetic, well-intentioned, well-read, and open-minded representatives—a few days or weeks later, all sales reps were obligated to present the title in question in a flash, if at all, to similarly overwhelmed store buyers.

In this pitiful exercise, guesswork piles on guesswork piles on guess-work. Finally, assuming the editors convince the sales reps who convince the store buyers to stock the book in question, the consumer has the final word, and the returns will soon stream in. The result? All lose. The author: it will be that much harder for her to place her next book. The store: its valuable shelf space is taken up by product that doesn't move. The publisher: it reimburses the store for the cost of those books, and must nonetheless pay the printer. The printer loses because it's operating in an environment populated by increasingly unhealthy clients. And the reader loses, as in their desperation the publishers and stores push more and more "product" into the world with less and less regard for its quality.

An Alternative

There's this thing called the Internet, this magical thing, which, with some work, enables a seller—a publisher—to reach a vast number of potential consumers—readers. It has been calling out to the book industry for some time now. In fact on Christmas Day, 2009, an historic milestone was reached (and ignored by most). On that day, for the first time ever, Amazon sold more electronic books than print books.

At OR Books, we decided to re-examine publishing from the ground up. We feel that there are certain elements of the profession worth keeping—editing, marketing, design work. Here's where we're different. We don't accept returns; our primary business is selling direct to consumers. We are platform-agnostic, and we issue our ebooks simultaneously with print editions. We don't have sales reps and don't solicit stores, but if the stores do come to us, we sell on a prepaid, non-returnable basis, at a flat discount (50 percent). We sell to third parties only out of necessity: we post our books on Amazon after selling them for a month or so on our own site exclusively. We don't have sales conferences; we promote our books on the Web through ads, emails, excerpts, promotional videos, author appearances, and only very occasionally in print publications. We then do our best to license the book to traditional publishers (which have the joy of dealing with bookstores and returns and ruinous discounts). We succeed in doing so about half the time. If we don't license the book to another publisher, more often than not we do just fine working with an author to build an audience. Our success does not depend on the first few weeks of a book's appearance on shelves, as is almost always the case with the traditional model.

The challenge for OR lies in marketing its titles. Thanks both to the advent of self-publishing—which I would argue has surged in recent years less because of technology than because of the proven incompetence of traditional publishing—and to the over-stuffed lists of the professionals, consumers see record numbers of new titles every season. Millions of new books are added to the lists every year. This is at once a challenge and an opportunity: the challenge is obvious (to make a book rise above the sea of mush). It is an opportunity because only a handful of these books are marketed with any seriousness. And a large portion of what OR saves by adopting a saner approach to inventory and sales goes into promoting its titles.

People call OR a "radical alternative" or an "experiment," but in many ways we're a throwback: we advocate a process wherein the publisher focuses on developing ideas into workable manuscripts, carefully editing them, and, above all, devoting substantial resources to marketing the finished product. These tasks were once the exclusive province of publishers, but in the last 20 years or so, development and editing have fallen increasingly to agents, while marketing has become the responsibility of authors themselves. We print only to fulfill orders, with a minimum of waste; we sidestep warehouses, wholesalers, and even—at least at the outset of a book's life—bookstores and online retailers, including Amazon.

If it sounds simple, it is. And the people quickest to understand our model have been agents and authors. Among them, we have found that the greater their exposure to traditional publishing, the more they're veterans of the industry, the more they're receptive to what we're doing. Consumers really don't care whether they buy from us or from Amazon, just as they don't care whether the publisher's name on the spine of the book they're buying is Random House or OR Books. The result is that we at OR Books have rather quickly acquired a stable of name-brand authors, represented by top agents, and that we've even begun convincing ourselves that there is a way for unsubsidized book publishing at the highest level to continue, and thrive, in the 21st century.

Give the author feedback & add your comments about this chapter on the web: http://book.pressbooks.com/chapter/or-books-john-oakes

24. The End of the Public Library (As We Knew It)? (Eli Neiburger, Ann Arbour District Library)

Eli Neiburger is Associate Director for IT & Production at the Ann Arbor District Library *in Ann Arbor, Michigan. He's the author of* GAMERS... IN THE LIBRARY?!, *published in 2007 by ALA Editions, and has written and presented extensively about libraries, content, and the Web. Find him on Twitter, he's* @ulotrichous.

The media explosion of the 20th century is imploding. As the text publishing industry is inevitably transformed by the Internet and left smoldering in a changed world, libraries—most particularly public libraries—are feeling the poke of a very sharp stick, with no carrot in sight. Created to store and organize the information of their communities, public libraries capitalized on the mass-market media explosion of the 20th century to aggregate and circulate commercial (and predominantly recreational) prefilled content containers. It was an irresistible opportunity to build new, unique value, and it worked so well that a majority of users think of their public libraries predominantly as a prepaid, only slightly inconvenient way to get temporary access to entertainment-filled containers.

The shakeouts of the digital text market have barely begun, but the players and battle lines are well-established. Following its traditional publishing plans, Big Text has a lot of risk floating out there, with distressingly few levers or knobs available to manage that risk. And there goes the public library, still trying to do business as usual, an anachronistic horse dragging an ice wagon past row after row of homes where shiny Frigidaires hum away.

Publishers know they can push libraries around a bit and we'll still eagerly line up for galleys each summer. They have to close whatever holes they can in their business models. Their nascent ebook businesses are at the mercy of many variables they can't control, circling a consolidation event horizon that has a jumpy look to it. The hoped-for return on big transitional investments is hanging in the balance. The public library, never a big part of publisher revenues, has become little more than an analog hole in the digital publishing business model.

Driven by a gut feeling but without much evidence, publishers are fretting that every library borrower is one less sale, especially as the user experience of buying an ebook and reading it once converges with the user experience of "borrowing" an ebook and reading it once. This ignores the fact and emerging evidence that most library borrowers were never considering a purchase, and that those library users are already among publishing's best customers. Also, while ebooks are over-priced, many publishers still have expensive processes to transition, and the early adopters are still lining up to help.

So, public libraries, faced with growing demand for ebooks, are stuck with few options, saddled with counterintuitive restrictions that our customers refuse to believe are beyond our control ("No, you don't understand, I want an ebook, and there's no waiting for ebooks.") crappy trust-chain focused tools, and library-specific licensing price points that, even while embracing publishers' restrictive terms, increasingly say "GO AWAY LIBRARIES."

On top of that, the net impact of the increasingly frictionless online market for text, the echo chamber of net-based media and the ever more rapid turnover of hotness means that the demand for hot things is more squished than ever into a taller, narrower peak. Meeting—or even denting—the demand for the new hot thing at public libraries is more out of reach than ever. Meanwhile, big companies are experimenting with commercial ebook lending libraries unfettered by the artificial scarcity forced on public libraries, and authors—if not publishers—are finding that being a part of it is a good idea.

Finally, there's the challenge of ownership. The first-sale doctrine took good care of us for years, but if the only thing that's for sale to public libraries are licenses and we're dependent on software trust-chains and continued operation of intermediaries for access to those licenses, how can libraries guarantee ongoing access to materials for our communities?

Something's got to give.

What to Do?

In many ways, our public library here in Ann Arbor, Michigan, is on the front lines of this phase change. The Ann Arbor District Library (AADL) has made significant investment in technology and in meeting the needs of 21st-century users, and our community has a voracious appetite for reading and media in all forms. For example, as early as 2008, AADL processed the most circulation transactions per capita, but was also in Amazon's top 5 that year for most books purchased per capita.[1] Readers borrow, and readers buy. They're not mutually exclusive or zero-sum in our community.

In addition, because of our investment in technology and in-house expertise, we've been able to set a high bar for usability of our catalog and online services. Today, our customers' expectations are simply not met by the ebook options available to us on the mass market.

We want to deliver digital content that's in demand, but we want to do it in a way that meets our users' expectations. In a system where there are no limits on borrowing or requesting physical items, that means leveraging the potential of digital distribution, not just offering digital services that are more restrictive than their physical equivalents. We also want to ensure compatibility by using standard, unencrypted file formats that any device

---

[1] http://bit.ly/MFq1kK

can display, without requiring proprietary software, support, or licensing servers.

You can see where this is a problem in the current publishing environment. We know that we have no leverage with big publishers or content platforms, so we developed a licensing model that works for our patrons, the library, and even the rights holder, provided that they are ready to do business in this century.

The AADL Digital Content Agreement is a starting point in negotiation with Independent Rightsholders or Creators. The Agreement establishes that the library will pay an agreed-upon sum for a license to distribute to authenticated AADL cardholders, from our servers, an agreed-upon set of files, for an agreed-upon period of time. At the end of the term, we can either negotiate a renewal or remove the content from our servers.

The licenses specifies that no DRM, use controls, or encryption will be used, and no use conditions are presented to the AADL customer. In fact, our stock license also allows AADL users to download the files, use them locally and even create derivative works for personal use.

This approach removes the complexity from digital distribution. It takes ebooks, audiobooks, music, and videos—all digital objects—back to what they truly are: files on a web server. Logged-in users can download this stuff. That's it. They don't have to return this information to the library or otherwise destroy it.

This tends to be where the rightsholders we work with either get it, or they don't. Users don't have to return the information to the library because library users have never had to return the information they got at the library, only the containers! Digital objects don't have to be returned to the library, because the library still has them. Digital content is indistinguishable from magic when unrestrained by a license.

So, this isn't a checkout. It's a download. Circulating bits makes no sense, and no business model can change that. When something can be infinitely duplicated, it cannot be made scarce in the process of distribution. This totally breaks the concept of a library, but the economics of sharing still make sense. In this case, the community is not pooling its funds to buy retail containers that are then shared. Instead, the community is pooling its funds to pay upfront to support rights holders whose releases they are interested in. The community receives the ability to take rubbings of these works for their personal collections.

Users get access to a completely hassle-free, expertly selected, and high-quality collection of files they can download. The standard agreement defines what AADL customers can do with these files. Libraries get sustainable, supportable cross-platform content that can immediately fill demand. And rightsholders get a stable, predictable revenue stream in the form of a few big, reliable checks instead of lots of little unpredictable ones. And if more libraries can get the technical, legal, and acquisition infrastructure to support this model, rightsholders can grow this revenue stream into a game-changer.

Why It Works

Of course, this download collection has little that anyone's ever heard of. The mass market stuff is just not available to license on these terms, and it may never be. But for creators who are making niche, quality content, this license can truly be a win-win. Instead of looking at the license fee as compensation for something like a one-time sale, the pricing works when the rightsholder considers how much revenue they would like to expect during the license term from our 54,000-odd cardholders. For niche creators, it's not hard for the library to beat that number, and all they have to do to get it is agree to the license and deliver the files to our server.

They're not releasing their content to the world (especially because it's already out there). They're just granting a year or so of downloads to these 54,000 people. They get more revenue than they would likely get from those people up front, and the library gets sustainable, usable digital content for its users. This approach also incentivizes the creation of further works by the rightsholder, as the library's interest in older works will lose value over time. This likely decline encourages creators to bring new work under the license at renewal. This helps keep the license fees up; it may even provide a path to something like ownership, where the library eventually acquires a license to permanently offer older files for download, with no external authority, infrastructure, or permissions involved.

While the business model here doesn't scale much past independent publishers, the fact is that the lines are pretty much drawn for digital distribution of mass-market content, and no matter who wins, libraries lose. We're not invited to any of these parties, simply because there is perceived to be no business case for licensing libraries to circulate digital content, beyond mining the temporary vein of transitional desperation. It could be the commercial market consolidates entirely under a paid lending model, and libraries are left with only independents who will still sell to us at all. It sounds apocalyptic to genre fiction buyers, but libraries have always been all about the long tail. The big peak is an interloper over the millennia we've been in business.

When everything is everywhere, libraries need to focus on providing—or producing—things that aren't available anywhere else, not things that are available everywhere you look. Developing relationships with independent publishers is nothing new for libraries. Together we can get unique, high-quality content in front of library users and grow the only business that really counts here in this century: *audience.*

A Glimmer of Hope

This approach offers an opportunity: we can rebuild the creator-consumer relationship, using the public library as the only needed intermediary. Wouldn't that just be awesome?

Anticipating a day when the app-storification of the entire content industry is complete, the library might be the only place left willing to pay real money for content, provided it's on our terms. When most basic content is distributed at prices below the impulse threshold, library licenses might be the only up-front money available once the speculative advance business finishes flaming out.

There is a transaction cost problem, both for the libraries who could conceivably need to do business with thousands of publishers or creators, and small rightsholders, who could conceivably need to do business with thousands of libraries. This could produce some new opportunities to aggregate the buying power of libraries while stabilizing and simplifying the revenue streams of the rightsholders. Instead of libraries stuck nowhere near the table with major media interests, libraries could become significant parts of more creators' businesses, jointly developing content relationships that benefit library users, publishers, and creators alike.

Digital content doesn't have to kill the public library. Libraries can diversify their value to their communities, continue to develop circulating collections of physical items that bring unique value to their communities, and aggregate the buying power of the community to keep independent artists producing good stuff for a real, paying audience. With licensing that embraces the digital format instead of resisting its potential, the library can give the user the experience of downloading free media, and the rightsholder the experience of selling paid media.

All we have to do to get there is to stop chasing blockbusters and take responsibility for our own legal and technical infrastructure. The future is ours to invent! Go Team Library!

Give the author feedback & add your comments about this chapter on the web: http://book.pressbooks.com/chapter/ann-arbour-district-library-eli-neiburger

25. Now Is the Time for Experiments (Ian Barker, Symtext)

Ian Barker is the Founder of Symtext and a proud contributor to this book. You can follow him on Twitter @irbarker. Symtext's Liquid Textbook platform is used by schools, educators, and publishers to provide educator-curated learning materials to students.

As a member of the educational technology community and as an entrepreneur, I view Clay Shirky's 2009 blog post, "*Newspapers and Thinking the Unthinkable*",[1] as required reading for those of us in the publishing industry. The post deals with the implosion of newspaper revenue and the utter lack of clarity on what is to become of newspapers both online and print, potential business models, even the future of journalism itself.

Shirky likens our age to that of Gutenberg, when the advent of the printing press sparked an overwhelming wave of societal change. That upheaval fundamentally undermined existing power structures and changed ways of thinking and behaving for people in the 1500s. Shirky

[1] http://bit.ly/18tDhy

effectively argues that—lucky us!—we are living through a time of equal transformation and uncertainty. He neatly captures the angst of an entire industry, offering scant solace:

> "In Craigslist's gradual shift from 'interesting if minor' to 'essential and transformative,' there is one possible answer to the question, 'If the old model is broken, what will work in its place?' The answer is: *Nothing will work, but everything might.* (Emphasis mine.) Now is the time for experiments, lots and lots of experiments, each of which will seem as minor at launch as Craigslist did, as Wikipedia did, as *octavo* volumes did."

I love this: "Nothing will work, but everything might." If ever there was a clarion call to people who want to change the game, this is it. And, much like the newspaper industry before it, book publishing across all sectors is facing tremendous pressure and uncertainty. Our much beloved Internet offers ubiquity, abundance, and immediacy. Devices and social tools have fueled an onrushing, demanding, attention-challenged digital generation that sits at the proverbial front door of educational publishers and educational institutions. We know the statistics, we see the effect on prices,[2] and we see the influence of digital book retailers.[3] It's a new world, but few if any of us are clear about where it's all leading.

Another indicator that educational publishing is in the throes of great change: venture capitalists, who once eschewed education as stolid, resistant to change, and a slow market to develop, are suddenly alert to an immense marketplace[4] in which two of the three things we most closely associate with education—schools and books—are both changing. Investment is flooding into educational technology, much of it aimed at speeding the reinvention of learning materials and education itself.

Burgeoning demand and high levels of investment create a new reality in which the pace and probability of radical change are increasing. It's impossible to believe that iPads, myriad competing tablets, social media platforms like Facebook, and technology developments yet to come won't

---

[2] http://on.wsj.com/Agp7tu
[3] http://nyti.ms/pnhCh9
[4] http://bit.ly/cbFiDa

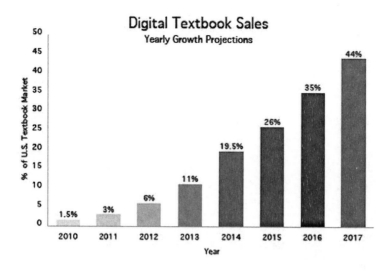

Figure 25.1. Digital textbooks reaching the tipping point in US higher education—A revised five-year projection (Source: http://www.nextisnow.net)

thoroughly disrupt learning materials publishing in the coming years. So, what to do?

For starters, it helps to look at this from Shirky's point of view—nothing *will* work, but everything might. In a time of constrained budgets and threatened revenue, uncovering something in a large set of possibilities that *might* work is far from easy. But, if we don't try, we don't learn; if we don't experiment, logically and scientifically, we gain no data and have no sound basis upon which to act. We can learn from observing others, but watching and doing remain latitudes apart. Now is indeed "the time for experiments, lots and lots of experiments."

> "What you do is what matters, not what you think or say or plan." From *REWORK: a better, easier way to succeed in business,*[5] a 37signals Manifesto

Let it not be said that we don't follow our own advice. At Symtext, we have been experimenting for years with business model variations, target market refinements, go-to-market strategies and product development. This

---

[5] http://bit.ly/9IjtB6

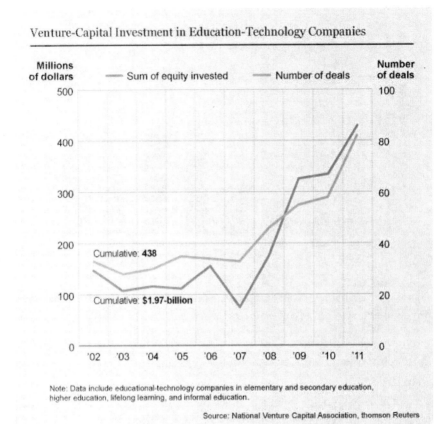

Venture-Capital Investment in Education-Technology Companies

Figure 25.2. The pace of investment in educational technology has increased dramatically

makes for business common sense—as a business meets the market, it learns and adjusts to make progress. We have made some pretty significant errors, but we have also learned an immense amount about what customers want in the educational marketplace.

Symtext is a collaborative social learning platform used by schools, educators, and publishers to provide "Educator Curated Learning Materials" to students. We call the platform within which these curated materials are delivered to students "Liquid Textbooks." Materials within a Liquid Textbook may be fee-based or open, text or multi-media, educator-authored or obtained from a major publishing house. All are fully rights managed for delivery online, offline, to specific devices as well as print-on-demand platforms.

We source, assemble, and distribute what would otherwise be "unbundled" learning materials: chapters, cases, presentations, videos, and self-authored materials. Compared with complete, generic works, our custom publishing solution generates higher rates of student purchase, gives publishers new commercialization opportunities, and offers schools a means to recapture income and data generated by learning materials.

For publishers, we parse materials and attach agreed-upon pricing and permissions (e.g., defining permissible markets and related processes, such as print enabled/disabled). We support multiple price/permission conditions per object, so that, for example, publishers can commercialize materials in one market while sharing them in another.

This customization also operates at the level of the individual. The Symtext platform can deliver a specific price/permission condition to a specific student. In addition to billing and royalty management, we manage student access via the learning management system (LMS) in place at an institution. Symtext can "white label" our platform while providing publishers and institutions with detailed metrics. Because we source broadly, we have also made sure that our platform can render poor quality digital files into searchable, highlightable (i.e., useful) content. These features are all part of solving the challenge of distributing world-class content to highly demanding and digitally literate schools, faculty, and students.

Students access and use remixed materials within Liquid Textbook, device-neutral, cloud-based, HTML5 compliant readers that support social interaction. Students can consume their learning materials, "hand-picked" by their professor, on whatever device they happen to be using. Using our platform, students can add notes or highlights that may be made available in real time to fellow students in their class or section. We see this native web, integrated, multi-platform approach as vital to providing a truly interactive and social learning experience.

Although some of these features have already been made available through things like annotatable PDFs, simply delivering these fixed objects is inadequate. Students are rejecting the notion that learning materials and the learning experience are in some way islands unto themselves, separate and distinct from their other activities.

Here's another way to look at it: Edmodo, which launched in 2007 as a sort of a Facebook for schools, reports a user base of over 6.5 million students. Their growth provides an indication that millions of students are already embracing social services. The point is less about what Edmodo does[6] (though it does directly affect publishers), but rather that students engage with educational platforms in ways that are consistent with their existing online behaviors.

Delivering PDFs isn't consistent, regardless of how fancy the wrap is. Collectively, we have to realize that the social web, the advent of brilliantly advanced devices, abundance replacing scarcity,[7] and the rise of curation fundamentally alter the demand side of the learning materials market. Students, schools, and professors want much more than what they are getting.

This is becoming more acutely the case, as seen in the rise of asynchronous learning, blended learning, team/group collaborative learning, green consumption patterns, cost concerns (value for money), and of course our insatiable craving for understanding, via the vast amounts of data produced by online systems. None of these trends support continuation of the textbook form. They do provide proof that where we are today is nothing compared to what tomorrow holds.

Suppliers of learning materials and providers of platforms to deliver these materials must together embrace these trends and capitalize upon them. Waiting—doing nothing—only deepens the future hole from which one must escape. Now is the time for experimentation.

There are negatives to online delivery and custom digital publishing, specifically. Based upon exit surveys, some students still prefer print. When it comes to designing a custom content package, a decent proportion of educators ironically describe themselves as "lazy": a clear impediment to wider adoption. Let's be charitable and call those reluctant educators "focused." We could interpret this feedback as an impenetrable attachment

---

[6] http://about.edmodo.com/
[7] http://bit.ly/a1Qdfu

to the textbook form. The textbook is, after all, in some respects an almost perfect expression of the print artifact.

At Symtext, we argue the opposite. Online presentation of learning materials is improving exponentially. As usability improves, resistance to electronic content is diminishing rapidly. We can't escape the trend:

> Over the next 5 years, digital textbook sales in the United States will surpass 25%[8] of combined new textbook sales for the Higher Education and Career Education markets.

We have found that professors are over-burdened with teaching, research, and administrative tasks. In response, we have partnered with publishers and schools' on-campus staff to help with Liquid Textbook assembly and delivery. Professors do no more than provide reading lists and add annotations.

We also specifically adopted the "universality" approach: in a custom assembly model, it's more important to be able to deliver anything an educator specifies over materials that are highly engineered. We have provided a means by which a wider universe of learning materials is available to educators, so they may in turn provide their learners with a superior educational experience at a minimum of fuss and expense. Although surveys show that students enjoy the highly engineered content available via platforms like Inkling, the vast majority of content available from educational publishers was not created in a way that can be used on such platforms, and much of it won't be created that way in the future.

At Symtext, we work to provide a platform that:

- enables professors to deliver superior learning materials
- allows publishers to strategically target elements of their repertoire
- supports a variety of commercialization techniques
- can successfully intersect with the larger, social web

Publishers with world-class content can use the Symtext platform to reach students on an unprecedented scale and at a substantially lower cost of acquisition. Given that we are all in the business of improving education, this approach provides all participants with an enormous win.

---

[8] http://bit.ly/JOIq5I

Apart from the overall move to digital learning materials, the Symtext approach is consistent with several trends. In other contexts we are all trained that we can get just what we need—tracks from iTunes, specific podcasts, articles from newspaper sites. While we have not yet seen the same concept break out in higher education, improvements in the user experience (UX) coupled with solutions to the problems of the over-burdened professor, should propel us faster in that direction.

This does not mean that demand for readily remixable learning objects—the unbundled textbook—will eradicate the textbook. People and markets are complex; nothing happens in a straight line. We hypothesize that a decline in *print* textbook sales presages the end of the textbook edition cycle and the arrival of versioning, in which chapters can be rapidly (perhaps even instantly, following proper review processes) be updated for end users. We also see the rise of curated selections of recommended chapters, subject to an ongoing process of review and improvement.

There are some fairly profound consequences for the learning materials market should versioning replace the textbook edition cycle. For starters, what of textbook rentals? Without an inventory of used textbooks, renting one would seem difficult! If we think of chapters and the ebooks we can easily create from them, what of the generic textbook? What new business models will emerge?

In a world where the production of learning materials can immediately respond to demand, how is pricing affected? Perhaps we can more easily move to blended pricing, "renting" learning materials we don't intend to keep and purchasing, in perpetuity, those we want to keep? From an admittedly biased perspective, the need for device-neutral platforms that enable seamless remixing across sources and support a social experience can only increase in size and importance.

Working with a variety of constituents in the education marketplace, we have yet to meet the professor, campus store manager, or head of IT who is interested in managing multiple publisher-specific platforms. In a similar way, we have yet to run into anyone who doesn't think that delivering content into the classroom won't become increasingly complex and increasingly custom in nature.

For publishers, it is increasingly impractical to be all things to all people. While there are exceptions, it is truly difficult to envision publishers becoming as skilled at developing software as they are at producing the reading materials upon which we all depend. But publishers must respond in some meaningful way.

As other chapters[9] of this book note, the production techniques publishers may adopt in response to this barrage of change are evolving quickly. At Symtext, our approach focuses more upon distribution. If we accept the premise that there are many delivery systems and business models from which to choose, but that waiting until The Answer manifests itself is just asking for trouble, then part of the answer must lie in drawing from Shirky's advice and conducting lots of experiments. While a complete answer may yet elude us, the gauntlet has been thrown down. Here's Shirky on publishing[10] from April, 2012:

> Publishing is not evolving. Publishing is going away. Because the word "publishing" means a cadre of professionals who are taking on the incredible difficulty and complexity and expense of making something public. That's not a *job* anymore. That's a *button*. There's a button that says "publish," and when you press it, it's done.

Words to provoke. Tools that trigger a deluge of "content" aren't analogous to the full suite of traditional publisher activities. In some respects, it makes these core activities even more valuable (e.g., curation). But the threat level is increasing. Understanding that what is most important is *doing*, conducting business model and technology experiments should be done quickly, iteratively, and with minimum risk. In an unpredictable and fast-changing environment, part of what publishers need to do is manage risk through the strategic deployment of capital. Lowering risk may include transferring development costs of new technologies to partners. Let new technologies emerge on someone else's dime.

Mitigating investment costs in new technology also means more capital left over for core publisher activities. Freed-up capital lets publishers place more markers in more places. Over time, expanding the breadth

---

[9] http://bit.ly/tbkvQi
[10] http://bit.ly/IOLX62

of experiments increases the probability that publishers will find the set of distribution activities that maximizes revenue. It also increases a publisher's ability to reach readers while reducing the likelihood that it will find itself playing catch-up. That's an experiment worth trying.

———————————

Give the author feedback & add your comments about this chapter on the web: http://book.pressbooks.com/chapter/symtext-ian-barker

26. The Forgotten Consumer (Jacob Lewis, Figment)

Jacob Lewis is the co-founder and CEO of Figment, an online community for teens and young adults to create, discover, and share new reading and writing. Before starting Figment, Jacob was the Managing Editor of The New Yorker *magazine, where he worked for more than 12 years, and* Conde Nast Portfolio. *He lives in Brooklyn, NY.*

The Inefficient Market

In the early 1990s, while in the port city of Brindisi, Italy, I came across some people on the street selling pirated versions of English-language books. The books were crudely bound and looked to be photocopied. But they were cheap and plentiful, and since I was getting on a long boat ride, I bought a couple.

On one hand, stolen content that benefits only the seller obviously isn't good for the book industry. But in their way, those stalls in Brindisi were models of smart publishing. They had created an incredibly efficient market. These sellers knew exactly who would be walking by—American kids backpacking around Europe with little money to spend and even less room in their bags—and they tailored their selection specifically to those customers.

Finding any kind of efficiency in today's publishing industry is difficult. Unlike the sellers in Brindisi, publishers (and most retailers) don't know who's going to walk by on any given day or what they might be interested in reading, let alone purchasing. There is very little information available for each product, including the forecasted market size and a title's potential for success. Information derived from sales is reactive, not predictive. Publishers play a guessing game with new genres, themes, and voices.

Historically, publishing has not been about data. It is about relationships and subjectivity—the imperious tastes of agents, editors, and buyers. The combination of overconfidence,[1] overreaction, representative bias, information bias,[2] and overreliance on individual taste all equal pretty poor business sense: publishers make their money back on a given book only 30 percent of the time. They begin with supply instead of demand. But understanding demand—whether you're creating new content, selling content, or even pirating content—is the key to an efficient market.

The problem is that publishers understand very little about their consumers and their consumption. In theory, consumer demand should determine how much of a product to make. But in publishing, every major production decision—cost of content, number of units, marketing spend—is set before a consumer is ever considered. In an industry that wants to sell billions of units every year to an amorphous demographic, issues of volume, price, and distribution are as connected to consumer demand as they are to production.

Content acquisition, editing, processing, and distribution all require capital and work. People are willing to pay for content, but publishers don't know where the demand is. As old models of pricing atrophy, an inefficient market like this one lacks the information needed to accurately predict demand and price products. The immediacy and transparency of a digital market can be used to determine and facilitate individual sales—*if* that

[1] http://en.wikipedia.org/wiki/Overconfidence
[2] http://en.wikipedia.org/wiki/Information_bias

information makes its way up to the publishers. Owning the consumer, not the content, may become the greatest asset.

Understanding demand and meeting it quickly would allow everyone to make better deals. Direct-to-consumer sales have never been an option for publishers, just as they aren't for most wholesale producers. It's not that surprising that a digital retailer—in this case, Amazon—began to see that owning consumer data could make them more than a simple middleman.

Unfortunately, the fight publishers have been waging with Amazon has never been, from the publisher perspective, about the consumer. Rather, they want to control price, and their solution—agency pricing, via Apple and others—has already brought accusations of collusion and price fixing from the Department of Justice.

But whether publishers can recognize and learn from their customers is unclear. The people who make books currently lack any intimacy with their prospective readers, even in a world of social networks. They set up fan pages and websites and wait for people to come to them. Finding consumers for any business is hard, more so when there is little brand identity (few people purchase books based on their respective publisher). Publishers need to discover their readers as much as readers need to discover new authors and books.

More than 300,000 books are put out each year—and more than 2.5 million self-published titles—with few opportunities for consumers to sort through them all, or for publishers to find communities of like-minded readers to sell to. Physical bookstores are dying, taking with them an opportunity to browse. Online retailers are demand-driven businesses. Imagine if they went to where the readers already are and allowed those readers to dictate what they wanted.

The coming transformation in publishing will not be about the move to digital content and distribution. It is about discovery—finding and understanding communities of consumers, increasingly through the use of technology.

A Community of Writers and Readers

I run a website called Figment, an online community that helps teens and young adults create, discover, and share new reading and writing. We enable our users to read amateur and professional stories and create their own unfiltered creative writing to share with their peers on Web and mobile platforms. Figment users can connect with their writing peers, provide feedback on each other's work, and discuss all things literary, from how to overcome writer's block to their favorite fictional villains.

In just over a year, we have built a community of more than 220,000 registered users. These community members have posted some 350,000 "books," from poems to multi-chapter novels. We're continuing to add 3,000 new people each week as well as about 1,000 new books every single day.

The idea for Figment came from a *New Yorker* magazine article written by my partner in the business, Dana Goodyear. Dana had gone to Japan to report on a phenomenon that exemplified both the collision of social networks and the digital transformation of books: the cellphone novel. Adolescent girls in Japan were writing, sharing, and reading full-length novels on their mobile phones. They had invented the first literary genre of the cellular age.

Japanese cellphone novels began organically. Cellphone screens were like blank sheets of paper, on which teens produced complex melodramas. Take this typical plot: Sixteen year-old May is in love with Yuya, who is in love with May's sister. May then falls in love with Taka. Her best friend also loves Taka and throws herself off a building. She recovers but without her memory, so May is free to love Taka, except that he turns abusive.

This may sound like a crude telenovela to you, just as it did to the Japanese literary establishment. But this story, published as a book after earning a massive digital audience, earned a spot on the bestseller list. The impulse to prejudge an idea or a plot is overtaken by the power of the community. The story may have been trite, but the storyline is not the point: it's about the power of a community of readers engaging with a story. It's about that story becoming a part of those readers' everyday lives through technology.

Publishers put out *this book* because a network of fans drove its success through fan communities. In Japan, fans of cellphone fiction see themselves as peers of the writers they admire, and they follow those authors and their works as if they were friends. There is an immediacy to the relationship between reader and writer. Delivered to a cellphone, a story is like a private email or text message: implicitly intimate by virtue of the distribution mechanism alone.

This kind of system—online communities of readers and writers sharing free content across multiple platforms—actually saved the Japanese publishing industry. In 2007, four of the top five books on the Japanese bestseller list originated as cellphone novels, all of which were available online for free. The things American publishers have been looking for—data about consumer preference and an understanding of the demand for their products—can both be found through Figment's community.

Contrary to conventional wisdom, today's young people are voracious readers: average book-reading times for American teens have actually increased over the past decade, from 21 minutes a day to 25 minutes a day. A group of kids eager to participate in the publishing process represents the future direct-to-consumer model. They will tell us all what they want to read, when, and how. The question is, will we give them what they want?

On Figment, we know who are our users are. We know how old they are, where they live, what they're reading, and who their favorite authors, books, series, and genres are. We know whether they abandon a book after a chapter or two, if there is seasonality to their reading habits, or if they're prejudiced toward particular authors, themes, or even character traits. We know how many of them hate *Twilight*, how many times they've read *Harry Potter*, and if steampunk is the coming wave.

But online communities of readers and writers, like Figment, allow authors, readers, and publishers to interact in the same space, strengthening and streamlining marketing efforts and book sales. The users of Figment write, comment, review, engage, follow along, play in the forums, and read. They are willing to test out new material and tell us if it's good. They read excerpts and proclaim if they're worthy of purchase. We can see if a story does well territorially, or if its reception depends on demographics or gender.

Long before we all discovered the distributive power of Facebook and

Twitter, teens were creating viral networks to share what they liked, by whatever technological means were available. These networks have, at times, driven certain books' success. But those networks have typically been diffuse and impossible to capture.

By curating a community of readers, Figment has begun to capture those organic networks, benefiting both kids looking for new books as well as authors and publishers looking for a new crop of readers. By centralizing all of an author's books and social media feeds, Figment gives authors new ways to brand and promote themselves. It also allows each author to create his or her own network. Figment users can follow authors on our platform and stay updated on what they do. The more authors and publishers engage with content and readers and writers, the better served Figment users are.

Figment users read and write on computers and mobile phones. These teens, like much of the content they consume, are "born digital," and they expect to be able to connect to stimulating material whenever they want, wherever they happen to be. Global teenagers increasingly choose to access the Internet and all of its reading, shopping, gaming, and socializing opportunities through cellphones, iPod touches, smartphones, laptops, PCs, TVs, tablets—any device that can connect to the Internet. They type, chat, and even *think* in a digital way. This is our future generation of content consumers. And the Internet, for all of its destructive capabilities, gives creators and distributors tremendous power in finding their audience.

The Power of Digital Content

But right now the industry doesn't give them what they want online. We don't go out of our way to put a wide variety of digital content in the hands of teens, on their devices. Very few young adult books are available as ebooks because very few young adults currently own dedicated ereaders. But that's bound to change as more content is delivered to a variety of devices, including the phones most kids currently own. In Europe, 41 percent of teenagers have used computers to read books. And in Japan, 86 percent of high school girls read novels on their phones. Over 75 percent of American teens own a cellphone or Internet-enabled mobile device, and 65 percent of American young adults access the Internet through their phones. They communicate, shop, watch movies, and create content on their devices, and they will learn to read on them as well. A recent Scholastic study showed that 60 percent of U.S. teens are eager to read ebooks.

Publishers have yet to really insert themselves into this market. Instead, publishers, like music companies before them, see digital production and distribution as a threat to their revenue and as a gateway to piracy and abuse. In order to retain control over distribution of their content, they often attempt to restrict legal digital access. Consider the failed attempt in 2009 to stagger the release of ebooks four months after the hardcover was out, or HarperCollins's astounding decision to restrict library ebook lending to 26 total views on any given purchase. To this day, Macmillan and Simon & Schuster refuse to sell ebooks to libraries at all.

Finding consumers who will pay for a product is difficult. But if the market is defined by sharing information, then allowing for some free distribution, especially through library systems, may be the best kind of loss leader.

There are plenty of lessons to be learned from the film and music industries, which have gone through cyclical attempts to restrict access to their material, whether to prevent sharing or stealing. Their efforts show us that if we don't give our consumers access to our content, then we facilitate a class of people willing to steal it and sell it as their own.

Piracy will always exist. But piracy doesn't occur just because books are digital. As the Brindisi sellers showed, it doesn't take much more than a Xerox machine to copy a book, and if someone were really inclined, it would be easy to enter the text into a word processor, just as it's easy to take a camcorder into a movie theater and copy a movie. Piracy doesn't occur because the process is easy—it occurs because there's an available and exploitable market. And it's more likely to occur if pirates are serving a market that has restricted access to the content it wants. The more we restrict access—whether by territory, by price, or by format—the more likely it is that we'll find our content in the wrong hands.

When I was traveling around Europe, I didn't know where I would find my reading material from country to country. The Brindisi sellers solved that problem. Today, in theory, there is no limitation to access or space.

Kids want to find and read good books. And they want iTunes-like instant gratification, a download with the tap of the finger. They want to sink into a good story, but they don't want to wait around for it.

Look at *Harry Potter*. Translators weren't given access to the English text before its release date, so there was a lag of several months before some translations hit the market. In France, the English edition reached the bestseller list—a first for an English-language book in France—before the French version was even out. There are unsanctioned editions in Sinhala and Tamil, in Sri Lanka, and as many as 16 different Persian translations.

The more we continue to try to restrict access to information and content, the more the market will demand it. In the US, publishers are frustrated and exasperated with Amazon for using a proprietary format for its ebooks. But when publishers limit access to their content by not making their content available in all formats or through library programs, is it really any different? Instead of being obsessed with retailers, distribution, and security, publishers would be better off getting obsessed with their readers, wherever they are.

The Promise of Digital Publishing

Publishing over digital platforms can increase readership, visibility, and marketability. It can also give content creators insight into what does and doesn't work. Digital distribution will allow for a more agile approach to publishing. But restricting content while other industries adapt to a global, online model is a sure way to do the unthinkable: block sales and stall growth.

There is a lot of content flooding the world today. Hundreds of thousands of titles are published every year, along with millions of self-published ones. Suddenly, everyone is both a producer *and* a consumer. If communities didn't exist for authors and publishers to engage with readers, it would be utterly confusing. Figment doesn't just facilitate this interaction, it encourages it. Already, we're seeing that readers are finding books not through editorial reviews or physical bookstores; they're finding that information online, in communities of other readers.

Figment works because reading is not necessarily a passive exercise.

It is a surprisingly social one. The kids on Figment tell each other every day what they want to write and read. Imagine if those same readers were telling publishers what they were willing to buy, and then had the ability to easily buy that book. That's a model of efficiency.

Gathering better information about reading habits, patterns, and preferences can drive the market for books—rights, translations, prices—to a place where guesswork can be eliminated. Online communities of readers engaging with stories and their authors, enabled by technology and emboldened by the participation of every member: these are good things for publishers. Readers, writers, and publishers would all benefit from meeting each other, and this congress will ultimately make the market more efficient. Just like those pirate sellers in Brindisi.

Give the author feedback & add your comments about this chapter on the web: `http://book.pressbooks.com/chapter/figment-jacob-lewis`

27. A Conversation That Can't Be Controlled (Sarah Wendell, Smart Bitches Trashy Books)

Sarah Wendell is the co-founder and current mastermind of Smart Bitches Trashy Books, *one of the most prominent communities examining romance fiction online. The site specializes in reviewing romance novels, pondering the history and future of the genre in digital and print form, and bemoaning the enormous prevalence of bodacious pectorals adorning male cover models. Sarah is also the author of* Everything I Know About Love, I Learned from Romance Novels *and co-author of* Beyond Heaving Bosoms: the Smart Bitches' Guide to Romance Novels, *which is used on syllabi at several universities including Harvard, Princeton, Yale, and DePaul.*

Because I'm a blogger (and boy, is that ever a visually ugly word), I tend to locate things in a very immediate sense of time. Usually I'm focusing on what's happening right now, what might happen in the future or taking a look at what's changed in the romance genre and its readership over the past 30-odd years. It's more difficult to write something that looks back over the past seven years I've been running *Smart Bitches, Trashy Books*, identify what I've learned, and where we've been.

I look at books, at readers, at trends, and cliches, and I honestly don't spend a lot of time looking at myself or my own statistics. So beginning this chapter, I'm almost compelled to locate the words I'm writing now in the events that are happening now, in March 2012. I suppose this is "dating" my chapter in a damaging way, but one thing I've definitely learned online, while also learning about publishing and the community of readers who thrive within it, is that the more things change, the more many try to keep things exactly as they are.

Right now, a published fanfiction called *50 Shades of Grey* is dominating the news. As I wrote on 2 March 2012,[1] this book has received the kind of attention publicists have fever dreams about. *Good Morning America* interviewed me for a segment that aired 13 March 2012. It focused on the fact that this book has reached record sales and top positions on bestseller lists purely through viral word-of-mouth exposure online and off. People are spreading the word about this book and creating astonishing sales, and there hasn't been any major advertising push from the publisher. I suspect that will change, now that Random House has paid a reported seven figures for the rights to the *50 Shades* trilogy. But the initial thrust of sales power came from readers talking to other readers.

Consumer interaction is, and has been, a powerful conversation that cannot be controlled.

That's what book blogging is at its best: a conversation about books that can't be controlled, not even by those who start it. People want to create content about the things they read. I can moderate heavily or even close comments, but if people have something to say, they will find a way to say it, even if the genesis of their thoughts is no longer a venue for continued interaction.

In speeches and panels about blogging and online reviewing, I have cited Clay Shirky's *Cognitive Surplus* several times. Shirky suggests that the excess brain energy we carry increases with each successive generation. As we build wealth and more of our daily chores and processes become automated, the potential creations of our harnessed surplus grow over time.

---

[1] http://bit.ly/zzE22r

I was grabbed by the idea embodied in the subtitle of Shirky's book: "Creativity and Generosity in a Connected Age." As consumers, we are more driven to create in response to what we consume, and we are encouraged by various forms of social media to interact and gauge our likes and dislikes against those of our friends, former friends, and casual online and offline acquaintances. The younger generations currently ascending into the ever-so-desirable advertiser demographics no longer passively consume entertainment. As Shirky notes:

> "Several population studies—of high school students, broadband users, YouTube users—have noticed the change. Their basic observation is always the same: young populations with access to fast, interactive media are shifting their behavior away from media that presupposes pure consumption. Even when they watch video online, seemingly a pure analog to TV, this generation now has opportunities to comment on the material, to share it with their friends, to label, rate or rank it, and of course, to discuss it with other viewers around the world."

That interaction is becoming second nature. For example, I rarely watch television without a laptop or smartphone nearby to talk about what I'm watching. I also do the same while reading. I consume entertainment with interaction tools close at hand.

Now, advertisers are driving collaborative creativity because it is more valuable for the products being promoted. Here's an example: on the highway circling the exit of the Lincoln Tunnel into and out of Manhattan, a route travelled by many thousands of people every day, huge billboards advertise products. One is almost always touting Absolut vodka. At one point, the text at the bottom of the billboard cautioned those reading to drink responsibly, then proclaimed the company's URL.

Now, the billboard directs folks to facebook.com/absolut.[2] Absolut probably spent a great deal of money on its destination website, but the interaction of fans of their product and the presence of those fans on their Facebook page is more desirable now. The interaction and the conversation

---

[2] http://www.facebook.com/absolut

and the content that result are more valuable than a one-way intake of information from one user looking at a website.

When I co-founded Smart Bitches in January 2005 with Candy Tan, I was seeking engagement that I didn't have an outlet for at that moment. Of course, I didn't know it at the time. Candy was someone I knew online through my now-defunct personal blog. She found my site after searching for raw cat food recipes—back when I had more free time, I made my own pet food. She used to leave long comments on my site, and we'd correspond very casually.

Then, after the tsunami of 2004, I emailed her, mistakenly remembering her as being from Indonesia. Candy is actually from Malaysia, and after telling me her family was all well and safe, we began emailing back and forth about random topics. Somehow the subject of romance novels came up. We both confessed to loving them and hating how much crap we took from people. As Candy wrote in *Beyond Heaving Bosoms*, our 2009 book, she could see people "revising downward" their estimation of her intelligence upon discovering she loved romance novels.

At some point in this conversation, we also mentioned how difficult it was to find concise and critical examinations of romance novels, especially when looking for new books to buy or borrow. One of us (we don't remember which) suggested we start a website of romance novel reviews. After a few bizarre suggestions of what we'd call it, *Smart Bitches, Trashy Books* was born. We wanted to harness the power of our English degrees and our dedication to criticizing and examining the books we loved and apply it to romance novels—a genre that isn't reviewed in most mainstream book review publications, or given much respect at all.

When I read Shirky's book years after starting the website, I realized that our creation of a blog was in part a step toward fulfilling our lack of outlet—using our cognitive surplus. We didn't know many romance readers. We wanted to talk to each other and anyone else who would listen about the romances we loved and the ones we didn't. Our public conversation in the form of a blog became a conversation for many others.

When we launched SBTB in 2005, we didn't advertise. Outside of our own circle of friends, we didn't do much in the way of announcements. I already had a personal online journal that I was running, and "Hey, I just started a blog" was about the extent of our promotion. Neither of us expected the site to take off the way that it did.

But through word of mouth and link sharing among romance writers and readers, our audience grew. It continues to grow over seven years later. We have readers in over 150 countries worldwide, and we receive traffic from just about every timezone. I think that in part reflects that same isolation I felt originally: many romance readers (90%+ of whom are women according to the Romance Writers of America) do not have friends with whom they can discuss the genre.

Some have written to me to tell me how relieved they are to have found our site, because they didn't have any people who served as recommendation resources for romance. Their romance reading was something of a secret, and preserving their secrecy while going online to find recommendations and discovering so many active communities of readers was a revelation for many. The most common email message I still receive is, "Where have you been all my life? I had no idea there were so many romance readers out there!"

The consumer's need to interact and create in response to the entertainment we consume is encouraged by television shows that direct us to Facebook in the end credits, and by movie promotions that encourage us to tweet about films using a hashtag to increase word of mouth. And even if that word is negative, it helps.

In the early years of our site, one thing that surprised me was how often we were described as "mean" when we gave a thoroughly negative review of a book. When a romance let us down, we ranted about it. And when we did, the traffic went up, and the hate mail increased. We were called mean and nasty for being so cruel about an author's hard work, even though most of the time, we were talking about a book, a product created for entertainment, and not the person who created it.

That drive to create in response wouldn't be present if creation itself weren't a personal endeavor. Creation is personal, from the creation of a book to the creation of the review of it to the comments on the book and the review from readers who liked or disliked either. But even a negative review is a positive thing: in my Amazon affiliate statistics, books that I've reviewed negatively, particularly books that have received low grades for being completely off the wall crazy in plot and dialogue, have outsold books to which I've given B and A grades.

One book, *The Playboy Sheikh's Virgin Stable Girl*,[3] by Sharon Kendrick, still appears on my sales reports a full two years after I gave it a D-. The author told me privately that the book has continued to sell marvelously for her. She credits my review, which highlighted some of the most over-the-top characters I've ever experienced in romance. In addition, she dedicated her next book to me.

That response is something of an outlier, though, because most often negative reviews garner outraged responses from authors and eager responses from readers. Our collaboration began because Candy and I could not find a critical and analytical site that examined romance novels. Now, there are many reader response blogs, not just devoted to romance, either. Not all of these readers react positively to the books they read, but I maintain that there is absolute value in the negative review. It allows readers to identify the rubric employed by that reviewer in evaluating content. Moreover, hype is much less effective than snark in terms of enticing sales, in my opinion. For one thing, hype is considered suspect by those on the receiving end—and this is especially true for me.

More importantly, negative reactions inspire curiosity because people learn about each other and themselves when they can identify what it is they label as "bad" or "not to their tastes." Imagine a review in which I am squeeing endlessly without a word of negativity about a book whose lead character eats pasta, does a lot of yoga, and finds herself. If I start spewing flowery prose about how this book Changed My Life, I bet you'd start to skim that paragraph.

But if I'm standing next to you, and I smell something in a plastic container and say, "This smells bad. Smell it," most likely you will totally take a big whiff, not only out of morbid curiosity, but because it's a compulsion to identify whether what's "bad" for me matches what's "bad" for you. The line of demarcation that defines "bad" is much more revealing than that which we consider "good."

Reviews offer that same function, particularly negative reviews. One of my favorite email messages was from a reader who said, "I love everything

---

[3] http://bit.ly/I9XADi

you hate, and hate everything you like." I found that to be a compliment of the highest order, because it meant that I was consistent, and that reader was happy reading the opposite of what I recommended.

Just as there are people who love role-playing games, watch television shows with intricate plots, follow reality television series or pursue artistic endeavors involving weaving, painting, or both, there are people who consume books as their entertainment. Creation is a human desire, I think. And because my favorite entertainment is books, and my favorite way to spend my leisure time is to read, the conversations I have with other romance readers about the books we love and hate is ongoing. It is out of the control of the author, the publisher, and even the blogger who might have started it.

Now that online and offline conversation have made *50 Shades of Grey* a huge bestseller, the power of that uncontrolled conversation is realized. It is realized not only in a seven-figure publishing deals for the author, but also by booksellers who can't keep the book on their shelves and must maintain a waiting list of customers looking for it, and by readers who want to join the conversation and have to read the book in order to understand the discussion. The more interaction there is, the more exposure, and the more exposure, the more profit.

Until recently, editors and sales teams saw book buyers—those individuals who decided what books to stock in their bookstores and supermarket bookshelves—as their customer. Moreover, editors and sales teams focused on what was coming out in six, eight, even twelve months from now, not what's on sale this week. Publishers as corporations are still trying to figure out how to best interact with and serve the reader, who is increasingly their customer.

As readers spend more time online interacting with one another, we learn how publishing works from authors, other readers, and even socially active people within the publishing industry. So when readers begin responding to the books they've read, they respond to the author and now to the publisher as well, and it hasn't been clear what the best response from a publisher might be. As more publishers sell directly—Random House just opened their author portal, which, among other things, offers discounts on Random House books—more publishers will experience being retailers and dealing with readers directly. That should be illuminating and create even more change in the world of reader interaction.

I gave a keynote at SXSW in 2011, and said, "Readers are a strange, sometimes unwelcome, sometimes baffling, sometimes irritating and yet absolutely important part of any conversation when it comes to the way the road to publishing is traveled." With so many new book blogs appearing each month—and a blogger-generated conference devoted just to them purchased by Book Expo America for the 2012 BEA convention— the conversation about books and the creation of debate and extended interaction and reviews will only continue to grow.

Readers, like any other consumer of media, are not content to passively consume. Allowing their consumption to become interaction, regardless of whether that interaction is laudatory, is part of selling books now. The reader's voice is important, as is her opinion and what she does next with her opinion. Listening to the reader and allowing the conversation to grow is essential—and is my favorite part of the *Smart Bitches* website.

Give the author feedback & add your comments about this chapter on the web: http://book.pressbooks.com/chapter/smart-bitches-trashy-books-sarah-wendell

About the Editors

This book was the result of collaboration among many people: writers, editors, developers, publishers, and others. Trying to wrangle this collection of talented people were Brian O'Leary and Hugh McGuire.

Hugh McGuire is a technologist and writer, who experiments and writes about the changing world of publishing. He is the founder of LibriVox, a free digital audiobook library, iambik audio, a commercial digital audiobook company, and PressBooks.com, a digital book production tool, upon which this book was built. You can find Hugh on Twitter at: @hughmcguire.

Brian O'Leary is founder and principal of Magellan Media, a management consulting firm that works with publishers seeking support in content operations, benchmarking and financial analysis. He writes extensively about issues affecting the publishing industry, including a research report on the impact of free content and digital piracy on paid book sales. You can find Brian on Twitter at: @brianoleary.

CPSIA information can be obtained at www.ICGtesting.com
Printed in the USA
LVOW131911161012

303109LV00001B/1/P